Vampire Films of the 1970s

Vampire Films of the 1970s
Dracula *to* Blacula *and Every Fang Between*

GARY A. SMITH

McFarland & Company, Inc., Publishers
Jefferson, North Carolina

ALSO BY GARY A. SMITH
AND FROM McFARLAND

The American International Pictures Video Guide (2009)

Epic Films: Casts, Credits and Commentary on More Than 350 Historical Spectacle Movies, 2d ed. (2004; softcover 2009)

Uneasy Dreams: The Golden Age of British Horror Films, 1956–1976 (2000; softcover 2006)

Frontispiece: William Marshall in *Scream Blacula Scream* (1973).

LIBRARY OF CONGRESS CATALOGUING-IN-PUBLICATION DATA

Names: Smith, Gary A., 1950– author.
Title: Vampire films of the 1970s : Dracula to Blacula and every fang between / Gary A. Smith.
Description: Jefferson, North Carolina : McFarland & Company, Inc., Publishers, 2016. | Includes bibliographical references and index. | Includes filmography.
Identifiers: LCCN 2016049635 | ISBN 9780786497799 (softcover : acid free paper) ∞
Subjects: LCSH: Vampire films—History and criticism. | Motion pictures—20th century—History and criticism.
Classification: LCC PN1995.9.V3 S66 2016 | DDC 791.43/675—dc23
LC record available at https://lccn.loc.gov/2016049635

BRITISH LIBRARY CATALOGUING DATA ARE AVAILABLE

ISBN 978-0-7864-9779-9 (print)
ISBN 978-1-4766-2559-1 (ebook)

© 2017 Gary A. Smith. All rights reserved

No part of this book may be reproduced or transmitted in any form or by any means, electronic or mechanical, including photocopying or recording, or by any information storage and retrieval system, without permission in writing from the publisher.

On the cover Robert Quarry in *The Deathmaster*, 1972, R.F. Brown Productions/World Entertainment Productions

Printed in the United States of America

*McFarland & Company, Inc., Publishers
Box 611, Jefferson, North Carolina 28640
www.mcfarlandpub.com*

To Julie Hirsch
who wanted to know
about vampires

Table of Contents

Introduction	1
The Rules About Vampires	9
1. Hammer, Dracula and Christopher Lee	11
2. Hammer's Other Vampires	20
3. Other British Vampires	29
4. American International	35
5. I Am Legend	50
6. Carmilla Karnstein	53
7. Elisabeth Bathory	63
8. Deadlier Than the Male	70
9. Asian Vampires	82
10. Santo and South of the Border Vampires	89
11. Zut Alors! The French Vampires of Jean Rollin	95
12. Vampires Italian Style	102
13. ¡Viva España!	107
14. Jess Franco	124
15. The Bottom of the Barrel with Al and Andy	130
16. Vampire Comedies	139
17. Vampire Porn	151
18. Vampire Oddities	156
19. Dan Curtis: *Dark Shadows* and Other Vampires	177

20. More Television Vampires	184
21. Full Circle	190
Appendix: Vampires in Print	199
Filmography	203
Bibliography	225
Index	227

Introduction

For over a century, vampires have been part of popular culture. These undead bloodsuckers have indeed lived up to their reputation as immortal. As of this writing, vampires have undergone a major media resurgence. The television series *True Blood* and *The Vampire Diaries* were big hits and enjoyed lengthy runs. The ten-episode *Dracula* series (2013–14) starring Jonathan Rhys Meyers has come and gone from the primetime TV schedule (*Variety* pronounced it "Undead on Arrival"). The *Dracula* series featured a revisionist version of the famous vampire looking much the same as the decidedly modern interpretation that Meyers gave of Henry VIII in *The Tudors*. As Henry he wasn't at all bad, but he was no Charles Laughton; he is also no Christopher Lee. Meyers' Dracula was a rather high-minded avenger out to destroy an evil organization that has plagued the world for centuries. Sort of like *Arrow* with fangs. And speaking of things CW, a *Vampire Diaries* spinoff series, *The Originals*, was also added to the CW network's roster of shows in 2013. For the record, all of these shows feature "sexy vampires."

From a physical standpoint, vampires have never had it as good as they do now. As evidenced by the aforementioned TV shows and the *Twilight* movie series, vampires are now young, good-looking, buff and angst-ridden. Swoon bait for teenage girls and far more tragic than terrifying. Some of the blame for this goes back to Anne Rice who, in her 1976 novel *Interview with a Vampire*, introduced a tragic vampire protagonist. Her reluctant bloodsucking hero, Louis de Pointe du Lac, suffers so much torment at the thought of taking the blood of a victim that sometimes you just want to slap him and say, "For Heaven's sake! Just get on with it!" By the time the novel finally made it to the screen

Introduction

Tom Cruise as Lestat and Brad Pitt as Louis in *Interview with a Vampire* (1994).

in 1994, it hardly seemed worth the wait, but then the movie appears to be far more concerned with "hair design" than fangs.

Stephenie Meyer, who wrote the series of *Twilight* novels on which the films are based, took the vampire legend even further from its origins. Meyer has admitted that when she started writing these novels in 2003, she had little knowledge of vampire mythology so she made up her own as she went along. She also has said that her Mormon faith has greatly influenced her writing. Consequently, her vampires are far removed from the previously accepted view of them as creatures of darkness and evil. Instead of suffering from Satanic influence, Meyer's vampires are predatory animals who must kill to survive. And this seems to be the idea that has stuck in the contemporary public consciousness. Another, more recent example is the disillusioned rock star, who is also a reclusive vampire, played by Tom Hiddleston in Jim

Jarmusch's feature film *Only Lovers Left Alive* (2013). He survives by buying blood from a blood bank. Personally, I long for the days when a vampire could sink its fangs into a willing or unwilling neck without a hint of remorse.

The year 2014 may have seen the end of *True Blood* on TV but a pair of new vampire series were there to fill the void. I won't discuss Guillermo Del Toro's FX series *The Strain* in detail here other than to say it goes so far afield as to eschew the standard vampire conventions almost entirely. Worms spreading vampirism? Whatever happened to fangs? Del Toro has said that he wanted to take the "romance" out of vampires and re-imagine them and he has certainly done that. In addition to myriad other classic horror elements, Showtime's *Penny Dreadful* had some truly horrific vampires which were more like animals than resurrected humans. Their victims, however, are in the time-honored mode and the Victorian setting is a welcome return to form. For Halloween 2014, Universal hoped to jump start a new series of their classic monster movies with the theatrical release of *Dracula Untold*. More large-scale action fantasy than horror film, the story presents Vlad the Impaler, well-played by Luke Evans, as the "heroic, romantic, tragic" figure that Christopher Lee always claimed he was. What he isn't is scary, a real liability in a movie with horror franchise aspirations. *Variety* deemed it "decorous but dull." *Dracula Untold* had impressive production values and a nifty sequence featuring an army of vampires, so it wasn't a total loss.

So much for what vampires have become. Now let's look at what they once were.

The roots of the vampire in popular culture can be traced to the works of two Irish novelists. The first is the 1872 novella *Carmilla* by Joseph Sheridan Le Fanu. The second is, of course, the 1897 novel *Dracula* by Bram Stoker. It is from these two pieces of literature that most of the cinematic vampire mythos has devolved.

The first motion picture featuring a vampire (as opposed to the silent screen femme fatale known as a "vamp") was the 1922 German film *Nosferatu: A Symphony of Horror*, directed by F.W. Murnau. This was an unauthorized version of Stoker's *Dracula* with the names of the characters changed in the hope that no one would notice that the story was basically the same. Unfortunately for the filmmakers, Stoker's widow Florence was still alive and she did notice. The ensuing lawsuit was resolved in her favor and she insisted that the *Nosferatu* negative

Bela Lugosi as *Dracula* (1931).

and all existing prints be destroyed. Happily for future generations of film historians and horror movie fans, several prints survived.

Two years later, a stage version of *Dracula*, written by Hamilton Deane, opened in England with the blessing of Florence Stoker. It was this stage version that came to Broadway in 1927, with some alterations

Introduction

by John L. Balderston, and was eventually filmed by Universal in 1931. *Dracula* made a movie star of Hungarian-born actor Bela Lugosi, who had originated the role on Broadway, and started Universal on a cycle of horror films that gives the studio its identity to this day. The following year, Danish director Carl Dreyer helmed the German-French co-production *Vampyr*, which was derived from J. Sheridan Le Fanu stories, including *Carmilla*. Now both of the major pieces of vampire fiction had been brought to the screen and the motion picture industry never looked back. Vampires were here to stay.

In the '30s and '40s, Universal continued to use the Stoker character in films and soon other studios created their own original, but often quite similar, vampires. Columbia's *The Return of the Vampire* (1944) starring Bela Lugosi as vampire Armand Tesla is a perfect example. He is Count Dracula in everything but name. By the time Dracula encountered Abbott and Costello at Universal in 1948, gothic horror films had waned in public popularity, and soon science fiction movies took their place.

In two 1957 horror movies, vampires were created by "science gone wrong." In *The Vampire,* a doctor mistakenly takes some experimental pills which turn him into the title character and in *Blood of Dracula*, an unhappy teenage girl is turned into a vampire by her unscrupulous science professor. Neither of these films stressed the supernatural elements which had dominated the vampire movies of the '30s and '40s. But things were about to change.

In 1957, Warner Bros. released a color horror movie made by the small British company Hammer Films. *The Curse of Frankenstein* was a tremendous worldwide financial success and gothic horror was back. As a follow-up, Hammer decided to make a new color version of the original Bram Stoker novel. *Horror of Dracula* (aka *Dracula*) came out in 1958 and was an even bigger success than the Frankenstein film. The new screen Dracula, Christopher Lee, was unlike any vampire seen in movies thus far. Tall and handsome, he could quickly turn into a snarling monster with bloodshot eyes and long fangs dripping blood. But along with the more graphic representation of the Dracula character, Hammer also introduced an eroticism which had previously been only hinted at in vampire cinema. Now there was an element of desire in both vampire and victim. The inclusion of sexuality marked a turning point in the depiction of vampires in both movies and literature.

At first Hammer had few imitators as far as their vampire films were concerned. *The Return of Dracula,* made in Hollywood and released the same year as *Horror of Dracula*, was a good film but fairly tame by comparison. During the next ten years, Hammer took the lead when it came to making vampire movies, although the Italians weren't far behind with such films as *Black Sunday* and *The Vampire and the Ballerina* (both 1960). Then in 1968, Hammer produced a movie which was obviously in the right place at the right time. *Dracula Has Risen from the Grave* was Hammer's fifth vampire film and the third to feature Christopher Lee as the count. Although it was no better or worse than their other vampire films, it went on to become (along with *She* and *One Million Years B.C.*) one of the company's three biggest moneymakers up to that time, winning Hammer the prestigious Queen's Award for Industry.

The success of this movie and the increasing popularity of the

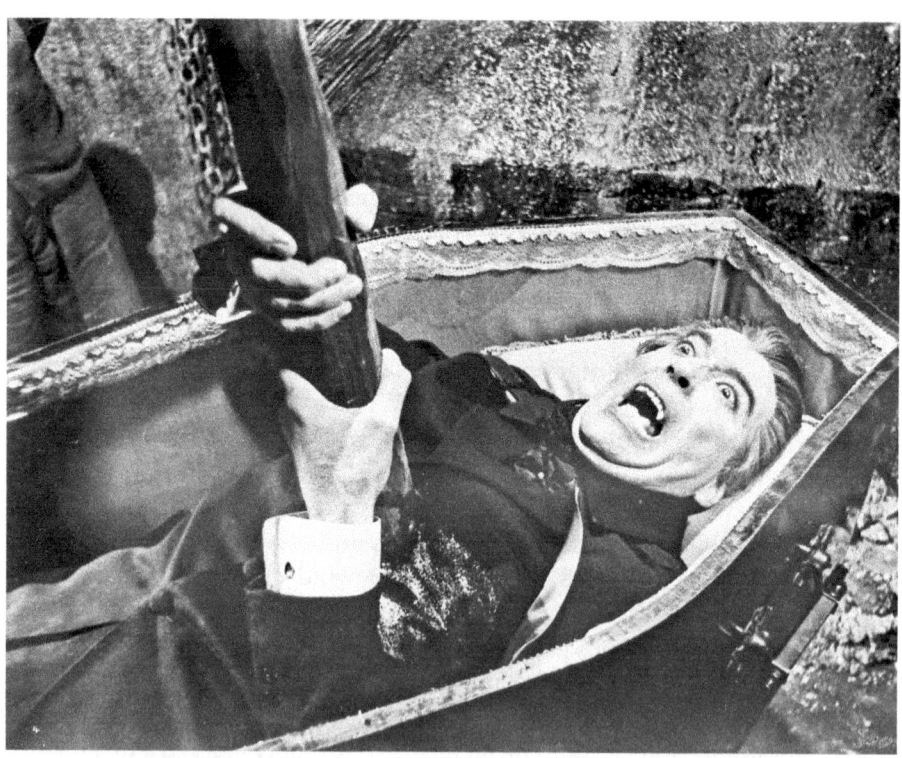

Dracula removes the stake from his heart in *Dracula Has Risen from the Grave* (1968).

daytime TV soap opera *Dark Shadows,* which featured vampire Barnabas Collins, seem to have been the major catalysts for the flood of vampire movies which followed and would continue throughout the next decade.

The '70s saw countless variations on the vampire theme as filmmakers everywhere jumped on the bloody bandwagon. There were black vampires, kung fu vampires, lesbian vampires, hippie vampires, canine vampires, comic vampires, and even some who managed to adhere to more traditional interpretations. It seemed as if a new vampire movie opened in cinemas every week, most of them offering some variation on the established formula. In *Blacula,* blaxploitation merged with vampires. *The Legend of the 7 Golden Vampires* had Far East vampires battling with kung fu fighters. The title *Zoltan, the Hound of Dracula* speaks for itself. Often creative, sometimes silly, but seldom dull, the vampire movies of the '70s were unique. They reflected turbulent times when minority groups were gaining rightful recognition and the Sexual Revolution was in full swing. Abundant female nudity became a major ingredient in '70s vampire movies, as did graphic bloodletting. On the *Let's Scare Jessica to Death* website, there is an interesting statement by the film's composer Orville Stoebar which comes close to summing up the entire genre of '70s vampire cinema. Looking back on the film and the decade in which it was made, he says, "The nation was mentally and morally ill in the early '70s of America. Director John Hancock used *Jessica* as a metaphor for our moral confusion of that time."

In the following pages I will attempt to give an overview of the vampire movies made during this period. Although the decade produced a number of embarrassments, it also yielded several bonafide classics of the genre. Like the '70s in general, it was a mixed bag. Some of these movies should be sought out and viewed while others should be avoided. But then, some of the worst ones are the most fun so who am I to judge? I leave that up to you.

The Rules About Vampires

The rules about vampires are that there *are* no rules. In *Captain Kronos Vampire Hunter* (Hammer, 1974), vampire expert Professor Grost explains to another character, "There are as many species of vampires as there are beasts of prey." With this comment in mind, it is easier to accept the various and sundry characteristics which seem to change from movie to movie.

In *Horror of Dracula* (Hammer, 1958), a vampire changing into a bat or wolf is dismissed by Dr. Van Helsing as "a common fallacy." Yet in *The Brides of Dracula* (Hammer, 1960), the same Doctor Van Helsing concedes that some of them can do just that.

In the Bram Stoker novel, Count Dracula can move about in the daylight, although his supernatural powers are reduced. The first vampire movie, *Nosferatu: A Symphony of Horror* (1922), shows Count Orlock being destroyed by the sun. This has been a standard means of destruction of cinema vampires ever since. In *Horror of Dracula,* Van Helsing emphatically states that vampires are allergic to light: "Sunlight fatal, repeat, fatal." The climax of the movie proves this in no uncertain terms as Dracula is reduced to a pile of dust when exposed to the sun. However, in *The Kiss of the Vampire* (Hammer, 1963), the vampires can go out on a cloudy day as long as they use an umbrella.

Sunlight isn't the only vampire exterminator. A wooden stake through the heart seems to be the favorite, although there always seems to be somebody ready to remove it and return the creature to life. Totally flaunting convention, Dracula removes the stake himself in *Dracula Has Risen from the Grave*. Decapitation is also popular and much more permanent. Sometimes burning a vampire works (*Black Sunday,* 1960) but sometimes it doesn't (*Lust for a Vampire,* 1971). Ditto with clear running water.

And those damn mirrors! Although a vampire is supposed to cast no reflection in a mirror, countless movie vampires have done just that. In *Curse of the Vampires* (1970) it is obviously done for dramatic effect but in the otherwise wonderful *Son of Dracula* (Universal, 1943) it is just a lack of attention to detail.

Perhaps the most puzzling "rule" of all is just how one becomes a vampire. In some movies it is by a long, slow process and in others it is just one nip on the neck. In literature, far more often than in films, the vampire must offer its own blood to the victim in order for that person to join the ranks of the undead. It's a fairly repulsive idea and the first time I remember seeing this in a movie was in *Dracula—Prince of Darkness* (Hammer, 1966). Christopher Lee uses a fingernail to slice open his chest and then invites Suzan Farmer to drink his blood. *Twins of Evil* (Hammer, 1971) provides yet another explanation when the vampire Count Karnstein tells his intended victim, "One who is dedicated to the Devil and his deeds will not die by a vampire's bite but will become one of the undead … a vampire! The good and the innocent die!"

As I said, there are no rules. A little logic, even in the illogical, would be nice but with these films, you just have to go with the flow and accept them on its own terms.

CHAPTER 1

Hammer, Dracula and Christopher Lee

Following the 1958 release of their landmark movie *Horror of Dracula* (aka *Dracula*), Hammer was eager to get another Dracula film underway. Christopher Lee (1922–2015), however, was reluctant to play the character again, although later Lee claimed that he was never asked by Hammer to return for the sequel. Whatever the case, it was decided to proceed without him and make Peter Cushing's Van Helsing character the link to the first movie. The resulting film was *The Brides of Dracula* (1960). An early title was *Disciple of Dracula,* which is far more fitting as the brides herein are of Baron Meinster (David Peel), not Dracula. The next Hammer vampire movie, *The Kiss of the Vampire* (1963), deals with a Bavarian cult of the undead whose chief vampire is Dr. Ravna (Noel Willman).

Christopher Lee eventually reprised the role of Dracula for Hammer in *Dracula—Prince of Darkness* (1966) and again in *Dracula Has Risen from the Grave* (1969). The latter proved so successful that, in its wake, Hammer made a new Dracula movie every year in addition to other vampire films not featuring the Stoker character. During the '70s, Hammer would produce 11 vampire films, in addition to an unrealized vampire project which would eventually hasten the company's downfall.

Taste the Blood of Dracula

Following the success of *Dracula Has Risen from the Grave* Hammer naturally wanted to make a follow-up right away. Christopher Lee announced that he was uninterested in playing Dracula again for Ham-

Christopher Lee in *Taste the Blood of Dracula* (1970).

mer. He felt the character was being misused in their films and that his talents were being wasted. Hammer had already faced this dilemma once and were undaunted by it. A Dracula film without Dracula had worked before and Hammer had every reason to think it would work again. Hammer had seen a young actor named Ralph Bates as Caligula in the 1968 Granda TV series *The Caesars* and they decided to put

1. Hammer, Dracula and Christopher Lee

him under contract and groom him as their next resident vampire. The new script was titled *Taste the Blood of Dracula* and in it, Dracula's latest disciple, Lord Courtley (to be played by Bates), drinks the blood of Dracula and becomes a vampire himself.

Everything was set to go but Warner Bros.–Seven Arts, who had released *Dracula Has Risen from the Grave* and would be releasing the forthcoming *Taste the Blood of Dracula*, felt that a Hammer Dracula movie without Christopher Lee wasn't really a Dracula movie at all. According to Christopher Lee, he only agreed to do the picture after James Carreras, the head of Hammer, guilted him into playing the part. Lee said Carreras told him that he would be responsible for putting a lot of people out of work unless he appeared in the film, which would be cancelled without his participation. Carreras also agreed to pay a hefty hike in Lee's salary. Now that Lee's presence as Dracula was assured, the script had to be rewritten to accommodate the character. This reduced Ralph Bates to the level of a supporting player rather than the lead but he still manages to make his performance as Lord Courtley a real scene-stealer. Linda Hayden, as a young girl who comes under Dracula's influence, gives an assured and engaging performance, one of the high points of the movie. This was the first of Hungarian director Peter Sasdy's three outstanding films for Hammer.

The Plot: Weller (Roy Kinnear), a London antiques dealer, is traveling by coach in the Carpathian forest when he comes across Dracula (Christopher Lee) impaled on an enormous crucifix. When the vampire disintegrates, Weller takes his cloak, ring and some of his now-powdered blood. In London, three upper-class gentlemen seek lower-class thrills unbeknownst to their respectable families. At a brothel, the dissolute Lord Courtley (Ralph Bates) convinces them to participate in a black mass ceremony held in a de-sanctified church. Courtley acquires the Dracula paraphernalia from Weller and, during the ceremony, invites the three men to drink the blood of Dracula. When they decline, Courtley drinks it himself and suffers a terrible reaction. Frightened of exposure, the men beat Courtley to death and flee. The corpse of Courtley transforms into Dracula and he sets forth to get revenge on the trio who murdered his acolyte, using the children of these men as the instruments of his wrath. One by one the men die violent deaths at the hands of their offspring. Paul (Anthony Corlan), the son of one of the murdered men, conceives of a plan to destroy Dracula in his lair by making the de-sanctified church holy again.

Scars of Dracula

Taste the Blood of Dracula continued the run of successful Hammer Dracula films. The company, which had in the past relied on financing from American companies, now began to feel the crunch as U.S. money was no longer readily available for British productions. In reaction to this, Hammer made a deal to make three films which would be financed by the British film distribution company ABPC. The first was *Horror of Frankenstein*, to be released on a double bill with the next installment in Hammer's Dracula series. *Scars of Dracula* began production in May 1970, the same month that *Taste the Blood of Dracula* hit cinemas in the United Kingdom.

Although disappointed with his part in the previous Dracula film, Christopher Lee agreed to appear in *Scars* because he felt that the script gave him far more to do. Roy Ward Baker was brought on to direct and the young lovers this time were played by the very appealing Dennis Waterman and Jenny Hanley. Although nudity is kept to a minimum, the violence and gore quotient is far higher than in any of the other Hammer Dracula movies. In another major departure from the series, this one does not pick up where the prior film left off. *Taste the Blood of Dracula* ended in a London cemetery but for *Scars of Dracula* we are back at Castle Dracula near Keinenberg, the setting for *Dracula Has Risen from the Grave*.

Released in the U.K. in October 1970, the *Horror of Frankenstein*-*Scars of Dracula* double bill did respectable business in England but, without the benefit of a major U.S. distributor, it fared badly in the U.S. when it was released there two months later by American Continental Pictures. *New York Times* critic Howard Thompson, unimpressed, penned a June 18, 1971, review of the double bill, dismissing *Scars of Dracula* as "garish, gory junk."

The Plot: Paul Carlson (Christopher Matthews), a reckless young Lothario, is caught trifling with the burgomaster's daughter and is forced to flee his hometown of Keinenberg. He seeks shelter at a nearby castle and is admitted by a beautiful woman named Tania (Anoushka Hempel) and her master Count Dracula (Christopher Lee). Ever-horny Paul takes Tania to bed but, as she attempts to bite him with her fangs, Dracula intervenes and kills her. When Paul fails to return home, his brother Simon (Dennis Waterman) and their friend Sarah (Jenny Hanley) go in search of him. After they are thrown out of the local village tavern for being too inquisitive, Simon and Sarah end up at the castle. Dracula gets one look at the lovely girl and wants her for his own. Simon and Dracula are fighting over Sarah on the battlements of the castle when a convenient bolt of lightning strikes Dracula and destroys him.

Dracula A.D. 1972

Despite declining to be involved in the production of *Scars of Dracula,* Warner Bros. had not given up on Hammer ... not yet, anyway. Noting the success of *Count Yorga—Vampire,* Warners approached Hammer with the idea of a Dracula film set in modern London. Hammer passed the idea on to screenwriter Don Houghton, who wrote *Dracula Chelsea 1972.* Not only did Warners approve the script, they commissioned a sequel as well.

The film went into production in September 1971 and reunited Christopher Lee and Peter Cushing in their first Dracula film since the original in 1958. Cushing was optimistic about the new project but Lee typically expressed concern about Hammer's treatment of the Dracula character. Canadian-born Alan Gibson was chosen to direct the film, which was now called *Dracula Today.* Gibson had previously worked for Hammer on their 1968 TV series *Journey to the Unknown* and the psychological thriller *Crescendo* (1970). Stephanie Beacham, Marsha Hunt and Caroline Munro supplied the requisite "Hammer Glamour." Christopher Neame, who had appeared in a small part in Hammer's *Lust for a Vampire,* was now given the choice role of Dracula's acolyte Johnny Alucard. Michael Coles plays a beleaguered Scotland Yard inspector who must suspend his disbelief about the existence of vampires.

After another title change, to *Dracula A.D. 1972,* the film was released in the U.K. in September 1972 and two months later in the U.S. Reviews were indifferent and audience attendance was even worse. According to Roger Greenspun of *The New York Times* (November 20, 1972), "Nothing much happens that couldn't have happened 100 years ago." Roger Ebert, in a typically snarky *Chicago Sun Times* review (December 13, 1972), used the film as an excuse to complain about "the general decay at Hammer Films" but had little to say about the movie itself. Apparently Count Yorga in modern Los Angeles was fine but nobody wanted to see Dracula in mod London.

Stephanie Beacham and Christopher Lee in *Dracula A.D. 1972* (1972).

In retrospect, what seemed like a terrible idea back in 1972, really isn't so dire after all. Now, so far removed from its contemporary setting, the swinging London of *Dracula A.D. 1972* seems as much a period piece as the Victorian settings of its predecessors. The main problem with the film is that Dracula is confined to the ruins of a gothic church and never really interacts with the modern world.

The Plot: In 1872, a runaway coach races through London's Hyde Park. Fighting on the top of it are Count Dracula (Christopher Lee) and his nemesis Lawrence Van Helsing (Peter Cushing). When the coach crashes, Dracula is impaled on the spoke of a wheel. Van Helsing watches as Dracula is reduced to ashes. Dracula's servant appears on the scene and collects some of the ashes, which he buries in a churchyard cemetery. Cut to modern London 100 years later. Johnny Alucard (Christopher Neame) and his hip friends, bored with crashing posh parties, go to a de-sanctified church where Johnny performs a black mass. One of the participants is Jessica Van Helsing (Stephanie Beacham), great granddaughter of Lawrence. Johnny Alucard is actually the descendant of Dracula's servant and he is using the black mass to resurrect Dracula from his ashes. Members of the group disappear and are later found drained of blood. Inspector Murray (Michael Coles) of Scotland Yard turns to occult specialist Lorrimer Van Helsing (also Cushing) for help. Lorrimer learns that Jessica is involved and suspects that Dracula has returned and is seeking revenge on his family. Lorrimer confronts Johnny in his home and discovers that he has also become a vampire. The two fight and Johnny is dispatched by exposure to sunlight and the clear running water of a shower. On a hunch, Lorrimer goes to the de-sanctified church where one of the bodies was found. There he finds a hypnotized Jessica laid out on an alter awaiting Dracula. Lorrimer stabs Dracula with a silver blade, throws holy water in his face, and pushes him into a pit filled with wooden stakes. Apparently Lorrimer Van Helsing believes that if something is worth doing, it is worth doing well.

The Satanic Rites of Dracula

Before *Dracula A.D. 1972* had proven itself to be a box office failure, the production of the sequel was already underway per the agreement between Hammer and Warner Bros. Initially the title was to be *Dracula Is Dead.... But Well and Living in London.* This was soon changed to the simpler but only slightly less ridiculous *Dracula Is Dead and Living in London.* Cushing and Lee returned, as did Michael Coles as Inspector Murray. The character of Jessica Van Helsing also came back, this time played by Joanna Lumley. Once again Don Houghton wrote the script and Alan Gibson directed. One of the main flaws of *Dracula A.D. 1972* was corrected as Dracula here has far more contact with the modern world: He assumes the identity of a business tycoon named D.D. Denham. In his scenes as Denham, Lee seems to be doing an imitation of Bela Lugosi's accent.

Shortly prior to the film's London release in January 1974, the title was changed to the far more palatable *The Satanic Rites of Dracula.* The title change didn't improve the film's prospects: It made disappointingly little money in England. Warner Bros., already smarting from the failure of *Dracula A.D. 1972,* decided not to release it in the

U.S. It was a pity not to give it a fighting chance as, in most respects, *Satanic Rites* is a better film than its predecessor. Lee has more to do and there are some memorable sequences, one in particular involving Joanna Lumley in a cellar full of vampire women. All things considered, it was a far more successful attempt to bring Dracula into modern times than *Dracula A.D. 1972*.

Several years later, Warner Bros. sold *Satanic Rites* to Max J. Rosenberg's company Dynamite Entertainment. The title was changed to *Count Dracula and His Vampire Bride* and it was finally given a paltry U.S. release in November 1978. Arthur Thirkell in *The London Daily Mail* found it to be "a horror movie with a touch of class," but *Variety* dismissed it as "silly, dull, and without a sense of humor."

The Plot: A branch of British Intelligence has been observing strange goings-on at the country estate Pelham House. Three high-ranking British government officials and a noted scientist, Professor Keeley (Freddie Jones), have been engaging in Black Mass rituals there. British Intelligence brings in Scotland Yard Inspector Murray (Michael Coles), who suggests they consult with occult specialist Lorrimer Van Helsing (Peter Cushing). Murray and Van Helsing's granddaughter Jessica (Joanne Lumley) go to Pelham House to investigate while Van Helsing pays a visit to Keeley. Jessica encounters five vampire women in the Pelham House cellar and she and Murray only just manage to escape the place. Meanwhile, Van Helsing discovers that Keeley has been developing a new and extremely virulent strain of the Black Plague, a project backed by a reclusive millionaire named D.D. Denham. A visit to Denham by Van Helsing exposes the tycoon as Count Dracula (Christopher Lee), who is engineering a plan to create a modern apocalypse which will destroy

Christopher Lee's finale for Hammer in *The Satanic Rites of Dracula* **(1973).**

mankind. Jessica is kidnapped as Dracula plans to perform a rite in which he will make her his immortal consort. Naturally, Van Helsing intervenes once again. His plans thwarted, an irate Dracula follows Van Helsing into the woods surrounding Pelham House and becomes conveniently enmeshed in the thorns of a hawthorn tree (Van Helsing has already explained that vampires abhor it because it represents Christ's crown of thorns). As Dracula struggles to free himself, Van Helsing grabs a wooden stake from a picket fence and drives it through Dracula's heart.

In the end, poor box office returns were more effective than any of the methods that Van Helsing used to destroy Dracula. While *Satanic Rites* was Christopher Lee's swan song as the count, Hammer would make another film featuring Dracula with another actor in the part.

Chapter 2

Hammer's Other Vampires

Although Dracula was their primary vampiric export, Hammer also dabbled with other fanged fiends in the '70s. Their Karnstein Trilogy and a film about Elisabeth Bathory are covered in other chapters in this book. That leaves three of Hammer's most unusual productions to be discussed here ... plus an unmade vampire film which was instrumental in causing the company to sink into financial ruin.

Vampire Circus

The idea for *Vampire Circus* came from producer Wilbur Stark and screenwriter George Baxt. Together they prepared a story treatment and presented it to Michael Carreras in early 1971. Michael was impressed but his father James, who ran Hammer, was not. He felt there was too much violence in the story and that it was certain to run afoul of the British censor. Michael persisted with *Vampire Circus* and hired Judson Kinberg to fashion a script from the story treatment. Stark was signed as producer and Robert Young hired to direct his first feature film. The movie began shooting in the late summer of 1971. Unfamiliar with Hammer's rapid style of filmmaking, Young fell behind schedule. When the six-week proposed schedule stretched into seven, Michael Carreras shut the production down. The filmed footage was given to editor Peter Musgrave and he was instructed to make do with what he had.

Although the finished film suffers somewhat from a rather rushed quality, not aided by an overabundance of characters, it is an imaginative and unique entry in Hammer's canon of vampire movies. Young provides many stylish directorial touches and Anthony Corlan, previously

2. Hammer's Other Vampires

the romantic lead in *Taste the Blood of Dracula*, makes a wonderfully feral gypsy vampire. *Vampire Circus* was released in England in April 1972 and six months later in the U.S. on a 20th Century–Fox double-bill with the much delayed U.S. release of *Countess Dracula*. Both films were heavily edited by Fox to get a PG rating; all the nudity and most of the bloodletting ended up on the cutting room floor. The Fox publicity campaign touted the double-bill as "The Greatest Blood-Show on Earth!" even though there was little blood on view in either movie.

Frederic Milstein said in his *Los Angeles Times* review, "Robert Young's true chiller, *Vampire Circus*, offers lots of real-looking teeth, believable gore and—save for a very lurid ending—a lot of pace, a certain sense of subtlety, and a definite, consistent style." Howard Thompson of *The New York Times* wrote, "Wise horror fans will skip *Vampire Circus*." Obviously this further proves that movies, like beauty, are all in the eye of the beholder.

The Plot: The vampire Count Mitterhouse (Robert Tayman) has been preying on the children of the village of Schtettel with the help of his human mistress Anna (Domini Blythe), wife of local schoolmaster Professor Mueller (Laurence Payne). When Anna abducts another child and takes her to the count, Mueller leads the villagers in an attack on the castle. In the ensuing fight, Mueller stakes Mitterhouse, who puts a curse on the people of Schtettel as he dies. The villagers torch the castle. presumably with Anna inside. Fifteen years later, a plague comes to Schtettel. Although roadblocks are set up to quarantine the village, the Circus of Nights suddenly appears, led by a gypsy woman (Adrienne Corri) and her companion Emil (Anthony Corlan).

Anthony Corlan as the gypsy vampire Emil in *Vampire Circus* (1972).

Despite its sinister atmosphere, the circus becomes a welcome diversion where the villagers can briefly forget their troubles. But then the townspeople mysteriously begin to die. The gypsy woman is actually Anna Mueller transformed and Emil is the cousin of Count Mitterhouse ... and a vampire. They have come to fulfill the Mitterhouse curse and return the count to life. Two of the circus performers are twins who are the vampire offspring of Anna and Count Mitterhouse. Eventually the evil purpose of the circus performers is discovered and the vampires are destroyed, but not before most of the characters involved have met with bloody deaths in the caverns beneath the castle.

Captain Kronos Vampire Hunter

In 1971, Brian Clemens and Albert Fennell scored a success producing *Dr. Jekyll and Sister Hyde* for Hammer. The following year, Michael Carreras invited them back to try their hands at a vampire story. Clemens, who had also written *Dr. Jekyll and Sister Hyde*, set to work on a script which would eschew the usual trappings of the Hammer vampire movies. In an interview with *ABC Film Review*, he said, "I sat through eight or nine vampire horror films and each had the same plot, the same basic story elements. I have tried to make *Kronos* as different as possible from these others." Clemens and Fennell were the team responsible for the popular TV series *The Avengers,* and Clemens decided to structure his story in the style of episodes from that show. So here we have John Steed and Emma Peel, in the persons of Captain Kronos and his sidekick Professor Grost, investigating mystifying murders while encountering odd characters and strange situations along the way, only in this case the main characters are vampire hunters, not secret agents.

At this point, Hammer desperately needed a hit, and a hit that could easily become a new series was even better. *Captain Kronos Vampire Hunter* seemed to possess all the elements destined for audience appeal and Hammer was already contemplating Kronos meeting Frankenstein and Dracula in future movies. In addition to writing and co-producing the film, Clemens also directed. He was given a larger budget and longer shooting schedule than usually afforded a Hammer film. A lot of hopes were riding on the picture and Michael Carreras wanted it done right. But as filming progressed, Carreras became disenchanted with Clemens' approach to the material. He felt that Clemens wasn't being faithful to the Hammer formula. Consequently, Carreras lost faith in the project and, upon completion, it was given a poor release in the U.K. It faired slightly better in the U.S. on a double-bill with *Frankenstein and the Monster from Hell*, which would become Hammer's last gasp of the type of gothic horror which had made the company famous.

Reviews were not kind. *Variety* called *Captain Kronos* "an uneven tease" and even the normally generous Kevin Thomas at *Los Angeles Times* thought it was "handsomely produced" but "tepid." However, the film quickly gained a cult following and it is now considered one of the best films of Hammer's later period. Indeed, it is hard to fathom the lack of enthusiasm from audiences, critics, and particularly Michael Carreras at the time of its release. Carreras had often said he hoped to steer Hammer in other directions and this would seem to have been a perfect opportunity to do just that.

The Plot: In the village of Durward, the mysterious deaths of several young women prompts Dr. Marcus (John Carson) to send for his friend Captain Kronos (Horst Janson). Kronos, a master swordsman, and his assistant Professor Grost (John Cater) are vampire hunters, and Marcus suspects that a vampire is responsible for the murders. Kronos and Grost conclude that a vampire is indeed the culprit but this is a vampire who drains people of their youth, not their blood. The deaths continue and Marcus himself is infected by the vampire's bite. His eventual death at the hands of Kronos and Grost reveals how the vampire may be destroyed, but first they must find out who it is. Their search leads them to the castle of Lady Durward (Wanda Ventham) and her children Paul (Shane Briant) and Sara (Lois Daine). There the mystery is finally solved and the vampire menace is eradicated.

The Legend of the 7 Golden Vampires

Was there ever a more troubled production in the history of Hammer horror than *The Legend of the 7 Golden Vampires*? I doubt it. What is most remarkable is that out of the madness came what I believe is one of the most inventive and entertaining of Hammer's '70s movies.

Golden Vampires came about from Michael Carreras' desire to expand Hammer's horizons and do something different, while still adhering to the formula which had made the company so successful. In January 1973, he took over ownership of the company from his father James Carreras. Michael had always leaned toward more exotic themes and locales. Many of the Hammer films with which he was previously involved attest to this: *The Mummy, The Stranglers of Bombay, The Terror of the Tongs, She, One Million Years B.C.,* etc.

Although Warner Bros. had been disappointed in the box office returns of *Dracula A.D. 1972* (*The Satanic Rites of Dracula* had yet to be released), they came to Michael with the idea that he should make another Dracula film for them. Kung fu films were then enjoying great popularity and Warner had recently financed a successful feature filmed in Hong Kong, *Enter the Dragon.* It was suggested that a Dracula film set in the Far East, and filmed in Hong Kong in conjunction with Shaw Brothers Studio, could be a viable project. At first Warner insisted that Christopher Lee and Peter Cushing be part of the package but, predictably, Lee refused to participate. This time, however, his absence was not a deal-breaker. Apparently kung fu was a more important element than Christopher Lee. John Forbes-Robertson, who had played the mysterious "Man in Black" in *The Vampire Lovers,* was hired to take on the part of Dracula. Don Houghton, who had written Hammer's two modern Dracula films, was given the duel tasks of writing the script and serving as producer. The talented and ever-reliable Roy Ward Baker was hired to direct. Peter Cushing returned as Van Helsing and popular martial arts star David Chiang played Chinese hero Hsi Ching.

In theory this must have all sounded very encouraging to Michael Carreras. But filmmaking in Hong Kong and England were worlds apart, and the production quickly dissolved into total chaos. The film ran over schedule and over budget.

Golden Vampires had its London premiere in August 1974 and went on to do big box office business in England and Asia. Oddly, Warner Bros. lost interest in it and declined to release it in the U.S. at all. American International offered to distribute the movie, but this never panned out. *Golden Vampires* went unreleased in the U.S. until 1978 when it was picked up by Max J. Rosenberg's new company Dynamite Entertainment. Rosenberg cut down the running time, eliminated and rearranged scenes, and changed the title to *The Seven Brothers Meet Dracula.* In a 1996 interview, Rosenberg told me with great relish, "[It] was a bad picture when we got it and an even worse one when we finished with it." Still, even in its bastardized form, the potential of the

2. Hammer's Other Vampires

Sacrificial maidens in the temple in *The Legend of the 7 Golden Vampires* **(1974).**

movie managed to show through to some extent. *Golden Vampires* is colorful and exciting, with a breadth of scope that many of the Hammer horrors lack. The martial arts action sequences are well integrated into the plot and never feel extraneous.

Warner's refusal to release the film in the U.S. hastened the demise of Hammer. Even Michael Carreras gave up on *Golden Vampires* and felt that "it wasn't such a good idea after all." A follow-up movie to be made in India, *Kali: Devil Bride of Dracula,* was not produced. Hammer never again was on strong financial footing after this film.

The Plot: In 1804, Transylvania's Castle Dracula is visited by a Chinese traveller, Kah (Chan Shen), high priest of the Temple of the 7 Golden Vampires in the Chinese village of Ping Kuei. Kah seeks the help of Dracula (John Forbes-Robertson) in resurrecting the dormant 7 Golden Vampires who will restore him to power over the village. Instead, Dracula assumes Kah's form and goes to China. A hundred years later, Professor Van Helsing (Peter Cushing) is lecturing on the legend of the 7 Golden Vampires to a skeptical audience at Chung King

University. Only Hsi Ching (David Chiang) is attentive. Ping Kuei is his ancestral village and, many years before, his grandfather was killed there while destroying one of the vampires. Hsi Ching convinces Van Helsing and his son Leyland (Robin Stewart) to journey to Ping Kuei to help him rid the village of the vampires who still plague it.

The expedition is financed by wealthy widow and adventuress Vanessa Buren (Julie Ege), who insists on going along on the trek. Accompanying them are Hsi Ching's six brothers and their sister Mai Kwei (Shih Szu). During the arduous journey, three vampires attack the group but are destroyed. When the expedition reaches Ping Kuei, the remaining three vampires, accompanied by their zombie minions, attack the village. Vanessa is bitten and turned into a vampire. As she bites Hsi Ching, he impales both Vanessa and himself on a bamboo stake. After two more vampires are destroyed, the last one abducts Mai Kwei and takes her to the Temple of the 7 Golden Vampires. Van Helsing and Leyland follow, dispatching the last vampire and rescuing Mai Kwei. When the danger seems over, Kah suddenly appears. Realizing who he really is, Van Helsing taunts Kah into resuming his true form of Dracula. The two long-standing enemies fight and Van Helsing impales Dracula with a silver spear. For the umpteenth and final time in a Hammer film, Dracula is reduced to dust.

Vampirella

You'd think that, after all the trouble Michael Carreras had with *The Legend of the 7 Golden Vampires*, he would have steered clear of making another vampire film. But such was not the case. In 1975, Hammer posed the question "What should we do now?" to readers of *Famous Monsters of Filmland* magazine. The response was: make a movie from the comic book *Vampirella*, which, like *Famous Monsters,* was a Warren Publication and a creation of Forrest J. Ackerman. Carreras thought this was a good idea and soon a full-page color ad on the back cover of *Famous Monsters* announced, "The movie you've been waiting for! *VAMPIRELLA*. A Major Motion Picture now in production from HAMMER FILMS. Coming your way in 1976!"

Christopher Wicking, who had written the scripts for Hammer's *Blood from the Mummy's Tomb* and *Demons of the Mind,* was hired to write the screenplay. Carreras approached Sam Arkoff at American International for the much-needed American funding and, initially,

2. Hammer's Other Vampires

Arkoff agreed to participate. Caroline Munro was considered for the part of Vampirella, the busty space vampire from the planet Drakulon, but she demurred because of the extremely skimpy costume that was a given for the role. Carreras, searching elsewhere for his leading lady, found her in *Playboy*: model Barbara Leigh.

Confident about the *Vampirella* project, Carreras attended the November 1975 Famous Monsters Monstercon in New York City accompanied by Leigh and Peter Cushing, who had been cast as Vampirella's sidekick, the magician Pendragon. The convention's souvenir book has an article about Carreras and his films which ends with the following quote: "And destined to top them all, Mr. Carreras promises us the shape of things to come: VAMPIRELLA!"

Barbara Leigh as Vampirella (1976) (courtesy Barbara Leigh).

Obviously Carreras' hopes were high. A year passed in which Gordon Hessler and John Hough were mentioned to direct (Hough being the final choice) and Wicking continued to refine the script. Then Arkoff withdrew AIP's financial support, in part because he felt that Leigh was not a sufficiently bankable personality to carry the picture. In 1976, I spoke with Dez Skinn, editor of *The House of Hammer* magazine, in his offices at Hammer House on Wardour Street in London. A poster for *Vampirella* was on the wall and I asked him about the status of the movie. He told me that Hammer was having difficulties obtaining the merchandising rights for the character from Warren Publications and he doubted at this point if the movie would ever be made. He was right: Hammer ended up footing the entire bill for developing a costly endeavor which came to nothing.

In 1978, Carreras announced Hammer's intention to make a movie called *Vlad the Impaler,* which had been a radio play written by Brian Hayles called *Lord Dracula.* Nothing much came of this project other than some vague discussions of who might play the lead. In 1979, a series of financial failures, including the large amount of money spent on *Vampirella,* put Hammer into Official Receivership, and the company was finished.

A version of *Vampirella* was eventually made in 1996 by Roger Corman's company Concorde for the Showtime cable TV network. Jim Wynorski directed Talisa Soto as Vampirella. It is so puerile and awful that, given the basic material, it makes one wonder if even Hammer could have done anything better with it. Obviously we'll never know.

Chapter 3

Other British Vampires

Although British producers were quick to capitalize on horror films in the wake of Hammer's early successes, vampire movies by other British companies were few and far between. The first of these was *Blood of the Vampire*, made by the producing team of Robert Baker and Monty Berman in 1958. The vampire in this gothic horror film is a scientist with a blood disorder rather than a conventional member of the undead. The 1965 Planet Films Production *Devils of Darkness* was the first British horror movie to place a vampire in a contemporary setting. *The Hand of Night* (1966) deals with a cult of vampires in Morocco while the 1967 Tigon-British Production *Blood Beast Terror* (aka *The Vampire Beast Craves Blood*) features a giant bloodsucking moth. Roman Polanski's *Dance of the Vampires* (aka *The Fearless Vampire Killers*, 1967) was an affectionate tribute to Hammer vampires. During this time period, Hammer produced five vampire movies of their own. The '70s film scene was dominated by Hammer vampires, and few other U.K. film companies attempted to compete.

Bloodsuckers

The 1970 British movie *Bloodsuckers* is a strange film with an even stranger production history. Based on Simon Raven's novel *Doctors Wear Scarlet*, it was filmed by director Robert Hartford-Davis as *Incense for the Damned*. Production stopped and started as money ran out and additional financing was secured. Post-production tampering by the producers included extensive editing, the addition of narration by Alexander Davion, the inclusion of a totally gratuitous psychedelic orgy scene (it runs a grueling seven minutes) and a pointless tacked-on ending. This caused Hartford-Davis to demand that his name be removed from the film entirely.

The germ of a decent movie is still there and it makes one wonder what Hartford-Davis' original film might have been like. Most likely it would have been much better than the fragmented mess we have now. *Bloodsuckers* certainly has an interesting cast and Desmond Dickinson's color location photography is often stunning. As it is now, it seems like two different movies. The first half, set in Greece, often plays like an espionage action film complete with Patrick Macnee, John Steed of *The Avengers*. The second half takes place at Oxford University and is more the stuff of a standard horror movie. In addition to top-billed Macnee and Davion, the film also stars Peter Cushing, Patrick Mower and Imogen Hassall, all of them Hammer veterans. Davion appeared in two Hammer horrors, *Paranoiac* and *The Plague of the Zombies*, before crossing the pond to play Ted Casablanca in the infamous trash-fest *Valley of the Dolls*. Mower appeared in Hammer's *The Devil Rides Out* and Hassall was in *When Dinosaurs Ruled the Earth*. She was a

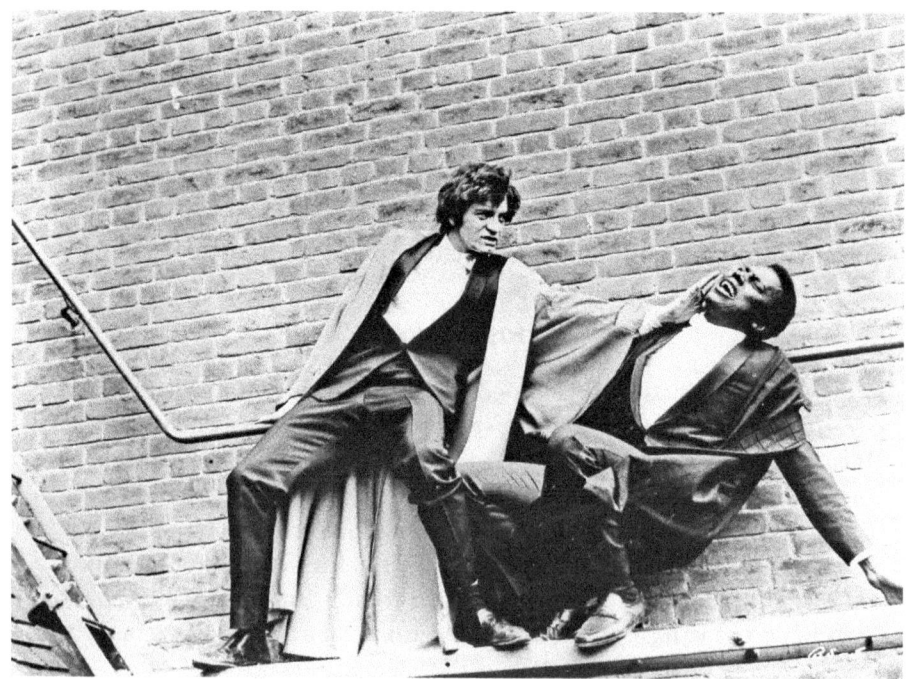

Patrick Mower attacks Johnny Sekka in *Bloodsuckers* (1970).

movie and television actress who was often a target of the British scandal tabloids. Tragically, she committed suicide at age 38 in 1980.

The Plot: Oxford professor Richard Fountain (Patrick Mower) goes on sabbatical to Greece to complete his book on Hellenic studies. When he fails to return, his friends Tony (Alexander Davion) and Bob (Johnny Sekka) and his fiancée Penelope (Madeleine Hind) go to Greece to find him. They learn from Brit expat Derek Longbow (Patrick Macnee) that Richard has fallen under the spell of jet-setting playgirl Chriseis (Imogen Hassall), the leader of a blood-drinking cult and possibly a vampire. Richard is eventually rescued by his friends but both Longbow and Chriseis are killed in the attempt. Richard returns to Oxford where he is pressured into marrying Penelope by her father, Oxford don Walter Goodrich (Peter Cushing). Richard begins to exhibit strange behavior and it becomes apparent that Chriseis' evil influence lives on. Occult expert Dr. Holstrom (Edward Woodward) tells Tony that vampirism is a sexual perversion and that Richard, who is apparently impotent, may be a homosexual sadomasochist. After an extremely hysterical outburst at an Oxford dinner honoring him, Richard bites Penelope in the throat, drinking her blood and killing her. Bob pursues Richard across the rooftops of Oxford. Richard falls and is impaled on an iron fence. The final scene shows Tony and Bob in a crypt about to drive stakes into both Richard and Penelope.

The House That Dripped Blood

Amicus Films was the closest thing to a rival that Hammer had in England but their approach to horror was quite different. While Hammer's films were often bloody and sexy, Amicus seldom showed blood; the glamour factor, so important to Hammer's success, was usually missing from the Amicus product. Amicus was the brainchild of American producers Max J. Rosenberg and Milton Subotsky, who had been drawn to England to make films because of the Eady Plan, a government subsidy provided to filmmakers in Britain to encourage the industry there.

The first horror movie under the Amicus banner, *Dr. Terror's House of Horrors* (1965), found inspiration in the famous 1945 Ealing Studios omnibus horror film *Dead of Night*. Noting Hammer's success (but only grudgingly acknowledging it), Rosenberg and Subotsky enlisted Hammer talent both in front of and behind the cameras. Thus,

Dr. Terror's House of Horrors was directed by Freddie Francis and starred Christopher Lee and Peter Cushing.

While vampires were a staple of Hammer, Amicus only dabbled with the subject occasionally. One of the *Dr. Terror's House of Horrors* stories was titled "Vampire" and starred a young Donald Sutherland as a man who suspects his new wife might be a vampire. The film was a moneymaker on both sides of the Atlantic. In the following years, Amicus produced more movies in the anthology format, *Tales from the Crypt* (1972) being the most famous and the most profitable.

The House That Dripped Blood (1971) was the third Amicus omnibus film and one of the best. It consists of four stories penned by Robert Bloch, the author of *Psycho*, who had previously scripted *The Skull* (1965) for Amicus. These four stories are presented within the framework of a police inspector investigating the disappearance of a film star. The actor lived in a house in which several mysterious incidents occurred involving prior tenants. In this book, we are concerned only with the final story, "The Cloak." For once Amicus decided to go the glamour route by casting Ingrid Pitt, who had just received a lot of attention for her role in Hammer's *The Vampire Lovers*. This was a smart move as her presence is the most memorable thing about the movie and got the production a lot of publicity at the time it was being made. First-time feature director Peter Duffell infused this sequence with a lot of humor which was met with approval by Subotsky but not by Rosenberg, who insisted that the humor be reduced. Although the approach did turn out comedic in some respects, "The Cloak" cannot be considered an out-and-out comedy as Duffell had originally intended. Nevertheless, this sequence has a much more

Ingrid Pitt puckers up for a kiss in *The House That Dripped Blood* (1971).

lighthearted touch than the three which precede it. It was also the sequence which garnered the most favorable critical comments. Roger Greenspun in his *New York Times* review (April 22, 1971) found the other stories "dull in development" but he singled out "The Cloak" as "a piece of quite charming silliness" and praised the inclusion of Pitt "for her face and figure." This is selling her contribution short but at least Greenspun could appreciate her on some level.

The Plot: Horror movie actor Paul Henderson (Jon Pertwee) rents a house near the movie studio where he is starring as a vampire in *Curse of the Bloodsuckers*. Unhappy with his costume, Paul buys a cloak from a vintage theatrical costumier. During filming the next day, Paul dons the cloak and really bites his co-star Carla (Ingrid Pitt), who walks off the set in a rage. That evening Paul puts on the cloak at home and at the stroke of midnight he sprouts fangs and begins to levitate. The next day at the studio, Carla is standoffish but agrees to forgive Paul if he will take her to dinner. Later, at Paul's home, he attempts to show Carla the effects of the cloak but nothing happens. Paul realizes that his cloak has been replaced by one from the studio just as Carla produces his cloak and puts it around her shoulders. As she rises into the air, she says through her fangs, "We loved your films so much we wanted you to become one of us forever."

The Vault of Horror

When Amicus' 1972 production *Tales from the Crypt*, based on the EC Comics, turned out to be a huge financial success, the company logically turned again to EC for inspiration. The result, *The Vault of Horror* (1973), has the same structure as the previous Amicus omnibus films but by this time the multi-story format was becoming very formulaic. Roy Ward Baker directed despite feeling that the movie was not his cup of tea. He thought the approach was too flippant. This opinion was shared by EC publisher William Gaines, who disliked the movie so much that he refused to give Amicus the rights to film any more EC stories. The U.S. version was also edited, reducing the shock value even more. In *The Vault of Horror,* the framing device has five businessmen, trapped in a basement room in their office building, trading stories about their nightmares. The first of these stories is "Midnight Mess."

The Plot: Rogers (Daniel Massey) traces his estranged sister (Anna

Massey) to the village where she now lives. Their father has recently died and left his fortune to her. Rogers stabs her to death and then goes to a nearby restaurant for a celebratory dinner. The menu is an odd assortment of "delicacies" and Rogers is the only patron who casts a reflection in the mirrors. As he begins to realize just what sort of restaurant it is, Rogers' sister walks in holding the knife with which he "killed" her. She smiles, showing her fangs, and joins the rest of the vampire diners in sharing her brother's blood.

In 1973 Amicus made the last of their anthology movies, *From Beyond the Grave,* this time basing the stories on the writings of R. Chetwynd-Hayes. After leaving Amicus Films, Subotsky continued to make horror films using the anthology format. In his last movie *The Monster Club* (1981), he again uses the stories of Chetwynd-Hayes. The most notable thing about this movie is that it is the only time Vincent Price played a vampire in his long career as a horror film star.

Chapter 4

American International

During the 1950s and '60s, American International Pictures, those premier purveyors of exploitation movies in the U.S., only dabbled in vampire films. Their sole vampiric output from the '50s was *Blood of Dracula* (1957), the plot being a variation of the company's big hit *I Was a Teenage Werewolf.* Sandra Harrison plays Nancy Perkins, a girl with a troubled family life and a chip on her shoulder, who is sent to the Sherwood School for Girls. Her science teacher, Miss Branding (Louise Louis), thinks that Nancy would be a perfect subject for her experiments which turn Nancy into a weird-looking vampire. There is little of the standard vampire lore here other than a discussion by some police detectives which involves a mention of Dracula, presumably to justify the title of the picture.

The next AIP vampire outing is one of the finest movies in all of vampire cinema. Produced in Italy in 1960 under the title *La maschera del demonio* (*The Mask of Satan*) and directed by the great Mario Bava, it was picked up for U.S. distribution by AIP, who changed the title to *Black Sunday*. The movie was a huge success. Four years later AIP, bought another Italian-made, Bava-directed film, *I tre volti della paura* (*Three Faces of Fear*). They changed the title to *Black Sabbath*. The film consists of three stories, one of which is "The Wurdulak," starring Boris Karloff as a 19th century Russian vampire.

During the '60s, AIP also released *Goliath and the Vampires* (1964) and *Planet of the Vampires* (1965) but, despite their titles, these were not vampire movies per se. The first is a sword-and-sandal film with a villain who drinks the blood of sacrificial virgins from a goblet, the second an outer space saga in which invisible alien entities drain men of their minds, rather than their blood. A more conventional vampire

Blood of Dracula **(1957) with Sandra Harrison and Jerry Blaine (pictured) was AIP's first vampire movie.**

was the green skinned femme fatale of *Queen of Blood* (1966). This egg-laying alien lives on the blood of the Earth astronauts who rescue her from a crashed spaceship found on another planet.

It wasn't until the '70s that AIP got into vampire movies in a big way with the milestone genre movies *The Vampire Lovers* (see the chapter on Carmilla), *Count Yorga—Vampire* and *Blacula*.

An ad for *Black Sunday* (1970).

Count Yorga—Vampire

In 1970, college pals Michael Macready and Michael Murphy had the idea of making a low-budget softcore porn movie called *The Loves of Count Iorga*. They secured the services of Marsha Jordan, who had previously appeared in such softcore films as *The Ramrodder* and *Lady Godiva Rides Again* (both 1969). Michael's father, actor George Macready, suggested that they try and get Robert Quarry to star in the picture. The idea intrigued Quarry but he felt that the movie would work better as a straight horror film and he agreed to appear in it only if it were made as such. Bob Kelljan wrote and directed the movie, which was shot on weekends and evenings at an eventual cost of just $64,000.

AIP purchased the distribution rights and retitled it *Count Yorga—Vampire*. According to the pressbook, the film had an enthusiastic reception at an invitational advance showing for the UCLA Cinema Department, alma mater of Macready and Murphy. After a fairly steady diet of gothic vampire movies from Hammer, the moviegoing public was apparently ready for a vampire film set in modern times and *Count Yorga—Vampire* went on to be a big success for AIP with a take of $1,300,000. I'm sure the movie was also helped by AIP's typically unsubtle ad campaign: "Almost Too Unbelievable, Unspeakable, Unbearable to Watch! Don't Dare Come Alone!"

The two main things differentiating *Count Yorga—Vampire* from other current vampire films are the setting (contemporary Los Angeles) and Quarry's performance, which at times verges on tongue-in-cheek. Nevertheless, he manages to maintain a successful balance between the humorous and the horrifying. The part earned Quarry horror star status and gained him a contract with AIP, where he was featured in five more films. Quarry later claimed that AIP was grooming him to be the next Vincent Price but this is debatable as both had their final roles for the company in *Madhouse* (1974). *Count Yorga* got some respectable reviews. Roger Greenspun in the *New York Times* (November 12, 1970) said the film "has snatches of seedy insight into the paraphernalia of vampirism and, in Robert Quarry, the best chief vampire I have seen in years." *Variety* (June 17, 1970) found it to be "a low-budget programmer with enough bite to turn an easy profit," which certainly turned out to be an accurate estimation.

The Plot: A crate arrives at the Port of Los Angeles and is transported by truck to a mansion on the outskirts of the city. A few weeks later, Donna (Donna Anders) enlists her neighbor Count Yorga (Robert Quarry), newly arrived from Bulgaria, to conduct a seance in the hope of contacting her recently deceased mother (Marsha Jordan). Among those attending the seance are Donna's boyfriend Michael (Michael Macready), Erica (Judith Lang) and Erica's boyfriend Paul (Michael Murphy). During the séance, Yorga brings Donna under his hypnotic influence. Later that night, he attacks Erica, drinking some of her blood. The next morning, Erica is examined by her friend, Dr. James Hayes (Roger Perry). He is puzzled by her considerable blood loss and the two tiny puncture marks on her neck. Then Paul comes home to find Erica eating her pet kitten. Hayes realizes that he must seriously consider the possibility that she has become the victim of a vampire. That night, Erica vanishes and Paul goes to Yorga's mansion in search of her. When Donna also disappears, Hayes and Michael decide to go to their rescue. What they find is a houseful of vampires including Donna's undead mother, who had been Yorga's first victim. During the ensuing fight between the living and the undead, there are more victims before Yorga is staked in the heart by Michael.

The Deathmaster

After the surprising success of *Count Yorga—Vampire*, Robert Quarry wanted to make another horror film before his AIP contract took effect at the beginning of 1971 (Quarry's contract stipulated that he could not appear in any non–AIP horror movies). His idea was to play a character similar to Charles Manson who, in addition to being a cult leader, is also a vampire. Originally the project was called *Khorda*. It would be produced by Quarry and his friend Fred Sadoff and directed by another friend, actor Ray Danton. The budget was set at $110,000. Filming got underway in November 1970 under the title *Guru Vampire* and went quickly and without problems. The problems came later.

When the film was completed, Quarry invited *Count Yorga* producer Michael Macready to a screening. Macready then contacted AIP chairman of the board Samuel Z. Arkoff and told him that Quarry had made a film which plagiarized *Count Yorga*. Arkoff threatened a lawsuit unless Quarry and company agreed to sell AIP the distribution rights to the movie. The film was sold to AIP for a pittance; AIP shelved it for almost two years before it giving it a poor release in August 1972

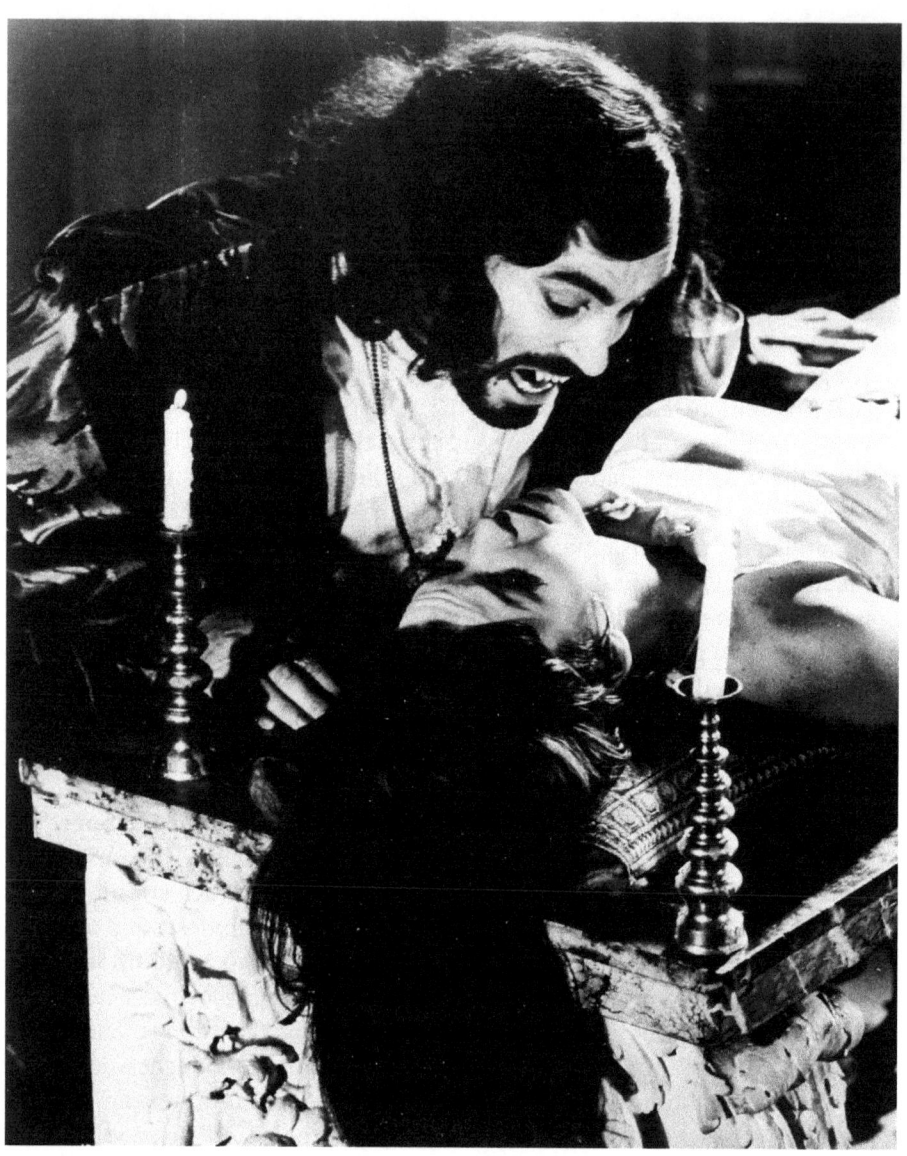

The Deathmaster **(1972) (Robert Quarry) claims another victim (Brenda Dickson).**

under the title *The Deathmaster*. Since "Deathmaster" was a term used to describe the vampire count in the advertising for the Yorga films, it was a logical title change to help connect it to Quarry's other movies. The film could just as easily have been called *Count Yorga—Hippie* as that is basically what it is. Quarry gives a very Yorga-like performance as Khorda, only this time he does it wearing a shoulder-length wig and a kaftan.

In later years, Quarry confessed that *The Deathmaster* had only been conceived with the intention of capitalizing on the first Yorga film to make a quick buck. In many ways, it comes across as just that, but there is still enough good and unusual about it, to make it worth watching. Not the least of which is seeing how the Topanga Canyon counterculture hippie community looked in the early '70s. This may well be the only filmed document of that place during this period of time.

In his *Chicago Sun Times* review (September 14, 1972), Roger Ebert was decidedly unimpressed. Although he thought that Quarry was "an old hand at the vampire game ... and knows all the tricks by now," he found the rest of the characters wanting: "They are so dumb that they have had to learn to speak English by watching old AIP exploitation movies, and their dialog is eight years out of date."

The Plot: A coffin washes up on the beach in Malibu and is taken to a large house in Topanga Canyon where a local hippie commune hangs out. It contains a mysterious Guru named Khorda, who also happens to be a vampire. He assumes leadership of the commune and all the members become his acolytes with the exception of Pico (Bill Ewing), who suspects all is not quite as it should be with Khorda. When Pico is attacked by a female vampire, he flees for his life. The only person he can convince of the truth is Pop (John Fiedler), the owner of a local store, and together they return to Khorda's hangout to try and rescue Pico's girlfriend Rona (Brenda Dickson). By now, all of Khorda's followers have been turned into vampires. When Pico finally stakes Khorda, the rest of his gang turn into piles of dust. Groovy!

The Return of Count Yorga

Nothing spawns imitation like success so in 1971 AIP commissioned the same team that made *Count Yorga—Vampire* to do a sequel (originally titled *Yorga Returns*). This time, thanks to AIPs involvement, the budget was nearly twice that of the original. Michael Macready returned as producer and Bob Kelljan once again wrote (with Yvonne Wilder) and directed what eventually became *The Return of Count Yorga*. Robert Quarry reprised his role of Count Yorga. Roger Perry also returns, this time as a different character but in name only as he basically does exactly what he did in the first film. The other returning actor is Edward Walsh, who once again plays Yorga's hulking manservant Brudah although he was supposedly killed off in the first movie.

Because of its larger budget, *Return* has better production values than its predecessor. The cast is good, though Mariette Hartley is a bit lethargic as the female lead. She seems to be in a trance long before Yorga actually puts her in one. There are a couple of wonderfully frightening set pieces but the pace seems slower this time around and the second half is mostly a retread of the original.

Although many of the necessary ingredients were in place, this film failed to find favor with audiences and critics. *Cinefantastique* reviewer Robert L. Jerome thought the larger budget was a handicap rather than an advantage: "As a follow-up film, it suffers a familiar stigma; too much money but too little inspiration.... [T]he crude, poverty-row vitality which made the original something of a 'sleeper' is absent." *Variety* (August 11, 1971), however, thought the film was an "excellent follow-up to *Count Yorga—Vampire*."

More films featuring Count Yorga were planned by AIP, including one in which Yorga meets Dr. Phibes, but the failure of *The Return of Count Yorga* to live up to box office expectations drove a stake into the heart of that idea.

The Plot: Despite his being staked in the heart at the end of the previous film, Count Yorga is alive and well (with no explanation whatsoever) and now living in the San Francisco area. The movie opens as Tommy (Philip Frame), a boy who resides in a nearby orphanage, chases a ball through the woods and into a neglected cemetery. As dusk falls, vampire women crawl out of their

Robert Quarry strikes a contemplative pose in *The Return of Count Yorga* (1971).

graves and begin to pursue him. Attempting to escape, he runs smack into Yorga. Later, a Halloween costume party is given at the orphanage. Yorga attends and meets Cynthia Nelson (Mariette Hartley), who works at the orphanage and lives with her family nearby. That night Yorga sends his horde of vampire brides to Cynthia's home where they slaughter her family and then carry her off to Yorga's mansion. Yorga hypnotizes Cynthia, making her forget the murder of her family, and keeps her a prisoner in his house. Her fiancée, Dr. David Baldwin (Roger Perry), begins to suspect the truth about Yorga and convinces the police to join him in confronting the vampire in his lair. After much mayhem, Cynthia comes to her senses and throws an axe into Yorga's heart. But the horror is not over for Cynthia and David.

Blacula

With their Count Yorga series terminated and *The Deathmaster* collecting dust on the shelf, AIP decided to try their hand at a new kind of vampire movie, one that would capitalize on the increasingly popular trend of blaxploitation films. *Cotton Comes to Harlem* (1970) and *Shaft* (1971) had already proven that there was a huge market for black action films so AIP decided to add horror to the mix. The producers approached actor-singer William Marshall to play the lead. He agreed, provided that he had some input as to how the character was portrayed. Although several of Marshall's obituaries claimed that he had created the character of Blacula, he didn't. He did refine what the writers had created and gave the character some much-needed dignity. It was Marshall who came up with the idea of naming the character Mamuwalde (in the original script he was Andrew Brown) and giving him a background as an African prince. William Crain was hired to direct his first feature film. He would go on to direct episodes on a number of popular TV series and the blaxploitation horror film *Dr. Black, Mr. Hyde* (1976).

Shot in Los Angeles with a budget of $500,000 in early 1972, *Blacula* has some of the same gritty atmosphere as the first Count Yorga film. In fact, the shots showing the arrival of the crate containing Blacula's coffin at the Port of Los Angeles and its subsequent transport by truck through the streets of Los Angeles are lifted from the beginning of *Count Yorga—Vampire*.

Despite the absurd-sounding premise, there is much in *Blacula* to recommend. First and foremost is William Marshall. An actor with a sonorous bass voice, he was already established as an opera singer and Shakespearean actor when he was cast in his first film role as a Haitian rebel in the underrated *Lydia Bailey* (1952). Throughout a lengthy and varied career, Marshall never failed to enhance every movie he appeared in. Looking back, it is odd to think he is now best remembered as Blacula and the "King of Cartoons" on the Pee-wee Herman TV show. *Blacula* also boasts a memorable supporting cast headed by the beautiful and talented Vonetta McGee in the female lead. Also worth mentioning is the inventive animated title design of Sandy Dvore which, accompanied by Gene Page's music, gets *Blacula* off to a snappy start.

Blacula was released in August 1972, exactly one year after *The Return of Count Yorga*. As with most AIP films, reviews were mixed. *Variety* (August 2, 1972) said, "William Marshall portrays title role with a flourish and gets first rate support right down the line." But Roger Greenspun at the *New York Times* (August 26, 1972) opined, "Anybody who goes to a vampire movie expecting sense is in serious trouble, and *Blacula* offers less sense than most." AIP laughed all the way to the bank because *Blacula* went on to become one of their biggest moneymakers of 1972, grossing over a million dollars. Never a company to overlook a good thing, AIP released, during the next five years, over 20 blaxploitation movies.

The Plot: *Blacula* opens with a prologue set in Transylvania in 1780. An African prince, Mamuwalde (William Marshall), and his wife Luva (Vonetta McGee) have come to Castle Dracula to try and convince the count (Charles Macaulay) to join them in their attempts to stop the African slave trade. Instead, Dracula turns Mamuwalde into a vampire and kills Luva. Cut to 1972 and two interior decorators (two of the worst gay stereotypes you're ever likely to see) buy the contents of Castle Dracula and ship it to Los Angeles. Among the artifacts is a large locked coffin which the decorators open, unleashing Blacula on the modern world. While flitting about town turning people into vampires, Blacula meets Tina (also Vonetta McGee), the spitting image of his dead wife. Blacula comes clean with Tina about his nocturnal habits and she agrees to become his consort. Meanwhile, police pathologist Gordon Thomas (Thalmus Rasulala) has been investigating the rash of vampire killings which all point to Tina's new boyfriend. During the final confrontation, Tina is shot by a policeman before Blacula can turn her into a vampire. In despair, Blacula walks out into the daylight and is destroyed by the sun.

Scream, Blacula, Scream

Considering the money *Blacula* made, a sequel was a no-brainer for AIP. Two suggested titles were *Blacula Is Beautiful* and *Blacula Lives Again* but a contest among AIP employees resulted in the final title of *Scream, Blacula, Scream.* Bob Kelljan, who had directed both of the Yorga films, was chosen over William Crain as director. Once again Sandy Dvore supplied the clever animated credits, this time accompanied by the music of Bill Marx, son of Harpo and composer for both Yorga films.

Cast-wise, the only hold-over from the original film was William Marshall. His co-star was the Queen of AIP blaxploitation movies, Pam Grier, who had already made a name for herself in *Black Mama, White Mama* and *Coffy* (both 1973). Grier is especially good in *Scream, Blacula, Scream*, showing a far move sensitive and vulnerable side than her AIP blaxploitation roles generally offered her. Don Mitchell, a regular on the *Ironside* TV series, was cast as the hero. The film "introduces" Richard Lawson, who has worked in film and TV ever since, including playing the recurring character Nick Kimball in the seventh season of *Dynasty.*

Under the direction of Bob Kelljan the *Blacula* sequel has a much darker tone than its predecessor; you'll hear no "Bloody Mary" cocktail jokes here. Also, Marshall gives a much more Yorga-like performance. Although the mix of voodoo and vampires is a good one, some of the scenes are a rehash of ones from the Yorga films. A subdued verbal confrontation between Marshall and Mitchell plays just like one between Roger Perry and Robert Quarry in *Count Yorga—Vampire.* The climactic police assault on the mansion Blacula shares with his vampire followers is just like the finale of *The Return of Count Yorga.*

On July 19, 1973, *New York Times* reviewer Roger Greenspun wrote, "Despite all its blood-letting, *Scream, Blacula, Scream* fails for lack of incident, weakness of invention, insufficient story." In the *Chicago Sun Times* (July 4, 1973), Roger Ebert said that Marshall and Grier "both have a lot of style; so much, indeed, that it stands out in this routine movie." Although the film was another moneymaker for

Blacula (William Marshall) prepares to strike Denny (Lynne Moody) in *Scream Blacula Scream* **(1973).**

AIP and the inconclusive ending seemed ripe for a sequel, no further Blacula films were forthcoming.

The Plot: Following the death of voodoo priestess Mamaloi, her mantle is bequeathed to Lisa (Pam Grier). This decision is challenged by the evil Willis (Richard Lawson). To get revenge on Lisa, he performs a voodoo ceremony which resurrects Mamuwalde (aka Blacula). The vampire immediately bites Willis and makes him his acolyte. At a party, Lisa and her boyfriend Justin (Don Mitchell) meet Mamuwalde and are impressed with his knowledge of African history. That same night, there are several murders, the victims drained of their blood. Eventually Mamuwalde reveals to Lisa that he is the vampire Blacula and begs her to use voodoo to exorcise him of the vampire curse. As Lisa performs the ceremony, the police, led by Justin, descend on Willis' mansion which is now filled with Blacula's vampire disciples. The voodoo ceremony is interrupted and the film ends as Blacula, still a vampire, screams in anger and frustration.

The Bat People aka *It Lives by Night*

The Bat People (1974) was conceived by writer-producer Lou Shaw, a frequent contributor of scripts for TV series and producer of the Americanized version of *Hannah, Queen of the Vampires* (1973). The film was originally called *Angel of Fear* and a song of the same title is played under the opening credits. Real-life husband and wife Stewart Moss and Marianne McAndrew play the movie couple Dr. John and Cathy Beck. Moss, a sort of poor man's Bradford Dillman, appeared frequently in film and TV prior to *The Bat People*. For McAndrew, it was the fourth and final film in her very brief movie career. She had been hired for the high-profile role of Irene Malloy in the 1969 movie version of the hit Broadway musical *Hello, Dolly!* Although she inexplicably got some positive recognition for her (awful) performance, the movie was an expensive disaster. Her next part was a supporting role in Russ Meyer's *The Seven Minutes* (1971), a considerable comedown. Surely the most notable thing about *The Bat People* is that it features Stan Winston's first monster makeup, but even that is a poor indication of what was to follow in his illustrious monster-creating career.

Stewart Moss as one of *The Bat People* (1974) ... the *only* one, in fact.

AIP picked up *Angel of Fear* for distribution and changed the title to *It Lives by Night*. After a brief release under this title, AIP had second thoughts and gave it a wider release as *The Bat People*. Whatever the title, the movie is a miserable, slow-moving endeavor which was not a success on any level.

The Plot: While on a belated honeymoon, Dr. John Beck (Stewart Moss) and his wife Cathy (Marianne McAndrew) stop off at Carlsbad Caverns on their way to the ski slopes. While they are nosing around the caves, John is bitten by a bat. Next stop, the infirmary where he is given an anti-rabies shot. His reaction is so violent that he is hospitalized for observation. That night, one of the nurses is bloodily murdered. Sheriff Ward (Michael Pataki), a nasty redneck, suspects Dr. Beck. While Ward relentlessly dogs Beck, he also tries to put the make on Cathy, who is repulsed by his advances. Several murders later, Ward brings Cathy back to the caverns where her husband, now fully transformed into a "bat person," has taken refuge. Ward is killed by a horde of bats and Cathy, now pregnant with a "bat baby," goes into the cave to join John.

Love at First Bite

American International struck gold with their vampire comedy *Love at First Bite* (1979). George Hamilton is Count Vladimir Dracula and even a pound of William Tuttle's white face makeup cannot conceal his unnatural tan, making him the healthiest looking vampire ever. Both Hamilton and Arte Johnson are intermittently amusing but Richard Benjamin is hammy and annoying. Susan Saint James, wearing a series of awful wigs, is badly miscast as a glamorous model. Making cameo appearances are Sherman Hemsley and Isabel Sanford from the popular TV series *The Jeffersons*. Michael Pataki, a '70s vampire alumnae, shows up briefly as a gangster.

Love at First Bite is basically a series of one-liners strung together by a minimal plot. Viewed now, it comes across as a collection of politically incorrect gags. There are black jokes, Puerto Rican jokes, gay jokes and Jewish jokes. Of course, the entire movie is one big vampire joke, but the Coalition Against the Defamation of Vampires hasn't protested yet. In her April 13, 1979, *New York Times* review, Janet Maslin said, "Some of the film's ethnic jokes skate by on very thin ice," but in general she found the movie to be "a scream." *People* (April 23,

1979) said, "Although the film is occasionally hilarious, many jokes thud." Both reviewers thought Hamilton was "delightful," which, on occavsion, he is.

The Plot: Count Dracula (George Hamilton) and his servant Renfield (Arte Johnson) are ousted from Castle Dracula by the Rumanian government who are going to turn the place into an athletic training center. They go to New York City, where the count hopes to meet fashion model Cindy Sondheim (Susan Saint James), who is the spitting image of Dracula's great lost love, Mina Harker. Cindy's psychiatrist boyfriend, Jeffrey Rosenberg (Richard Benjamin), is the grandson of the vampire's old nemesis Dr. Van Helsing. Dracula tries to get the girl and the psychiatrist tries to kill Dracula. And that's about it for the plot.

George Hamilton is Dracula in *Love at First Bite* **(1979).**

Chapter 5

I Am Legend

Richard Matheson's 1954 novel *I Am Legend* begins in the future year 1976, after a plague has turned the world's population into vampires. The one "normal" man left alive, Robert Neville, spends his time hunting down and killing the vampires.

In 1957, Hammer Films bought the rights and hired the author to write the screenplay. The film was to be called *Night Creatures*. Hammer submitted the script to the British Board of Film Censors for approval, and they rejected it outright. Hammer decided not to make the movie. A few years later, Hammer producer Anthony Hinds sold the property to American producer Robert L. Lippert. Lippert turned the script over to William Leicester for revisions and then unsuccessfully attempted to get Fritz Lang to direct. When Sidney Salkow was signed to direct, Matheson wanted nothing more to do with the project. He used the pseudonym Logan Swanson for his writing credit so he could distance himself from the movie but still get paid for his contributions.

Although the novel was set in Los Angeles, Lippert decided to cut costs and film in Italy (no location is established in the movie itself). The finished film was released in 1964 as *The Last Man on Earth* and stars Vincent Price as Robert Morgan (not Neville). The vampires in it are shambling, zombie-like creatures who are still repelled by the traditional garlic and mirrors and dispatched by a stake in the heart.

Matheson felt that Price was miscast but Price is excellent in a role which is largely silent with his voiceover narration. The stark black-and-white photography works to the film's advantage by stressing the bleakness of the surroundings. All things considered, *The Last Man on Earth* would turn out to be the most satisfying movie version of *I Am Legend*.

The Omega Man

The second screen adaptation of *I Am Legend*, *The Omega Man* deviates greatly from the source novel. This was the second of three nihilistic science fiction films starring Charlton Heston, the first being *Planet of the Apes* and the last *Soylent Green*. *The Omega Man* abandons the traditional vampire element almost entirely. The plague victims become night-prowling albinos who dress in black capes and act like a post-apocalyptic version of the Spanish Inquisition. Since this is the '70s, there is also a Blaxploitation element in the person of Rosalind Cash ("Up against the wall, you mutha! Or I'll bust yo ass!"). She is Heston's love interest and the object of one of cinema's earliest interracial love scenes. Roger Ebert, in his January 1, 1971, *Chicago Sun Times* review, opined, "The ghouls, alas, are a little too ridiculous to quite fulfill their function in the movie." Ebert also makes an uninformed comment at the end of his review: "*The Omega Man* is based on an uncredited novel by Richard Matheson. I wonder if it was *I Am Legend*, a very good work about the last normal man left in a world of vampires." Duh, Roger.

The Plot: In 1975, germ warfare between China and Russia results in a plague which destroys most of the world's population. Two years later, former military scientist Col. Robert Neville (Charlton Heston), immune to the plague, is spending his days in Los Angeles watching the movie *Woodstock* and his nights fighting "The Family." Members of the Family are plague survivors who have mutated into nocturnal albinos. They are led by former TV newscaster Matthias (Anthony Zerbe). He and his people are determined to kill Neville who, to their way of thinking, represents all that went wrong in the past. When Neville is captured by the Family, he is given a hasty trial and condemned to be burned at the stake in Dodger Stadium. At the last minute he is rescued by Lisa (Rosalind Cash) and Dutch (Paul Koslo), the guardians of a group of children who have also survived the plague. The children lack Neville's immunity, so there is the possibility of them turning into mutant albinos. Lisa's younger brother Richie (Eric Laneuville) is slowly converting already and she wants Neville to use his scientific expertise to try and reverse the process. Neville succeeds in making a serum from his blood that cures Richie, who then goes to the Family to tell them of the cure. Not interested in a cure, they kill Richie and set out to destroy Neville and all he stands for. Lisa suddenly and inexplicably mutates, although it has already been established that this is a slow process. She betrays Neville to the Family, and Matthias kills him with a spear. Neville dies in the position of the crucified Christ. Dutch and the children drive off with the antidote he has concocted.

Although *The Omega Man* should probably have put the novel to cinematic rest once and for all, there was still enough life left for yet another version in 2007. Although it uses the title *I Am Legend*, this version is based more on *The Omega Man* than the source novel, from which it deviates even further. This time Will Smith is Robert Neville, a military scientist trying to find a cure for a manmade virus which has killed most of the world's population. The vampire factor has again been jettisoned in favor of mutants, herein called "Darkseekers" because they can't stand the light. These CGI-rendered mutants are bald-headed, carnivorous creatures who move fast and have ridiculously big mouths. Once the Darkseekers take center stage the movie deteriorates rapidly. This is unfortunate because the film does have a very effective first hour with Smith and his dog roaming the deserted streets of New York City. A few months before the theatrical release of *I Am Legend*, Asylum Films, those infamous purveyors of cheap direct-to-video ripoffs, released *I Am Omega*, which attempted to cash in on the Smith movie and follows the same basic plot line.

CHAPTER 6

Carmilla Karnstein

J. Sheridan Le Fanu's novella *Carmilla* was originally serialized in *The Dark Blue* magazine beginning in late 1871. The following year, it was included in Le Fanu's five-story collection *In a Glass Darkly*. It relates the tale of a young girl, Laura, and how she falls prey to female vampire Carmilla Karnstein. Not only does Carmilla drink Laura's blood but it is intimated that she is a sexual predator as well.

Prior to the 1970s, *Carmilla* served as the inspiration for three films, none of which were straightforward story adaptations. The first was Carl Dreyer's 1932 *Vampyr*, which uses elements from *In a Glass Darkly* including the idea of a predatory female vampire. Roger Vadim's *Blood and Roses* (1960) tells of a modern woman named Carmilla, possessed by the spirit of her vampire ancestor. This is the most beautiful cinematic interpretation of the story if not the most faithful. *Terror in the Crypt* (*La cripta e l'incubo*, 1964) uses more plot elements from *Carmilla* than its predecessors but still fails to be true to the source. At times this film seems to draw as much influence from Mario Bava's *Black Sunday* as it does from the original novella as both movies present a close association between witchcraft and vampirism.

The Vampire Lovers

One of the most influential vampire movies of the '70s is *The Vampire Lovers* (1970). Not only did it spawn a subgenre, the lesbian vampire film, but it marked a turning point for Hammer Films as well with its emphasis on overt sexuality. Hammer had introduced the erotic element to vampire movies years before but *The Vampire Lovers* took it to a new level.

The idea for *The Vampire Lovers* originated with British producers Harry Fine and Michael Style and writer Tudor Gates. They approached Hammer's James Carreras with it, and he in turn set up a deal for a co-production with American International. This was to be the only co-production between these two titans of exploitation cinema. Gates then set about writing a script which would be a faithful adaptation of *Carmilla* but would also stress the sexuality only hinted at in the original story. In the source material, the lesbian element is only suggested but

Ingrid Pitt as Mircalla Karnstein in *The Vampire Lovers* (1970).

Gates' script wallops you over the head with it. So much so that both the British movie censorship board and AIP had some misgivings about its production. But Hammer's track record for producing quality movies eventually allayed their fears to some extent.

Finding an actress to play the lead role was of paramount importance. Carreras met starlet Ingrid Pitt at a party and, after interviewing her, all involved agreed that she would be perfect for the part. Such was her appeal that, although Pitt would only make two films for Hammer, she remained ever afterward associated with the studio in fans' minds. She was proud of that association for the remainder of her life.

Roy Ward Baker, who had already helmed three Hammer features, now directed his first gothic horror film. In his hands, what could have been crass and exploitative material was instead filmed with taste, style and humor. *The Vampire Lovers* opened in October 1970 in both England and the U.S. In A.H. Weiler's February 4, 1971, *New York Times* review, he said, "*The Vampire Lovers*, praise be, does manage to be a departure from a hackneyed, bloody norm. It also is professionally directed, opulently staged and sexy to boot." Other critics were less kind but audiences apparently didn't care as the film went on to make money for both Hammer and AIP.

The Plot: A countess (Dawn Addams) and her daughter Marcilla (Ingrid Pitt) are guests at a party given by General Spielsdorf (Peter Cushing). When the countess is called away unexpectedly, Marcilla is invited to stay on as a houseguest. Spielsdorf's niece Laura (Pippa Steel) and Marcilla quickly become devoted companions. Laura soon falls ill and dies. News of her death reaches Roger Morton (George Cole) and his daughter Emma (Madeline Smith), who was Laura's best friend. While horseback riding, Emma and her father witness a coach accident and a young woman passenger, Carmilla (also Ingrid Pitt), is taken to the Morton home to recover. Carmilla is actually Mircalla Karnstein, a member of a family of vampires thought to have been destroyed years before. Emma soon succumbs to Carmilla's amorous advances, falling under her spell as the life is drained out of her. In the end, Morton and Spielsdorf join forces to destroy the vampire before she can kill Emma.

Carmilla on Stage

The end of 1970 proved to be a popular time for *Carmilla*. A month after the October opening of *The Vampire Lovers*, LaMama, the innovative experimental theatre group in New York City's East Village, premiered their multimedia opera *Carmilla: A Vampire Tale*. It was written and directed by Wilford Leach with Ben Johnston composing the score. In this avant-garde production, Laura and Carmilla are seated together on a large settee. The other characters play their parts as faces carved into the wood of the couch. The opera opened to good reviews (*The New York Times* called it "fantastic") and it ran for six weeks. During that time, the show built a considerable reputation and a cult following. It was revived at LaMama in 1972, 1976, 1986 and 2003.

Lust for a Vampire

The Vampire Lovers was a hit on both sides of the Atlantic. James Carreras had anticipated this and plans for a follow-up were in the works while the first film was still in post-production. It had been hoped that AIP would again participate financially but they declined. The new script, again by Tudor Gates, was called *To Love a Vampire* and Terence Fisher was set to direct with Peter Cushing in the important supporting role of history professor Giles Barton. Before filming got underway, Fisher was hit by a car while crossing a street and hospitalized. Cushing was also forced to bow out because of his wife's declining health. Jimmy Sangster replaced Fisher as director and Ralph Bates took over the Barton part. To play Carmilla Karnstein, Hammer's latest star discovery was the stunningly beautiful Danish actress Yutte Stensgaard.

According to writer Gates, shortly before the film's release, producer Michael Style decided to change the title to *Lust for a Vampire*, which Style felt was more exploitable. It may have been more exploitable but it is a much less appropriate title considering the storyline's strong romantic angle. Roger Greenspun pointed this out in his *New York Times* review (September 4, 1971): "It is love, not lust, that Richard makes to Mircalla outside the castle, and it is love that makes her hesitate long enough to take a burning stake in her bosom while she is being exorcised at the end." Sangster professed no love for this film,

Count and Countess Karnstein (Mike Raven and Barbara Jefford) have Carmilla (Yutte Stensgaard) under their control in *Lust for a Vampire* (1970).

but it is not the lamentable misfire he claimed. With the pastel color scheme, leisurely pacing and lush background score, *Lust for a Vampire* often seems more like a gothic romance than a horror film. As such, it is certainly unique in Hammer's canon of vampire movies.

The Plot: Using the blood of a young peasant girl, Count and Countess Karnstein (Mike Raven and Barbara Jefford) resurrect their daughter Carmilla (Yutte Stensgaard). Under the name Mircalla, she enrolls at a girls' finishing school for located near the ruins of Karnstein Castle. There she can prey on other students at will. One of her teachers, Giles Barton (Ralph Bates), is fascinated by the history of the Karnsteins and, while researching the subject, he comes to realize who Mircalla really is. When he confronts her with this knowledge and offers to become her disciple, she kills him. Richard Lestrange (Michael Johnson), another teacher, falls in love with Mircalla and she responds in kind. When the truth about the vampire family is discovered, the villagers set fire to Karnstein Castle where a burning stake pierces Mircalla's heart and destroys her.

Twins of Evil

When producer Michael Style saw the Collinson Twins in *Playboy* magazine, he approached Tudor Gates with the idea of writing a vampire story centered on twin sisters. James Carreras was impressed with the idea and Gates was given the go-ahead to write the screenplay with the proviso that there would be a leading role suitable for Peter Cushing. Along with several other sets of twins, Mary and Madeleine Collinson were interviewed, and they got the parts. Peter Cushing was signed to play the puritanical vampire hunter Gustave Weil, Damien Thomas was cast as Count Karnstein, and Katya Wyeth played the small but pivotal role of Mircalla Karnstein. *Twins of Evil* is often lumped into the lesbian vampire genre but, unlike the prior two films, it has no lesbian element. Upon release, the film got some enthusiastic reviews. Foremost among them was Kevin Thomas, who said in his *L.A. Times* review (August 25, 1972) that *Twins of Evil* was among Hammer's "most sophisticated horror pictures."

The Plot: When their parents die, Frieda and Maria Gellhorn (Madeleine and Mary Collinson) are sent to live with their Aunt Katy (Kathleen Byron) and Uncle Gustav (Peter Cushing) in the village of Karnstein. The twins learn that their uncle is the leader of a fanatical

Evil twin Frieda (Madeleine Collinson) kills Dennis Price in *Twins of Evil* (1971).

religious group, the Brotherhood, that seeks out women suspected of being witches or vampires and burns them at the stake. Maria is afraid of her uncle but Frieda defies him by allying herself with the evil Count Karnstein (Damien Thomas). Karnstein has recently been turned into a vampire by his undead ancestor Mircalla and he quickly makes Frieda his vampire consort. When the Brotherhood discovers Frieda drinking the blood of a victim, she is taken to jail and sentenced to be burned. Karnstein switches Maria for Frieda and the innocent sister is nearly executed before the deception is revealed. Gustav leads the villagers in an assault on Karnstein Castle. Frieda is beheaded and Count Karnstein is staked, but at the cost of Gustav's life.

The Hammer Karnstein Chronology

The timeline of the three Hammer Karnstein films has raised some questions. Rather than seeing the movies as separate entities with a similar theme, some fans prefer to tie them together into one cohesive whole. I recently re-viewed the trilogy and made a few notes regarding the chronology of the stories.

The *Vampire Lovers* prologue takes place in 1794. The story proper is set several years later, placing it in the early 1800s. The dates on Mircalla Karnstein's tomb are 1522–1546.

Lust for a Vampire is set in 1830. The dates on Carmilla Karnstein's tomb are 1688–1710.

Although it is often assumed that Yutte Stensgaard plays the same character as Ingrid Pitt in the first film, this isn't accurate. The Carmilla of *Lust for a Vampire* is a descendent of Mircalla in *The Vampire Lovers*. In the film, Karnstein historian Giles Barton explains that children were often given names which were anagrams of relatives.

Twins of Evil is actually a prequel to the two other films, set in a year never specified. (The movie's *Hammer House of Horror* comic book adaptation places it in the 17th century.) The only date shown in the film is on a bust of Mircalla Karnstein: "Died 1547." Although the date is one year off from that shown in *The Vampire Lovers*, I think it can be assumed that this Mircalla is the same character as the one in the first film. Too bad Ingrid Pitt didn't come back to make a cameo appearance in the part.

Hammer's Unfilmed Karnstein Project

After the release of *Lust for a Vampire,* Hammer announced that the follow-up would be *Village of the Vampires.* Tudor Gates wrote a brief story outline before it was decided to proceed with *Twins of Evil* instead. Anticipating that a fourth Karnstein movie would be produced by Hammer, Gates wrote a detailed treatment for *Village of the Vampires,* which he now called *The Vampire Virgins.* But after *Twins of Evil,* Hammer never made another Karnstein film.

In 1990, an actress friend of mine was eager to make a vampire movie. She told me that she wanted it to be in the style of the Hammer Karnstein films, which she loved. I knew that Gates had mentioned a fourth Karnstein story many years before so I contacted him to see if I could get a copy of the script. Here, in part, was his reply:

> *Vampire Virgins* does not exist in script form but in a lengthy story outline, almost a treatment. I would have sent it to you with pleasure but, checking through my files, I could not find it. I know it must be around somewhere.

> It remains an ambition of mine to write a fourth Karnstein story and I have a feeling that the time is right. I think the new generation of horror films has rather lost its way. I am convinced that a new "Hammer"-style horror (though not under Hammer) would be a big hit, rekindling today's audiences' imaginations in the way those films used to do.
>
> Even if I can't find the storyline, it is absolutely clear in my mind and I could script it tomorrow. Should I find it, I will send you a copy, of course.

Gates was true to his word and a few years later I did receive a copy of the treatment. In February 1999 I got this final letter from him regarding *The Vampire Virgins*:

> It may just be that *Vampire Virgins* will shortly go into production. Not with Hammer—which is now really nothing more than a library—but for a new American company.
>
> They have indicated they would be prepared to finance the script development and I am hoping to tie this matter up very soon.
>
> If all goes well, the plan is to go on and make more horror films—to be a new Hammer, in effect—and this has long been an ambition.
>
> So ... let's keep our fingers crossed for *Vampire Virgins*.

Tudor Gates died in 2007 and the story was never filmed.

The Plot: The elders of the village of Karnstein hire bounty hunters Kurt Manning and Johann Mayer to rid them of the vampires which plague the town. They promise to pay 100 marks for the head of every vampire the hunters bring them. Kurt and Johann live up to their part of the agreement and bring the elders the heads of 11 vampires. When the elders renege, Kurt retaliates by kidnapping four of the village daughters to hold for ransom. He sequesters them in the ruins of Karnstein Castle. Unknown to Kurt, Count Karnstein still lives and he wastes no time turning the girls into vampires. The girls quickly begin to prey on the men of the village. Now Kurt and Johann must hunt down the four vampire girls and Count Karnstein or face hanging by the villagers.

The Blood Spattered Bride

The oddest movie adaption of *Carmilla* has got to be the 1972 Spanish production *The Blood Spattered Bride* (aka *La novia ensangrentada: The Bloody Bride*), written and directed by Vicente Aranda. Aranda was noted in his country for employing an experimental style in his filmmaking. He was a pioneer in helping to establish the avant-garde movement in Spanish cinema during the late '60s. Although he had been making movies since 1964, *The Blood Spattered Bride* was the first of his films to receive widespread international distribution, eventually getting a U.S. release in 1974 on a double bill with *I Dismember Mama.*

Carmilla's story is barely discernible within the framework of the often confusing plotline, no doubt a reflection of Aranda's avant-garde preferences. *The Blood Spattered Bride* seems more concerned with the perils of marrying the wrong man than with vampires. The sexually naive bride is so fearful of her hyper-masculine husband (who is never named) that a lesbian relationship with a female vampire becomes a welcome alternative. The film is definitely an example of style over substance and it takes the sexual elements far beyond what Hammer had done in their Karnstein trilogy. Following *The Blood Spattered Bride*, Aranda's films would often focus on sexually explicit themes but he never returned to the horror genre to express them. In *The Blood Spattered Bride,* the vampire is Mircala-Carmila Karstein instead of using the correct spellings of the names.

The Plot: Newlywed Susan (Maribel Martin) is taken by her husband (Simón Andreu) to his ancestral home, a large chateau in the forest. Once there, his increasingly violent sexual demands frighten Susan and she eventually withholds sex from him entirely. While searching the chateau's cellar, she finds a painting of Mircala Karstein and learns that 200 years ago, she was a bride who killed her husband on their wedding night and then disappeared. Shortly thereafter, Susan sees a mysterious woman in the forest who also visits her in her nightmares. While wandering on a nearby beach, the husband comes across a naked woman who is apparently suffering from amnesia. He takes her to the chateau and Susan recognizes her as the woman in her dreams. Her name is Carmila. Susan and Carmila become close, excluding the husband entirely. Carmila encourages Susan to hate her husband by saying, "He has pierced your flesh to humiliate you. He has spat inside your body to enslave you." When the husband discovers bite marks on Susan's neck, she reacts violently and tries to stab him with the dagger Mircala used to murder her husband. Carmila and Susan leave the chateau and the husband discovers them naked together inside a coffin at the site of Mircala Karstein's tomb. He shoots the coffin full of holes with his rifle and then cuts out their hearts.

Although the 1978 Mexican film *Alucarda—The Daughter of*

Darkness incorporates some basic ideas from *Carmilla,* the movie is about witchcraft and demonic possession, not vampires. The story involves two teenage girls in a Catholic convent who become possessed by demons. Because of the title, the film has often been mistakenly included on lists of movies in the vampire genre.

Chapter 7

Elisabeth Bathory

The Hungarian Countess Elisabeth (or Erzsebet) Bathory (1560–1641) is one of the most notorious "historical vampires," second only to Vlad Tepes (1431–1477), prince of Wallachia, whom Bram Stoker used as the model for the character of Count Dracula. Infamously known as "The Bloody Countess," Bathory reportedly tortured and murdered 650 women, often bathing in their blood with the belief that it helped preserve her youth and beauty. Her noble rank prevented her execution so, as punishment for her crimes, she ended her days imprisoned within her own castle.

Her exploits were a prime subject for horror movies and in the permissive era of the '70s her character found incarnation in a variety of motion pictures, none of which comes close to representing the unbelievably gruesome facts of her real life story.

Countess Dracula

The idea for the first movie based on the Bathory saga began with historian Gabriel Ronay, who had done considerable research on the historical figure. He took his findings to Hungarian producer Alexander Paal who, with fellow Hungarian Peter Sasdy, wrote a story treatment which they presented to James Carreras at Hammer. *The Vampire Lovers'* success and the popularity of its star Ingrid Pitt had Hammer searching for another suitable property in which to feature her. An Elisabeth Bathory movie seemed the perfect vehicle. Jeremy Paul was hired by Hammer to write a screenplay from the Paal-Sasdy story. Paal was hired as producer and Sasdy, who had previously directed Hammer's stylish *Taste the Blood of Dracula*, was signed to direct.

Paul's screenplay eschews the more gruesome aspects of Bathory's crimes and instead concentrates on the countess' obsession with regaining her youth via bathing in the blood of virgins. Consequently, instead of a representation of the historical facts about Countess Bathory, the script is concocted from a few facts and a lot of fantasy. After reading the script, Pitt was disappointed at the lack of horror elements. In later years she told author Wayne Kinsey, "There wasn't enough horror in it. It had beautiful sets and costumes but there was no horror." This seems to have been the general consensus as far as audiences were concerned when the film was released in England in February 1971. With the title *Countess Dracula*, moviegoers expected a typical Hammer horror, which it was not, and it ended up being a box office disappointment for the company. But British reviewers were more complimentary to the film than they were to the majority of Hammer's productions. *Monthly Film Bulletin* went so far as to compare the movie's "romantic imagery" to Keats.

No one was more disappointed with the outcome than Ingrid Pitt, who discovered, upon viewing the finished film, that all of her dialogue had been re-dubbed by another actress. Although Pitt felt that her performance had been ruined, she is still wonderful in the role and she never looked more beautiful. In addition to Pitt and a fine supporting cast, *Countess Dracula* also has much to recommend it from a technical standpoint. The production is one of Hammer's most atmospheric and opulent-looking, with art director Philip Harrison making brilliant use of sets left over from *Anne of the Thousand Days* (1969). Also worthy of praise are the outstanding costume design of Raymond Hughes and the beautiful background score by Harry Robinson.

Ingrid Pitt as Elisabeth Bathory in ***Countess Dracula*** **(1971).**

Countess Dracula remained unreleased in the U.S. until October 1972 when 20th Century–Fox double-billed it with Hammer's *Vampire Circus*. Howard Thompson gave *Countess Dracula* a very good review in *The New York Times* (October 12, 1972), saying in part, "The horror uncoils steadily, cushioned by a kind of stylish relish on all sides, including the acting."

The Plot: The recently widowed Countess Elisabeth (Ingrid Pitt), a bitter, cruel old woman, is greatly feared by her subjects. When she injures a maidservant in a fit of anger, she is splashed with the girl's blood. It turns out to have a miraculous rejuvenating effect on her skin. Elisabeth kills the girl and bathes in her blood, which restores the beauty she had enjoyed in her youth. Impersonating her own absent daughter Ilona (Leslie Anne Down), Elisabeth sets her sights on a handsome young soldier, Imre Toth (Sandor Eles), and soon they become lovers. The restorative effects of the blood are temporary and Elisabeth must kill again and again to maintain her youthful appearance. All of this takes its toll on Elisabeth's sanity, which eventually costs Imre his

Countess Dracula (1971) (Ingrid Pitt) **is surprised in her bath of blood.**

life. Finally exposed as the monster she is, an aged Elisabeth awaits the hangman in a prison cell as the peasant women outside revile her as "Devil Woman" and "Countess Dracula" (thereby justifying the title of the movie).

Daughters of Darkness

The year 1971 continued to be a good one for Elisabeth Bathory. Six months after the release of *Countess Dracula*, "The Bloody Countess" was back on the screen in the Belgian film *Daughters of Darkness* (*Les Lèvres rouges/The Red Lips*), directed by Harry Kumel, set in contemporary times. French actress Delphine Seyrig plays Countess Elisabeth Bathory as a sort of vampiric lesbian Auntie Mame. Beautiful and eccentric, this Elisabeth is actually a vampire who has lived through the ages by drinking the blood of her victims rather than bathing in it. John Karlen, who played Willie Loomis on TV's *Dark Shadows*, co-starred.

Stylish, gruesome and erotic, the film took audiences by surprise and became a cult favorite. In many ways it recalls the dreamlike lyricism of Roger Vadim's *Blood and Roses* (1960) and the female protagonists of both films meet a similar fate. Contemporary *Daughters of Darkness* reviews were generally positive. Howard Thompson (*New York Times*, May 29, 1971) found the film to be "subtle, stately, stunningly colored and exquisitely directed." Roger Ebert (*Chicago Sun Times*, April 6, 1972) gave it a typically jokey and dismissive review but did concede that it was "a fairly stylish vampire movie." The film's reputation has grown over the years and now it is rightly considered a classic example of screen horror. Stunningly gowned by Bernard Perris, Delphine Seyrig deserves the most praise for her unforgettable portrayal of that self-admitted "outmoded character," the ageless Countess Bathory.

The Plot: Stefan (John Karlen) and Valerie (Danielle Ouimet), newlyweds en route from Switzerland to his home in London. miss the ferry and must spend the night in a deserted seaside hotel at Ostend, Belgium. Two other guests arrive, Countess Elisabeth Bathory (Delphine Seyrig) and her young companion Ilona (Andrea Rau). The countess attempts to ingratiate herself with the couple but Valerie is distrustful. A series of murders has occurred in the nearby city of Bruges; the victims, all young women, have been drained of blood.

Valerie realizes that her husband and the countess are hiding some very sinister secrets. When Stefan accidentally kills Ilona, he and Valerie become further entrapped by the countess' machinations and there seems little hope of escape for either of them. After murdering Stefan, the countess and Valerie, who has become her new companion, drive off together. The rising sun causes Valerie to crash the car, with fatal results for one of them.

The Legend of Blood Castle

Delphine Seyrig as Countess Bathory in *Daughters of Darkness* (1971).

The Legend of Blood Castle (1973) is one of those European horror movies that makes very little sense. This might work in a film by Mario Bava where the cinematic elements compensate for the poor script but *The Legend of Blood Castle* also suffers from pedestrian direction and an almost total lack of atmosphere. This Spanish/Italian co-production was directed by Jorge Grau, a Spanish director who would make his mark on horror cinema the following year with the excellent zombie film *Let Sleeping Corpses Lie*. *The Legend of Blood Castle* was known in Italy as *Le vergini cavalcano la morte* (*The Virgins Ride Death*) and in Spain as *Ceremonia sangrienta* (*Blood Ceremony*). Whatever the title, it is a mishmash of ideas that don't really gel. It reinforces what a good film Hammer's *Countess Dracula* is.

The Plot: In 1807, the villagers of Cajlice, Hungary, use a virgin boy on a white horse to lead them to the grave of a vampire. When the grave of a recently deceased local doctor is opened, his corpse is in a position indicating he was buried alive. A stake is driven through his heart and the corpse is put on trial to determine whether he was a vampire. One of the jurors is the Marquess Karl Ziemmer (Espartaco

Santoni). His wife, Erzsebet Bathory (Lucia Bosé), Marquise of Cajlice, is a descendant of the infamous "Bloody Countess" and, like her ancestor, dreads growing old. Erzsebet strikes a servant girl and her blood splatters on the Marquise's hand, making the skin momentarily smooth and youthful. The blood of a dove fails to yield the same results so, with the help of her faithful servant Nodriza (Ana Farra), Erzsebet gets the blood of a little girl, which has the rejuvenating effect. Karl is a sadist more interested in his falcons than his wife. Determined to share something with her husband, Erzsebet concocts a scheme in which Karl will appear to have died and returned as a vampire. He will bring the local village girls to the castle where Erzsebet can bathe in their blood. The plan satisfies Karl's sadism and provides the blood that Erzsebet needs. Soon the villagers are fearing that another vampire is in their midst. When Karl brings home the village innkeeper's pretty daughter Marina (Ewa Aulin), Erzsebet suddenly becomes jealous and stabs him to death as he is killing the girl. Now it is Karl's corpse which must go on trial for vampirism. Erzsebet confesses their scheme and, as Karl's accomplice in murder, she is walled alive within her castle.

Immoral Tales

Countess Erzsebet is also featured in the 1974 anthology film *Immoral Tales* (*Contes immoraux*), made in France by Polish director Walerian Borowczyk. "Bathory," the third of its four erotic stories, stars Paloma Picasso, the youngest daughter of Pablo, as the countess. It is her only film role to date. Borowczyk based this account of Countess Bathory on the 1962 prose work *Erzebet Bathory la Comtesse sanglante* by French poet Valentine Penrose. In "Bathory," a group of young peasant women are brought to the castle to admire the exquisite gown of the countess. Instead they rip it and themselves to shreds, thereby supplying the countess with the blood she must bathe in to insure her eternal youth. It's all very odd, to say the least.

Thirst

The 1979 Australian film *Thirst*, a deft combination of science fiction and horror, deals with a cult of vampires who abduct a descendant of Elisabeth Bathory. Coming at the end of the vampire cycle of the '70s, it offers a refreshing new take on the genre. *Thirst* was the theatrical debut of Rob Hardy, a director with a huge body of TV work before and after. Extensive location photography was done in Melbourne at Montsalvat, an artists compound created by Justus Jorgensen in 1934 (and now a popular tourist destination). The movie adaptation of Anne Rice's vampire novel *Queen of the Damned* (2002) also used Montsalvat as a location.

Leading lady Chantal Contouri had already appeared in the Australian comedy vampire film *Barry McKenzie Holds His Own* (1974). Contouri also starred in producer Antony I. Ginnane's previous film *Snapshot* (aka *The Day After Halloween*), and he hoped that *Thirst* would make her an international star. She later appeared frequently in TV soap operas and was last reported managing a restaurant in Adelaide. David Hemmings and Henry Silva were cast to give the film more international appeal. *Thirst* is an amazingly good-looking film, particularly considering the meager budget of 750,000 Australian dollars.

The Plot: Kate Davis (Chantal Contouri) is abducted from her home and taken to a remote research facility. This is "The Farm" of the Brotherhood, an organization of vampires with 70,000 members worldwide. It is run by Dr. Fraser (David Hemmings), Mrs. Barker (Shirley Cameron), Dr. Gauss (Henry Silva) and the mysterious Mr. Hodge (Max Phipps). Kate has been taken because she is a direct descendent of Elisabeth Bathory and they want her to be the organization's symbolic figurehead. Kate is told that there is nothing supernatural about the Brotherhood but that it is made up of a super race of the ultimate aristocrats, of which she is one. The Farm is a dairy where young, complacent human "cows" are repeatedly drained of blood which is then packaged in milk cartons and shipped to Brotherhood members. Mrs. Barker cheerfully tells Kate, "The dairy brings our lifestyle up to date." Kate witnesses a symbolic ritual in which a vampire with glowing red eyes and silver fangs drinks the blood of a human sacrifice. Repulsed, she attempts to escape from the Farm but is quickly recaptured. Since she will not voluntarily join their ranks, Kate is put through a series of hallucinatory treatments to break down her resolve. Afterwards, Kate is returned to her home and for a while it seems as though she has accepted her new lifestyle. But when she again resists the blood urge, she and her boyfriend Derek (Rod Mullinar) are both taken back to the Farm in one last desperate attempt to convert her.

Chapter 8

Deadlier Than the Male

Carmilla and Elisabeth Bathory were not the only lethal ladies in movies with a predilection for the blood of their own gender. In *Dracula's Daughter*, the 1936 sequel to *Dracula*, vampire Gloria Holden seduces a down-on-her-luck streetwalker (Nan Grey) and drinks her blood. This scene was pretty racy stuff for the time. *Blood and Roses* (1960) also had some subtle Sapphic undertones but it wasn't until the '70s that female vampires finally let it all hang out, both literally and figuratively. After the 1970 release of *The Vampire Lovers*, female vampires bared their fangs and their breasts with equal regularity. Female nudity became so frequent that it was often laughable and the lesbian angle, only hinted at in *Dracula's Daughter* and *Blood and Roses,* was now as commonplace an element as wooden stakes and crosses.

A prime example of this silliness occurs in the otherwise sexually tame *Count Yorga—Vampire*. Count Yorga sits on a tacky makeshift throne in his basement and wills two female vampires to "get it on" for his amusement. The scene cuts abruptly before anything really happens so perhaps this was a leftover from when *Count Yorga* was still being conceived of as a softcore porn film. Nevertheless, what remains of the scene is totally gratuitous. But don't think for a minute that female vampires went exclusively for the ladies. There were plenty of male victims too. The Sexual Revolution made it possible for filmmakers to take advantage of a newly permissive attitude in motion pictures. And the U.S. ratings system, established in 1968, made sure the kiddies didn't get exposed to anything that was too "permissive." I was just old enough by 1970 to see it all!

8. Deadlier Than the Male

The Velvet Vampire

The *Velvet Vampire* of the title is Diana Le Fanu (Celeste Yarnell), a nod to *Carmilla* author J. Sheridan Le Fanu. Like Countess Bathory in *Daughters of Darkness*, Diana insinuates herself into the lives of a young married couple, but this time the setting is a sprawling desert residence rather than a deserted seaside hotel. It has been suggested that *The Velvet Vampire* is a typical Roger Corman–New World Pictures ripoff, made to cash in on the success of *Daughters of Darkness*. This seems unlikely considering it would have been rather difficult for Corman to gauge the success of a movie that hadn't even opened yet. Since the latter didn't show up in U.S. theaters until a few weeks after *The Velvet Vampire*, it would seem that the plot similarities are mere coincidence with both films a reflection of the sexual attitudes of the time.

Velvet Vampire director Stephanie Rothman already had some experience with Corman and vampires. Corman bought a 1963 thriller made in Yugoslavia and hired Jack Hill to write and direct additional scenes in order to release it as *Blood Bath*. In Hill's version, mad artist William Campbell dips the bodies of his murdered models in wax. Unhappy with the final result, Corman brought in Rothman to rewrite some of the material and direct additional footage. In Rothman's rewrite, the artist turns into a vampire. *Blood Bath* was released on a 1966 AIP double bill with the space vampire movie *Queen of Blood*. It later showed up on TV under the title *Track of the Vampire*.

In 1970, Rothman directed *The Student Nurses* which turned out to be a big success for New World Pictures. Corman wanted her to do a follow-up but instead Rothman presented him with a script called *Through the Looking Glass*, written by Maurice Jules, her husband Charles Swartz and herself. Corman liked the script but hated the title, which was changed to the far more exploitable *The Velvet Vampire*.

In the end, Corman was not satisfied with the finished film as he felt it lacked the necessary exploitation elements for this type of picture. It is easy to understand his disappointment as the movie seems to have art house, rather than grindhouse, pretensions. There is plenty of nudity (both male and female) but action and gore are kept to a minimum. Actually *The Velvet Vampire* is a near-perfect example of a particular style of sleazy '70s filmmaking. It has an amateurish quality due to crude, overlit cinematography and uniformly bad acting. The dialogue

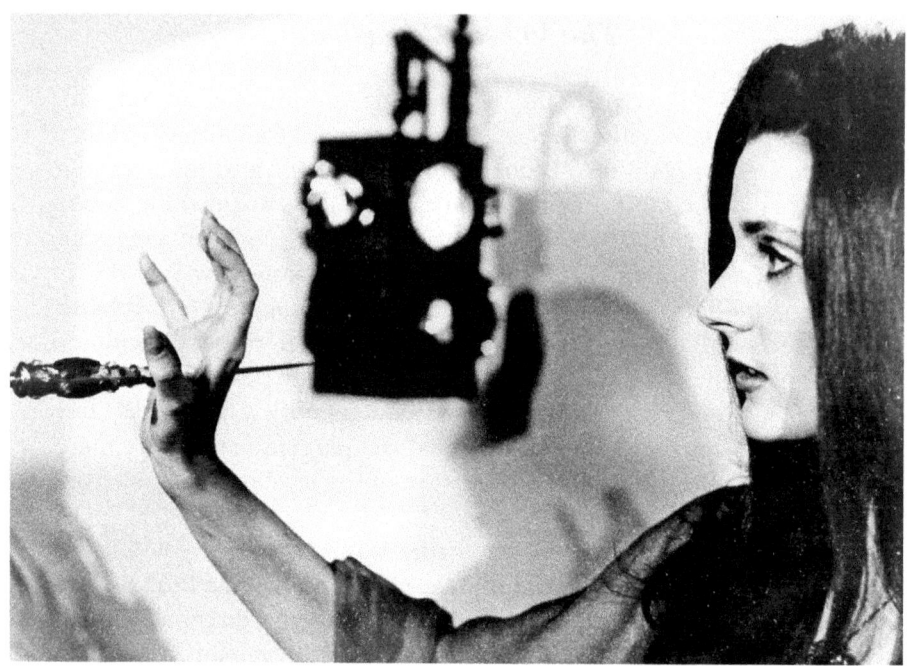

Diana Le Fanu (Celeste Yarnell) gets the point in *The Velvet Vampire* (1971).

is delivered in exactly the same flat style by all the cast members. Perhaps this was intentional, but to what purpose? Nevertheless, like so many of the low-budget productions from this period, it is still compelling and, with the desert setting, it does try to be a little bit different. *The Velvet Vampire* was released by New World Pictures in October 1971 on a double bill with the Italian horror film *Scream of the Demon Lover*.

The Plot: Lee and Susan Ritter (Michael Blodgett and Sherry Miles) meet a beautiful woman named Diane (Celeste Yarnall) at an art opening held at the Stoker (wink!) Gallery. Diane seems immediately taken with Lee and invites the couple to visit her at her desert home for the weekend. Annoying airhead Susan suspects Diane's motives and doesn't want to go but eventually gives in. Upon arriving at her remote home, the couple meet Diane's devoted manservant Juan (Jerry Daniels), who claims to have been taken in as a child by Diane, although they appear to be about the same age. The dates on the tombstone of Diane's deceased husband, Victor Le Fanu, would also indicate that she is much older than she looks. Although it first appears that Diane has

Celeste Yarnell attempts to put the bite on Sherry Miles in *The Velvet Vampire* (1971).

invited them so that she can seduce Lee, it later seems as if she is also trying to put the make on Susan. Diane kills both Juan and Lee by biting their necks and drinking their blood. She then pursues an escaping Susan on a Greyhound bus bound for Los Angeles. While Susan is being chased through historic Olvera Street, she notices that Diane is repelled by the huge cross monument erected there. Susan and some cross-wielding tourists surround Diane and force her into the direct sunlight, which kills her. Susan is safe at last ... or is she?

Let's Scare Jessica to Death

Let's Scare Jessica to Death (1971) is a film which never manages to live up to the sensationalism of its evocative title. It is, instead, a rather sedate affair which Roger Greenspun of the *New York Times* quite rightly called "Hippie Vampire" in his August 28, 1971, review. Filmed in Connecticut, the movie has a late '60s vibe complete with one character warbling a folk song. The settings are rural and lovely and the performances, except for Zohra Lampert, are laid back to the point of somnambulism. Lampert gives a performance so overwrought that it has to rank as one of the most eccentric ever captured on film. The writers claimed Le Fanu's *Carmilla* was their inspiration but finding a connection to that story is a bit of a stretch. *Let's Scare Jessica to Death* seems more of a ghost story with the vampire element thrown in for the sake of exploitation. The original title was *What Killed Sam Dorker?* which would shift the focus to a relatively minor incident in the movie and wouldn't make a lot of sense. Whatever the title, the movie is certainly an odd one. Not popular with critics or audiences at the time of its release, it has since enjoyed a loyal cult following.

The Plot: Duncan (Barton Heyman) moves his mentally fragile wife Jessica (Zohra Lampert) from Manhattan to an island farm in rural Connecticut. Their friend Woody (Kevin O'Connor) goes with them to help work the apple orchard on the farm, which is known by the townspeople as "the Old Bishop Place." When the three arrive at the farmhouse, they find it occupied by a squatter named Emily (Mariclare Costello). Emily is going to leave but Duncan and Jessica ask her to stay and live there with them. The townspeople, who all have strange wounds, don't take kindly to the newcomers ("Damn hippies!"). A local antiques dealer, Sam Dorker (Alan Manson), is more friendly. He tells Duncan and Jessica that legend has it that in 1880, Abigail Bishop drowned in the cove near the farm and came back as a vampire. After that, everything starts to go downhill fast for Jessica. Swimming in the cove, she sees a red-haired figure in white beneath the waters, beckoning to her. She later finds the bloody body of Sam Dorker in the woods. When she tells Duncan, he assumes she is having another mental breakdown and dismisses her story.

Jessica finds a photo of the Bishop family in the attic and notices that Emily bears an uncanny resemblance to Abigail. That's because Emily is actually Abigal, come back to feed on the townspeople and now set on making Duncan, Jessica and Woody her next victims. In the end, Jessica alone manages to escape the island in a rowboat, in voiceover saying, "Madness or sanity.... I don't know which is which."

Lemora

The 1973 film *Lemora* follows the '70s trends of female vampires and amateurish productions. This Southern gothic vampire tale (filmed in Pomona, California) is subtitled "A Child's Tale of the Supernatural." It is also known as *Lemora: The Lady Dracula*. It was made by former UCLA students Robert Fern and Richard Blackburn. Their inspiration was *Count Yorga—Vampire,* which was made by UCLA alums Michael Macready and Michael Murphy. The finished film premiered at Claremont College in the San Gabriel Valley and the reception was so poor that Fern and Blackburn immediately sold their rights to *Lemora* to try and recoup some of the cash they had spent making it. Two years later it was finally given a U.S. theatrical release by the Media Cinema Group, who cut it from 113 to 80 minutes.

Upon its release, the movie was condemned by the Catholic Legion of Decency for being "anti–Catholic." Why this movie should have been singled out for that dubious "honor" is anyone's guess. It is no more irreligious than any other vampire movie and the Catholic Church never figures into the story at all. *Lemora* is also far more subdued in terms of sex and violence than the majority of the other vampire movies being made at the time. Perhaps it was a slow day for the Catholic Legion of Decency.

Exploitation genre favorite Cheryl Smith (later known as Cheryl Rainbeaux Smith) had her first major role in *Lemora*. Although she was 18 at the time the movie was filmed, she easily passes for the 14-year-old girl of the script. She is also quite effective in the part. The pivotal role of Lemora is played by an untalented actress named Lesley Gilb. A more charismatic actress in the lead would have helped immensely. The scenes with Lemora tend to fall flat when they should have been the highlights of the movie.

The Plot: In the 1930s South, sweet and innocent Lila Lee (Cheryl Smith) is known as the "Singing Angel" at her community church. She is being raised by the Reverend (Robert Blackburn) because, three years before, her gangster father killed her mother and the mother's lover and then went into hiding. Lila receives a mysterious letter from a woman named Lemora (Lesley Gilb) which says that her father is alive and he wishes her to join him in the nearby town of Astaroth. Lila leaves a letter for the reverend telling him of her plans to meet her father, then takes a bus to Astaroth. When the bus breaks down, the driver is set upon by werewolf-like creatures from the forest. Lila flees and comes upon the house where Lemora lives with a gaggle of annoying, feral children. Her father is also there but he has been turned into one of the forest beasts. Lemora, who is a vampire, repeatedly tries to seduce Lila, but the young girl always evades her advances. The climax has the clutch of vampire men who protect Lemora fight the beasts of the forest and both factions are slaughtered in a prolonged slow-motion battle. Now only Lemora and Lila are left. Lemora bites Lila on the throat and drinks her blood. When the reverend finally arrives and attempts to rescue his young ward, it is too late: Lila puts the bite on him too.

Hannah, Queen of the Vampires

Hannah, Queen of the Vampires (1973) started out as a Spanish movie filmed in Turkey, written by Ricardo Ferrer and directed by Julio Salvador. The original title was *La tomba de la isla maldita* (*The Tomb of the Damned Island*). After Salvador completed filming, American co-producer Lou Shaw, the man who gave the world *The Bat People* a few years later, decided that additional footage should be shot for an English language version. Even though Shaw wrote only a few new scenes, the American version gives him solo writing credit for the entire movie. Actor-turned-director Ray Danton, who helmed *The Deathmaster* the previous year, was brought in to film new footage in California. The work of both directors is skillfully melded into the movie so that for the most part it is difficult to tell which is the new Danton footage. The one obvious exception is a prologue which gives away the identity of a cowled man in black before the movie proper even begins. Closeups of Mark Damon, obviously inserted later, reveal him to be the villain of the piece long before the intended climactic revelation. Why the decision was made to do this is a puzzle as it ruins the only surprise in the movie. One real gaffe in continuity has Jack La Rue, Jr., show up as an angry villager at the end of the movie when his character had been murdered earlier in the film. And his death isn't just a throwaway scene, it's a plot point. The movie is also known by the titles *Young Hannah, Queen of the Vampires* and *Crypt of the Living Dead*.

The Plot: Chris Bolton (Andrew Prine) arrives on Vampire Island to bury his archaeologist father, who was killed in an accident while researching the tomb of 13th-century noblewoman Hannah (Teresa Gimpera). Chris is shunned by the local villagers but welcomed by fellow Americans Peter (Mark Damon) and his sister Mary (Patty Shepard). To recover his father's body, Chris must move Hannah's sarcophagus. The villagers believe that Hannah was a vampire and that tampering with her tomb will bring her back to life ("She's smart ... 700 years smart!"). As it turns out, they are right. The lid of Hannah's tomb is removed and within she slumbers, looking the same as she did centuries before. For most of the film Hannah rests in her tomb wearing a cheap Mardi Gras tiara, fluttering her eyelids and breathing deeply. When she finally rises, she silently swoops around in her white gown, sometimes turning into a wolf (well, a dog, actually). Most of the vampire action is confined to the last 15 minutes as Hannah bites would-be acolyte Peter and then attacks Chris. Chris throws a lantern at her and she bursts into flames. The now smoldering vampire is surrounded by villagers with wooden stakes and torches who put an end to her once and for all. Or do they? A half-baked epilogue lets us know that evil Hannah lives on.

Vampyres

In 1974, Spanish director Jose Ramon Larraz (credited on-screen as Joseph Larraz) came to England to make *Vampyres*. At first glance, this movie might appear to be a pastiche of ideas gleaned from several of the vampire films which had recently preceded it. It has the nudity of *The Vampire Lovers* (and then some!), the gritty modernity of the AIP vampire films, and the dreamy eroticism of *Daughters of Darkness* but it also has its own special grim atmosphere of dread and doom. *Vampyres* was filmed mostly at Oakley Court, that oft-used manor house location familiar to all fans of British horror flicks. Anulka (Dziubinska) and Marianne Morris star as the lesbian vampire couple Miriam and Fran. Anulka was a *Playboy* Playmate of the Month a year before *Vampyres* was made and this was her first film role.

In keeping with the tenor of the times, sex plays an important part in *Vampyres*. There are copious amounts of both male and female nudity and some fairly strong sex scenes. The major motivation of one of the female vampires seems to be sex rather than blood. The male victims all meet their doom because of their hopes for a little nookie from the two beautiful protagonists.

Although it is generally well thought of now and has a large cult following, Tim Lucas' 1975 *Cinefantastique* review (Vol. 4; No. 3) dismisses *Vampyres* as "a generally poor horror entry. ... [T]he film is unintentionally funny, without continuity, and poorly acted." I find *Vampyres* to be one of the most intriguing entries in '70s vampire cinema.

Anulka and Marianne Morris are *Vampyres* (1974).

The Plot: A pre-credits sequence shows two beautiful naked women making love. The shadowy figure of a man appears and shoots them both dead. Several years later, a young couple, John (Brian Deacon) and Harriet (Sally Faulkner), are on a vacation. As they drive along a country road looking for a spot to park their trailer, they see a woman hitchhiking while another woman hides behind a tree. Harriet finds this disturbing but John makes light of it. They set up camp not far from a supposedly deserted mansion (Oakley Court). Harriet later sees the two women walking from the house and into the forest. These women are Miriam (Anulka) and Fran (Marianne Morris), vampires who pose as hitchhikers to pick up men whom they lure to the mansion and then kill for their blood. Fran is picked up by businessman Ted (Murray Brown).

> TED: Are you English? You don't look English. What are you then?
> FRAN: If I told you, you wouldn't believe me.

After a night of intense lovemaking, Fran decides not to kill Ted and instead keeps him as her sex slave and occasional snack. Miriam disapproves of the situation but she later gets over it and participates in a "three-way" with Fran and Ted. Each morning Fran mysteriously disappears and poor besotted Ted spends the day vainly searching the house for her. When nosy Harriet discovers Miriam and Fran's secret, the vampires go on a bloody killing spree, which includes John and Harriet, and then flee to parts unknown. The morning after, a weakened and bewildered Ted is awakened in his car by a realtor who is showing the empty mansion to some prospective American clients who hope the house is haunted.

Mary, Mary, Bloody Mary

The big question about *Mary, Mary, Bloody Mary* (1975) is whether or not Mary is a vampire. She is cold to the touch and drinks blood but doesn't have any of the other characteristics usually associated with vampires. This Mexican-American co-production was made entirely on location in Mexico by director Juan López Moctezuma, who went on to make *Alucarda* two years later. A typical example of '70s exploitation cinema, *Mary, Mary* includes the prime ingredients of nudity, lesbianism, blood and car chases. A fragile-looking John Carradine's brief appearance at the end prompted *Variety*'s reviewer to comment that his presence made "the bloodbath climax a laughable one."

The Plot: A series of gruesome unsolved murders ("The body count is staggering") has the Mexican police baffled, so they bring in American FBI agent Cosgrove (Arthur Hansel) for an assist. Mary (Cristina Ferrare), an American artist traveling through Mexico in her van, picks up good-looking hitchhiker Ben Ryder (David Young) and the two begin a romance. Ben doesn't know that Mary has a compulsion which causes her to stab men and drink their blood. Another killer, dressed in black and wearing a mask, employs the same method of murder. Greta (Helena Rojo), an art gallery owner with sapphic designs on Mary, attempts to seduce her and instead becomes Mary's next victim. This causes the police to consider Ben the prime suspect with jealousy as his motive. A climactic car chase has Mary and Ben in the van being pursued by the man in black, who is in turn being chased by Cosgrove. The big reveal is that the man in black is Mary's father (John Carradine). When dear old dad attempts to kill Mary, Ben shoots him. Mary then turns on Ben, kills him and drinks his blood. The film ends with Mary being consoled by the police over the death of her boyfriend.

Vampire Hookers

When you see the title *Vampire Hookers,* at least you know what kind of movie to expect. If the title wasn't enough of a hint, the poster tagline reads "Warm Blood Isn't All They Suck." *Vampire Hookers* (also known by a variety of other titles including *Cemetery Girls, Sensuous Vampires* and *Twice Bitten*) positively defines the term "grindhouse cinema."

Made in the Philippines, this 1978 film is poorly photographed in 16mm complete with the harsh lighting, post-synched dialogue and generally wretched performances so prevalent in '70s exploitation movies. *Vampire Hookers* was made by the incredibly prolific Filipino director Cirio H. Santiago, who is probably best known for directing that classic of Blaxploitation cinema, *TNT Jackson* (1974). Trust me, *Vampire Hookers* isn't nearly as good.

Lines like "Coffins are for being laid to rest, not being laid" seem positively brilliant when compared with the fart humor which abounds. When the pace lags for a bit, quick cut to Pavo (Vic Diaz), the moronic hulk who serves the vampires, and listen to him fart. In fact, the last shot in the movie is of Pavo farting. But now that I think about it, that does sum it all up rather perfectly. Then there is poor John Carradine, dressed in a white suit with Panama hat, as the poetry-spouting vampire Richmond Reed. When he tells you he was born in 1775, you can easily believe him. He hasn't aged well at all.

The Plot: Tom (Bruce Fairbairn) and Terry (Trey Wilson), horny sailors on liberty in the Philippines, meet their commanding officer, CPO Taylor (Lex Winter), at a bar for a drink. Taylor soon deserts them for a hooker named Cherish (Karen Stride) who lures him to her home, located in a cemetery mausoleum. There Taylor is confronted by vampire Richmond Reed (John Carradine) and his two other vampire brides (Lenka Novak and Katie Dolan). When it's discovered that Taylor has gone missing, Tom and Terry are sure he has met with foul play. They follow Cherish when she takes another sailor to the cemetery. Tom goes into the mausoleum where he sees the sailor strung up by his feet and being drained of blood. Tom and Terry try to enlist the help of the navy and the local police but nobody believes them. Tom goes back to the mausoleum on his own and is taken prisoner but, instead of drinking his blood, and since it is the '70s, the three vampire girls decide to have a "four-way" with him. This scene goes on and on complete with slow motion, "artful" camera setups and a sleazy pop music background. While Tom is busy having slo-mo sex, Terry is busy gathering up garlic and crosses to fight the vampires and save his buddy. As previously mentioned, it all ends with a fart.

CHAPTER 9

Asian Vampires

Although most Asian countries have a variation of the vampire in their folklore, the Far East horror movies made in the '70s reflected the traditional European version of the vampire, with the Hammer vampire films in particular as a major influence. In 1974, Hammer's *The Legend of the 7 Golden Vampires* (covered in detail elsewhere in this book) brought the vampire to China but the representation was far more European than Chinese. Although Hong Kong cinema thrived at this time, vampire movies were not part of the output until *Encounters of the Spooky Kind* (1980). This film was produced by Sammo Hung who, five years later, introduced the popular *Mr. Vampire* film series which is still being made today. Chinese vampires are unique in that they hop instead of walk.

The Philippines have their own special brand of vampire called the Aswang. This is a flying female creature who sucks the blood of her victims through her tongue. The first Filipino motion picture with sound was 1933's *Ang Aswang* (*The Vampire*), which was remade in 1992 and again in 2012.

In 1964, the prolific Filipino film director Gerardo de Leon made *Blood Is the Color of the Night* (*Kulay dugo ang gabi*), which features vampires cast in the European mode. This strange movie makes little sense but it is notable for its surrealistic use of color. It was shown in the U.S. in 1966 as *The Blood Drinkers* and re-released in 1971 as *The Vampire People*. The plot concerns a wealthy woman (Mary Walter) who, after many years, returns to the family mansion, accompanied by her comatose daughter Katrina (Amalia Fuentes) and Katrina's vampire lover Dr. Marco (Ronald Remy). Marco plans to resurrect Katrina by transplanting into her the heart of her twin sister Charito (also

Ronald Remy is a bald vampire in the Filipino horror movie *The Blood Drinkers* (1964).

Fuentes). Marco is presented as a Dracula type, complete with fangs and a cape. What sets him apart are a shaved head and sunglasses.

Curse of the Vampires

Two years after *Blood Is the Color of the Night*, Gerardo de Leon made another lyrically titled vampire film, *Whisper to the Wind* (*Ibulong mo sa hangin*). This time the director abandoned the surrealistic approach he had taken previously. The result is a far more conventional horror movie, but de Leon still manages to bathe many scenes in strikingly colorful light patterns. *Whisper to the Wind* is known by several other titles including *Creatures of Evil* and *Blood of the Vampires*. In the U.S. it was released as *Curse of the Vampires* on a 1971 double bill with another Filipino horror movie, *Beast of Blood*.

De Leon became one of the most highly acclaimed directors in the Filipino film industry. In 1982 he was posthumously awarded the title National Artist of the Philippines. Not bad for a director whose credits include titles such as *Women in Cages* and *Mad Doctor of Blood Island*.

The Plot: After Don Enrique Escudero (Johnny Monteiro) suffers a heart attack, he decides to let his son Eduardo (Eddie Garcia) and daughter Leonore (Amalia Fuentes) in on a family secret: Their mother Dona Consuelo (Mary Walter), who died several years before, came back as a vampire. Ever since, her grief-stricken husband has kept her imprisoned in the hacienda cellar. Horrified by this news, Leonore breaks off her engagement to Daniel Castillo (Romeo Vasquez). Eduardo goes to the cellar and attempts to reason with his vampire mom but she attacks and bites him. In a departure from standard vampire lore, the next day Eduardo admires his new fangs in a mirror. Then he goes out and attacks his fiancée Christina (Rosario del Pilar), who is the sister of Daniel. Eduardo hastily marries Christina and turns her into a vampire. Dona Consuelo escapes her cellar prison and is pursued by Don Enrique and a family servant. They drive a stake through her heart and burn her body. Don Enrique returns to the hacienda and is confronted by Eduardo, who bares his fangs. It's all too much for Don Enrique, who has a heart attack and dies. With her father dead and Eduardo behaving oddly, Leonore asks Daniel to take her away. Eduardo tampers with the carriage and the resulting accident kills Daniel and badly injures Leonore. With his dying breath, Daniel vows to Leonore that he will watch over and protect her. When Eduardo attempts to bite the bedridden Leonore, the spirit of Daniel appears and they duel with rapiers. Despite Daniel's disembodied attempts to protect her, Leonore is bitten by Eduardo, Christina and the three family maids, who have also become vampires. The family doctor and the priest arrive at Leonore's bedside just in time to see her turn into a vampire. They flee but return with the local villagers, a group of nuns and enough Catholic iconography to fill the Vatican. Eduardo, Christina and the maids retreat to the cellar. The villagers set the hacienda on fire and the vampires are destroyed. As the house burns, the spirit of Daniel appears and plunges a crucifix into the heart of Leonore, freeing her from the vampire curse. The last shot shows the spirits of Daniel and Leonore reunited on a hill, sort of like a Filipino version of Heathcliff and Cathy.

Japan's Bloodthirsty Trilogy

Japan's Toho Studios are primarily known to fans of fantastic cinema for their Kaiju monsters, most famously Godzilla, but they also produced a trio of memorable '70s vampire movies. These have come to be known as "The Bloodthirsty Trilogy." There is no plot connection between the films but all three share a vampire theme and were directed by Michio Yamamoto in collaboration with writer Ei Ogawa.

Japanese cinema was no stranger to the supernatural as films such as *Onibaba* and *Kwaidan* (both 1964) prove. But these were taken from stories based on Japanese myths. In 1956, Toho produced a movie called *The Vampire Moth* which involves a series of vampire-like murders. A clever detective eventually proves they are the work of a criminal mastermind rather than a supernatural entity. The first Japanese horror movie to present a Westernized version of an actual vampire was the 1959 Shintoho Production *The Lady Vampire*. In it, a vampire named Shiro Sofue (Shigeru Amachi) is a Dracula type who lives in a very non–Japanese-looking castle. Like *The Lady Vampire,* the Bloodthirsty Trilogy seems more firmly rooted in the Western horror tradition than the Japanese and tries to emulate the gothic horrors of Hammer and others of that ilk.

The first film in the trilogy, 1970's *Legacy of Dracula* (aka *The Bloodthirsty Doll*), is the least conventional of the three. The inclusion of the vampire element seems more like an afterthought added to an excellent ghost story. Director Yamamoto began his film career in 1957 as an assistant director on Akira Kurosawa's *Throne of Blood*. *Legacy of Dracula* was Yamamoto's third film as a director and his approach is atmospheric and subtle in its depiction of horror. The movie instills in the viewer a feeling of unease and dread. Vampire lore is mostly ignored in favor of the favorite Japanese theme of a vengeful spirit. The Japanese title is *Fear of the Ghost House: Bloodsucking Doll*.

The Plot: Kazuhiko Sagawa (Atsuo Nakamura) goes to a remote Western-style gothic mansion to meet Yuko (Yukiko Kobayashi), a girl he met and fell in love with in Tokyo. When he arrives, he is greeted by Yuko's mother, Mrs. Nonomura (Yôko Minakaze), who reveals that Yuko died two weeks before in an automobile accident. That night, Kazuhiko sees Yuko and follows her to her grave in the forest where she begs him to kill her. When Kazuhiko's sister Keiko (Kayo Matsuo) doesn't hear from her brother for several days, she asks her boyfriend Hiroshi (Akira Nakao) to help her find him. At the mansion, Mrs. Nonomura tells them that Kazuhiko left several days before. Hiroshi finds Kazuhiko's bloodstained cufflink at Yuko's grave. A local doctor (Jun Usami) tells them the tragic history of the Nonomura family and

Mexican lobby card for Japanese film, *Lake of Dracula* (1971).

says that Yuko "was born under an unlucky star." Returning to the mansion, Keiko finds the body of her brother and sees the ghost of Yuko, a spirit who cannot rest until she rights the wrongs done to her family 20 years before.

Lake of Dracula (aka *The Bloodthirsty Eyes*, 1971) has all the trappings of the Western-style vampire movie, in particular the Count Yorga films. While *Legacy of Dracula* often has the feel of a traditional Japanese ghost story, and Mrs. Nonomura is always shown wearing a kimono, there is nothing of Japanese culture evident in this movie. *Lake of Dracula* is not as subtle in its horror effects, and the overall outcome is less original than its predecessor. But it is still an interesting take on vampires.

The Plot: Five-year-old Akiko is playing with her dog on the beach when the dog suddenly runs away. Akiko follows it through a cave and into the forest where she sees a large, decaying mansion. Inside, she sees a dead woman and a man with fangs and glowing golden eyes.

Eighteen years later, the memory of these eyes still haunts Akiko (Midori Fujita) although she believes it was all a dream. She now lives with her sister Natsuko (Sanae Emi) in a house near Lake Fujimi. One day a crate is delivered to the caretaker of the lake community. The return address is simply **Dracula**. The caretaker opens it and finds a coffin. He is later attacked by a man in black. The next day, a young woman found on the road near Lake Fujimi is taken to the hospital. Akiko's boyfriend, Dr. Saeki (Choei Takahashi), examines her and determines that she is suffering from a loss of blood. That night, Dracula (Shin Kishida) comes to the hospital. While attempting to get to him, the woman falls to her death from an upper story. Akiko sees Natusko go into the forest in the middle of the night. There she gives herself to Dracula. Natsuko brings Dracula to their home where he tries to put Akiko under his spell. The timely intervention of Saeki prevents this. Saeki and Akiko attempt to get Natusko, who has been drained of blood, to the hospital but she dies before they arrive. Placed on an autopsy table, she comes back to life as a vampire and flees to join Dracula. Saeki hypnotizes Akiko and she relives the horrible event which took place in her childhood. Together Saeki and Akiko return to her hometown of Noto where they retrace her steps and end up at the forbidding mansion of Dracula for a final showdown with the vampire.

There was a three-year gap between *Lake of Dracula* and *Evil of Dracula* (aka *The Bloodthirsty Roses,* 1974), the final film in the Bloodthirsty Trilogy. During that period, director Michio Yamamoto and his writer collaborator Ei Ogawa must have watched all the current vampire movies and then incorporated most of the standard horror elements into this last movie. *Evil* is far less plot-driven and more action-oriented than its predecessors. Unlike the two previous movies, there is female nudity which shows the vampire's bite on bare breasts rather than the neck. Shin Kishida, who played Dracula in *Lake of Dracula,* returns as the main vampire in *Evil.* This was Yamamoto's last theatrical feature film. After directing a few television episodes in 1975 and 1976, he apparently left the Japanese film industry.

The Plot: Mr. Shiraki (Toshio Kurosawa) goes to a remote area of northern Japan to take a teaching position at the Seimel School for Girls. When he arrives, he learns that the wife of the school's principal has recently died in a car crash. Shiraki meets with the principal (Shin Kishida), who says he is planning to resign and that Mr. Shiraki will become the new principal. His first night at the school, Shiraki hears singing; when he goes to investigate, he is attacked by a vampire woman (Mika Katsuragi) whom he later recognizes from a painting as the principal's dead wife. Shiraki is ready to dismiss this all as a bad dream until he learns from the school's doctor (Kunie Tanaka) that in the past few years several students have mysteriously disappeared. When most of the students leave the school between terms, Shiraki agrees to look after the three girls who have stayed behind. A scream in the night sends him rushing to the dormitory where he sees the principal, who is a vampire, attacking one of the girls. The vampire jumps out the window and runs into the forest. When the girl dies, Shiraki goes to the local police with his suspicions. The police question the principal but he convinces them that he is not guilty of any wrongdoing. Now only Shiraki can protect the two remaining girls from the vampires.

Chapter 10

Santo and South of the Border Vampires

Santo (Rodolfo Guzmán Huerta), The Man in the Silver Mask, was the most famous of all the masked Mexican professional wrestlers (aka "luchadors"). His luchador career began in the 1930s and spanned nearly 50 years, gaining him legendary status in his country. In 1958, fellow wrestler Fernando Osés asked Santo to appear as his sidekick in two movies to be shot in Cuba. The resulting films flopped but in 1961 Santo starred solo in *Santo vs. the Zombies*. A tremendous success in Mexico, it launched Santo's film career. He appeared in over 50 films, and met more monsters than Abbott and Costello. Among his many horrific opponents were Dr. Frankenstein and his daughter, Dracula, mummies, werewolves, vampires, zombies, witches and Martians.

Santo and the Vengeance of the Vampire Women

By the time *Santo vs. the Vampire Women* was filmed in 1962, Mexico had already made impressive contributions to vampire cinema. Germán Robles had starred as Count Karol de Lavud in *The Vampire* (1957) and *The Vampire's Coffin* (1958). Robles later appeared as the vampire Nostradamus in a series of films beginning with *The Curse of Nostradamus* (1960). And then there is the delirious *World of the Vampires* (1961) which has to be one of the strangest vampire movies ever made. Guillermo Murray is Count Sergio Subotai, and in this film vampires are destroyed by the power of music. Carlos Agostí, who appeared in several of the Santo films, played the vampire Count Siegfried Von

Frankenhausen in *The Bloody Vampire* (1962) and *Invasion of the Vampires* (1963).

It is easy to understand why *Santo vs. the Vampire Women* is highly rated by Mexican horror film aficionados. Wonderfully atmospheric, it is far more of a true horror movie than most of the other films pitting Santo against monsters. It also has some memorable set pieces such as a hand mirror reflecting the true decaying visage of a vampire woman and one of the vampire henchmen bursting into flames when faced with a huge cross. *Santo vs. the Vampire Women* was one of only four Santo movies which were dubbed into English and consequently it received a wider distribution outside of Mexico. The film was retitled *Samson and the Vampire Women* for the U.S. release because the character of Santo had little or no recognition in the States. It went on to become the most financially successful Santo movie up to that time.

Santo, the most famous luchador of them all.

Hoping to repeat the success of *Santo vs. the Vampire Women*, the famous luchador kicked off the '70s with the color film *Santo and the Vengeance of the Vampire Women* (1970). Although this was not a sequel to the previous movie, there are a number of plot similarities. Aldo Monti, who played Dracula in two Santo films, is herein cast as Police Inspector Robles. Fernando Osés, who gave Santo his start in movies, is a henchman of the mad doctor. Three years prior to this, Osés played vampire Baron Brakola in *Santo vs. Baron Brakola*.

The Plot: In a pre-credits sequence, the vampire countess Mayra (Gina Romand) is staked in her grave. Two hundred years later, Dr. Brancov (Victor Junco) has Mayra's coffin taken to his laboratory where, using the blood of a go-go dancer, he restores her to life. Mayra vows to kill the only living descendant of the man who destroyed her vampire companions. This turns out to be the masked wrestler Santo. Mayra and Dr. Brancov attend a wrestling match and she attempts to use her hypnotic influence to have Santo's opponent kill him, to no avail. Mayra goes to Santo's home and tries to stab him while he sleeps (still wearing his silver mask, of course) but that attempt also fails. Mayra now decides to populate the world with the undead and, to this end, turns everybody she can get her hands on into vampires. Santo destroys her vampire disciples by setting fire to their coffins and he drives a stake through Mayra's evil heart.

Santo and Blue Demon vs. Dracula and the Wolf Man

In 1968, Santo first met Dracula, very effectively played by Aldo Monti, in *Santo and the Treasure of Dracula*. Story-wise, this is one of the most interesting of the Santo films, and it also has an equally interesting production history. In this film, Santo is a masked, crime-fighting scientist who has invented a way to transport people back in time to a previous life. Using his invention, which looks very similar to the one in the television series *The Time Tunnel*, he sends his girlfriend Luisa (Noelia Noel) back to her past life. Unfortunately, in this past life she happens to be the victim of Dracula. The first half of the movie is basically a retelling of Bram Stoker's *Dracula* and Santo and his pals are able to view it all on a TV in the laboratory. After showing Luisa his fabulous treasure, Dracula is staked and she is transported back to the laboratory by Santo. The remainder of the movie has Dracula revived in modern times while Santo and a criminal called Black Hood attempt to locate his treasure.

Two versions of *Santo and the Treasure of Dracula* were filmed simultaneously. The other one was titled *El vampiro y el sexo* (*The Vampire and Sex*) and featured alternate scenes of the female cast members in the nude. Later, the producers had second thoughts, fearing that this might tarnish the heroic reputation of Santo; the sexy version received only a limited release before it was shelved and forgotten. In 2011, *El vampiro y el sexo* prints were discovered in the vaults of Cinematográfica Calderon, the company that had originally produced both

Mexican poster for *Santo and Blue Demon vs. Dracula and the Wolf Man* (1973).

versions. Ever vigilant of his father's image, Santo's son, Jorge Guzmán Rodriguez, unsuccessfully attempted to prevent it being from shown at the 2011 International Horror Festival in Mexico City.

A year after the release of *Santo and the Treasure of Dracula*,

Santo and wrestler Blue Demon (Alejandro Muñoz Moreno) faced a wolf man, vampire, mummy, zombie and Frankenstein's Monster in *Santo and Blue Demon Against the Monsters,* one of the silliest luchador films ever made. In 1973, Santo and Blue Demon tag-teamed against monsters in *Santo and Blue Demon vs. Dracula and the Wolf Man* and this turned out to be one of the masked wrestler's most popular outings. Aldo Monti reprises his role as Dracula. A departure from the accepted vampire mythos in this movie is that no religious iconography is used to ward off the supernatural creatures. Instead, the magical Dagger of Boidros that repels them and which plays an important part in the story.

The oddest aspect of this film are the phony wrestling matches. Unlike previous luchador films, there is no attempt made to incorporate them into the story. They are shot against a blue background with no audience, which gives them a rather surreal quality. There are three matches, at the beginning, middle, and end of the picture. Eventually the staged wrestling match sequences would become less prevalent in the Santo films but they consume a considerable amount of footage in this one.

The Plot: Eric (Alfredo Wally Barron), the hunchbacked servant of Dracula (Aldo Monti), resurrects his master and Rufus Rex (Agustin Martínez Solares) the Wolf Man. Together they plan to conquer the world by turning everyone into either wolf men or vampires. Before they can do this, Dracula wants revenge on the descendants of Cristaldi, a wizard who tried to destroy him. Eric has already taken the life of Professor Cristaldi (Jorge Mondragon) and used his blood to bring Dracula back to life. This leaves the professor's niece, daughter and granddaughter to face the vengeance of Dracula. The Cristaldis call on Santo and Blue Demon to protect them. The two wrestlers have their hands full as Dracula and Rufus Rex have a cavern full of wolf men and vampires eager to fight them. There is also a pit filled with handy wooden stakes. You can easily imagine the bloody outcome.

The Vampires of Coyoacán

Santo and Blue Demon weren't the only lucadores to face vampires. In 1974, masked wrestlers Mil Máscaras (Aaron Rodriguez) and Superzan (Mora Veytia) took on *The Vampires of Coyoacán* (*Los vampiros de Coyoacán*). The most interesting aspect of this film is that

Germán Robles, who had starred as the vampire Count Karol Lavud in *The Vampire* and *The Vampire's Coffin*, returns as a Van Helsing–type vampire hunter. The movie has some interesting touches including a surrealistic Satanic altar set and bat monster makeup for the main vampire, played by Mario Cid (who also wrote the original story).

The Plot: As is the norm with this type of film, it opens with an interminable tag team wrestling match: Mil Máscaras and Superzan competing against El Greco and Tony Salazar for 15 minutes. Immediately afterward, Mister Tempest, another masked wrestler, fights El Espectro (Franquestein aka Nathanael León). Mister Tempest is killed; afterwards, a vampire enters the room where his body is laid out and drinks his blood. I expected this to later figure into the plot (perhaps a masked vampire wrestler?) but it is never referred to again.

Mil Máscaras and Superzan are asked to come to the home of Dr. Thomas (Carlos López Moctezuma) and his ailing daughter Nora (Sasha Montenegro). Dr. Wells (Germán Robles), called in to examine Nora, notices the mark of the vampire on her throat. Baron Bradok (Mario Cid), who has recently moved into a nearby mansion, shows up to inquire about Nora's health. Dr. Thomas tells him that she must rest and see no more visitors. The baron returns to his mansion where his zombie-like servant El Espectro and four fanged dwarf vampires are delivering the coffins of Bradok's two male vampire cousins. While the cousins are busy murdering some local prostitutes, Bradok goes to Nora and, after drinking her blood, attempts to kidnap her. He is stopped by Dr. Wells, Mil Mascaras and Superzan. Leaving Superzan to look after Nora, Dr. Wells and Mil Máscaras go to Casa Bradok where they are subjected to a dose of poison gas and attacked by and the dwarf vampires. The spellbound Nora eludes Superzan and joins Baron Bradok in his mansion. Surviving the obstacles put before them, Dr. Wells and Mil Máscaras secretly witness a Satanic rite in which Nora is converted into a vampire. Finally realizing that Nora is gone, Superzan turns to the police for help. Dr. Thomas goes to Casa Bradok, where he becomes Nora's first victim. Dr. Wells and Mil Máscaras discover the vampires' coffins and set them on fire. Nora throws herself onto the blazing pyre. With their coffins destroyed, the vampires have nowhere to retreat when the sun rises, and they vanish in a puff of smoke. Dr. Wells and his two luchador best buddies walk off into the sunrise.

Chapter 11

Zut Alors!
The French Vampires of Jean Rollin

The vampire films of French director Jean Rollin are a subgenre unto themselves. Rollin got his start working on short industrial documentaries and later, after he joined the French army, military recruiting films. After his army stint, Rollin continued to make short films without much success or recognition. In 1968 he made his first feature film, *The Rape of the Vampire* (*Le Viol du vampire*), which was actually two short films combined. The first half of the movie, *The Rape of the Vampire*, is about four sisters who live in a castle and believe they are vampires. A psychoanalyst and his two companions come from Paris to treat the sisters and prove to them that they aren't vampires, although in reality they are. The second half of the movie is *Queen of the Vampires* in which the one remaining vampire sister is pitted against a vampire queen. Upon its release in France, *The Rape of the Vampire* drew extremely harsh criticism for its eroticism and incoherent content from both reviewers and audiences. Rollin later said that during showings, audiences threw things at the screen.

The Nude Vampire

Discouraged by the poor audience and critical reception to his first feature, Rollin gave up filmmaking for a couple of years. Having learned no lesson with *The Rape of the Vampire*, his next film was *The Nude Vampire* (*La Vampire nue*, 1970). The plot involves a suicide cult and industrial espionage which, combined with a mutant vampire theme and S&M costuming, becomes another fairly incoherent stew. Although this film did not provoke the critical outrage which greeted

Rollin's former opus, it was not a notable success. Perhaps the inclusion of too many disparate elements was off-putting to audiences. With *The Nude Vampire*, most of Rollin's formula was already in place and the vampire films which followed would all share the familiar imagery of crumbling castles, spooky cemeteries, deserted beaches and much female nudity.

The Shiver of the Vampires

Apparently Rollin ascribed to the old adage "If at first you don't succeed, try, try again": His next offering was *The Shiver of the Vampires* (*Le Frisson des vampires*, 1971). The third time was the charm and Rollin finally had a minor hit with this surreal blend of female nudity, blood and horror. It is far better made than Rollin's two previous ones, which were amateurish to say the least. Jean-Jacques Renon's photography is excellent and the outrageous color schemes during some sequences are very effective. The background score by the rock group Acanthus is unusual and fits the odd mood of the film quite well. And mood is what this film is primarily about.

The Plot: Antoine (Jean-Marie Durand) and Isle (Sandra Julien) are newlyweds on their way to a honeymoon in Italy. Isle wishes to first make a stop at the castle of her two eccentric cousins, whom she has not seen since childhood. Antoine is told by a village woman that the two masters of the castle died the day before and are already entombed. Isle insists on paying her respects. At the castle, the couple are greeted by servant girls (Marie-Pierre Castel and Kuelan Herce) who invite them to stay.

That night, Isle tells Antoine that she wants to sleep alone. At midnight she is visited by Isolde (Dominique), a vampire woman who bites her on the neck. The next evening Isle's two cousins (Jacques Robiolles and Michel Delahaye) appear at dinner and inform the couple that the report of their death was only a joke. Disturbed by this turn of events, Isle wants to sleep alone again and, while Antoine goes to bed with "blue balls," she has another visit from Isolde. As it turns out, the cousins were vampire hunters who have now been turned into vampires themselves (although they dress and act more like campy queens). Now they want Isle, their last living relative, to join them in immortality. Antoine convinces the servant girls to help him. While the girls destroy Isolde, Antoine catches up with the fey, bloodsucking cousins

11. Zut Alors!

on a beach where they are draining the blood from Isle. Caught in the rays of the rising sun, the vampires and Isle perish, leaving Antoine alone. Free of their masters, only the servant girls have a happy ending and dance off into the sunrise.

Requiem for a Vampire

Jean Rollin's next film was *Requiem for a Vampire* (*Les Vierges et vampires/Virgins and Vampires*), also made in 1971. In content it is really no better or worse than his preceding films, but audiences and attitudes were changing and what had once been unpalatable had now

Marie Pierre Castel and Phillipe Gaste make love in *Requiem for a Vampire* (1971).

been elevated to the level of art in some circles. From a technical standpoint, *Requiem for a Vampire* is a definite step backward for Rollin as Renan Polles' cinematography has none of the polish of the camerawork in *The Shiver of the Vampires*.

Requiem's first half has very little dialogue and appears to be Rollin's attempt to emulate the French New Wave Cinema with its loose narrative structure and abstract style. In the second half, he returns to familiar territory complete with his usual excesses of female nudity, lesbianism, rape, and torture. To accommodate countries where censorship was more strict than in France, he shot both clothed and unclothed versions of some scenes. As a result, *Requiem* was given a wider release and went on to become one of Rollin's most commercially successful films. It was released in the U.S. in 1973 as *Caged Virgins*, an edited version dubbed into English.

The Plot: The movie opens with a car chase as two young girls dressed as clowns, Marie (Marie- Pierre Castel) and Michelle (Mireille Dargent), and their male companion attempt to escape a pursuing car. Gunfire is exchanged and the male companion is fatally shot. (The explanation given later is that the girls were attempting to escape from a school costume party. What the...?) After eluding the pursuing car, the girls set fire to their car and the body of the man inside. Then they set off walking aimlessly across the countryside. In a cemetery, Michelle is nearly buried alive when gravediggers fail to notice she has fallen into an open grave. After this narrow escape, the girls walk some more, this time through a forest full of bats. They end up at the ruins of a chateau. Exploring it, they find a bed covered with furs and immediately doff their clothes and begin to make love. (Beds covered in furs are a recurrent image in Rollin's vampire films.) They later discover a chapel full of skeletons dressed in cowls and a woman, wearing what appear to be novelty shop fangs, playing an organ. At the woman's behest, three thugs attempt to rape the girls, but then another woman cracking a whip puts a stop to it. The girls are taken to a dungeon where half-naked women are chained to pillars. The thugs immediately rip the clothes off the chained women and proceed to rape them. This scene seems to go on forever and eventually ends with a rather shocking closeup of one woman's abundant pubic patch with a bat attached to it. After this charming interlude, Marie and Michelle are introduced to a scrawny man (Michel Delessale) wearing more novelty shop fangs and a cape. They are told that he is "the last vampire" and in order to perpetuate his line, he must initiate two virgins into the vampire sect. Marie and Michelle *are* virgins, although they dress and act like tramps. He bites the girls on the neck to make them obedient to his will and tells them that during the day they must hunt victims and bring them back to the chateau so he can drink their blood in the evening. The next day, Michelle get right into the spirit of things by stripping off her clothes and luring a horny man into the chateau. He chases her for an interminable amount of time, accompanied by jaunty French farce music. Marie goes back to the cemetery, meets handsome young Frederic (Phillipe Gaste) and invites him to the chateau. After having a change of heart, she asks him to make love to her. He happily obliges. She then hides Frederic to keep him safe from the kooks in the chateau. That night, the girls are about to be initiated as vampires when it's discovered that Marie has lost her virginity. The old vampire sighs and says that it is better this way as he is tired of his undead life anyway. He tells the girls to take Frederic and leave. Frederic calls Marie a bitch for having gotten him involved in this mess and runs away. The girls trot off hand in hand while the old vampire returns to his tomb to die.

Lips of Blood

After *Requiem for a Vampire,* Rollin made two non-vampire horror movies, *The Iron Rose* (*La Rose de fer,* 1973) and *Demoniacs* (*Les Demoniaques,* 1974), then returned to vampires with *Lips of Blood* (*Lèvres de sang,* 1975). Production was problematic from the start as shortly before filming began, Rollin's financial backer pulled out. This forced him to cut down the shooting schedule and delete several planned sequences. At its present running time of 87 minutes, *Lips of Blood* is just long enough and doesn't wear out its welcome. In retrospect, the backer may actually have done Rollin a favor. I had often heard that *Requiem for a Vampire* is considered Rollin's most "accessible" movie for the uninitiated, but I found *Lips of Blood* superior in every way—although it is certainly atypical of his work. There is still a considerable amount of nudity but only brief sexual activity and no torture other than a nude woman being led off in chains. Bloodshed is also kept to a minimum. Rollin appears in the film as a cemetery caretaker beset by vampire women.

The Plot: At a party, Frederic (Jean-Loup Philippe) sees a photo of a castle in ruins and it sparks a childhood memory. In flashback we see 12-year-old Frederic come upon the castle at night. He is invited in by a pretty young girl dressed in white (Annie Brilland) who lets him spend the night and then sends him away before dawn, telling him never to return. Adult Frederic has no memories of his childhood after his father died; when he questions his mother (Natalie Perrey) about the castle, she denies that the incident ever happened. Frederic finds the photographer (Claudine Beccaire) who took the photo of the castle and she agrees to tell him its whereabouts if he will meet her at an aquarium at midnight. To pass the time, Frederic goes to the cinema (*The Nude Vampire* is showing) and there he sees a vision of the girl in white beckoning to him. He follows her to some ruined buildings and discovers four coffins. He opens one and a huge bat is inside. Frederic flees in terror before the other coffins open to reveal four vampire women (two of whom are Rollin favorites, the Castel Twins). When Frederic finally gets to his midnight rendezvous at the aquarium, he finds that the photographer has been murdered. Eventually he buys a postcard of the castle from a blind girl and it reveals the location. Frederic goes to the castle, as do the four vampire women. There he discovers a chamber with a wax effigy of the girl in white and a sealed coffin. Suddenly his mother appears and in a lengthy and convoluted expository scene explains how the girl in white is a vampire who killed his father and four village girls before being sealed in her coffin. The mother and two male accomplices have staked the four vampire women and now she tells Frederic that he must open the coffin of the girl in white and cut off her head. She leaves Frederic and oversees the burning of the vampire women's bodies. Frederic appears with the head of the girl and throws it in the flames. But Frederic has deceived his mother: The head was from the wax figure. He returns to the castle where the girl in white awaits. As they embrace, she bites him on the neck and makes him her vampire consort. In the last scene, Frederic and the girl climb naked into her coffin on the edge of the ocean. The waves will carry the coffin to a distant island where they will seduce the wealthy sailors who land there.

Using the pseudonym Michel Gand, Rollin also made a version of *Lips of Blood* retitled *Suck Me Vampire* (*Suce-moi vampire*). Released in 1976, it includes hardcore sex scenes. *Suck Me Vampire* runs only 71 minutes and in it Jean-Loup Philippe, again as Frederic, narrates a story about the sexually perverse nature of vampires. In this version, the photographer (Claudine Beccaire) plays a far more important role.

Some of the characters and incidents from the original film reappear and some new ones are added, mostly the porn scenes. In the end, you get to see Frederic being given a blow job by a girl with fangs. Ouch!

Fascination

During the next four years, Rollin primarily directed hardcore porn movies using the names Michel Gentil and Robert Xavier. He made his next vampire movie, the extremely tedious *Fascination*, in 1979. By the time I got to *Fascination*, my "fascination" with Rollin had diminished and my patience with his style of filmmaking was exhausted. *Fascination*'s only positive factor is that Rollin does at least try something different. Unlike his previous vampire movies, this is a period film (set in 1905) and these vampires are not supernatural beings but a cult of women who drink blood. True to form, there is a lesbian love scene on a fur-covered bed.

The Plot: Mark (Jean-Marie Lemaire) is a thief who has stolen gold and cheated his gang out of their share of the loot. Hoping to escape the gang, Mark takes refuge in a chateau where he finds two lovely young women, Eva (Brigitte Lahaie) and Elisabeth (Franca Mai). Eva eventually kills the pursuing gang of thieves with a scythe and convinces Mark to remain at the chateau for a reunion with a group of women that evening. The five other women arrive, led by Helene (Fanny Magier), and at midnight Mark is to join them in their ritual. Elisabeth, who has fallen in love with Mark, shoots Eva. While the other women drink the dying Eva's blood, Mark and Elisabeth flee. She explains to him that the women have gathered to drink the blood of a human sacrifice ... him! Then, for rather vague reasons, Elisabeth shoots Mark and returns to the women.

During the remainder of his incredibly prolific career, Rollin returned to the vampire genre two more times: *The Two Orphan Vampires* (*Les deux orphelines vampires*, 1997) and *The Fiancee of Dracula* (*La Fiancée de Dracula*, 2002). The formula never changed.

CHAPTER 12

Vampires Italian Style

Italian cinema has produced a distinguished roster of vampire movies beginning in 1957 with the first Italian horror movie, Riccardo Freda's *I vampiri* (aka *The Devil's Commandment*). In this seminal work, Gianna Maria Canale plays a modern-day Elisabeth Bathory type kept youthful looking by the blood of young women. Freda's collaborators on this film went on to make notable vampire movies of their own. The cinematographer and co-director of *I vampiri* was Mario Bava, who directed one of the great vampire movies of all time, *Black Sunday* (*La maschera del demonio*, 1960). The *I vampiri* writer Piero Regnoli went on to write and direct *The Playgirls and the Vampire* (*L'ultima preda del vampire*, 1960). This movie is noteworthy as the first in a trilogy of Italian vampire films starring Walter Brandi, who became a sort of Italian Christopher Lee; he also appeared as a vampire in *The Vampire and the Ballerina* (*L'amante del vampire*, 1960) and *Slaughter of the Vampires* (*La strage dei vampiri*, 1962). Other memorable Italian vampire-themed films of the '60s were *Atom Age Vampire* (*Seddok*, 1960), *The Vampire of the Opera* (*Il monstro dell'Opera*, 1961) and *Terror in the Crypt* (*La cripta e l'incubo*, 1964).

By 1970, the golden days of Italian gothic horror were mostly over. The Italian horror scene was now dominated by the giallo thrillers which had begun rather inauspiciously with Mario Bava's *The Girl Who Knew Too Much* (1962) and come into full bloom with Dario Argento's *The Bird with the Crystal Plumage* (1969). The vampires and vengeful ghosts of previous Italian horrors had been replaced by psychopaths with black leather gloves and razor-sharp knives. Still, two noteworthy vampire movies showed up in the early part of the '70s.

The Night of the Devils

The Family of the Vourdalak is a novella written in 1839 by Aleksei Tolstoy, second cousin to the great Leo Tolstoy. Three years later, Aleksei wrote another supernatural-themed story called *The Vampire* but it was so critically reviled that its author refrained from publishing three other vampire stories he had written. *The Family of the Vourdalak* had its first screen adaptation as an episode in Mario Bava's *Black Sabbath* (1963), entitled "The Wurdulak." Boris Karloff starred as Gorca, head of a 19th-century Russian peasant family who goes to kill the Turkish bandit terrorizing the countryside. This bandit is also a Wurdulak, a vampire who drains the blood of the people he loves most. Gorca accomplishes his mission but returns to the family as a Wurdulak himself.

The second screen adaptation of *The Family of the Vourdalak* was Giorgio Ferroni's 1972 film *The Night of the Devils* (*La notte dei diavoli*). Excellent but largely overlooked, it remained mostly unseen in the U.S. until its 2012 DVD release. Ferroni's version is set in contemporary times; by giving the story a modern setting, the director was able to make a horror movie more in keeping with the turbulent decade and filmgoers' changing tastes. *The Night of the Devils* never reaches the stylistic heights of the Bava version but it does stand on its own considerable merits. It stars Gianni Garko, who played Dracula seven years later in the abysmal farce *Dracula Blows His Cool*. Garko, a prolific figure in Italian genre movies, drew early recognition in sword-and-sandal films, most notably as David in *Saul and David* (1964). When that genre petered out, Garko garnered his greatest fame as a star of numerous Spaghetti Westerns.

The Plot: A man named Nicola (Gianni Garko) is found wandering in a remote area at the edge of a forest. He is suffering from total amnesia and is sent to a mental institution. When a young woman, Sdenka (Agostina Belli), comes to see him, he goes berserk at the sight of her. A short time before these events, Nicola had been on his way to the German town of Zehdenick to close a lumber-buying deal. Driving through a heavily forested area, he wrecked his car when a woman suddenly appearing on the road forced him to swerve to avoid hitting her. Nicola went to a dilapidated farmhouse in the middle of the forest to ask for help. It was getting close to nightfall and the family agreed to help him but not until the next morning. Nicola sensed that the family was terrified of something. What they feared was a supposed witch (Maria Monti), prowling the forest at night. Actually she was a Vourdalak who has already taken the life of one member of the family. The next day, the father, Gorca (William Vanders), set out to find and kill the witch. His eldest son Jovan (Mark Roberts) told him that if he did not return home by six that night, they would not let him into the house. Gorca returned as the clock struck six, bearing the severed hand of the witch as proof he had killed her. That night, Gorca took one of his grandchildren into the woods. Jovan realized that his father was now a Vourdalak and drove a stake through his heart. Witnessing this, Nicola fled in his repaired car, promising to return for the beautiful daughter Sdenka. In Zehdenick, Nicola speaks with a retired policeman who tells him that the family has lived in fear of a Vourdalak who haunts the forest. Nicola returns to the house to discover that all of the family have now been afflicted by the curse of the undead. He barely manages to escape with his life.

The Devil's Wedding Night

The Devil's Wedding Night (*Il plenilunio delle vergini/Full Moon of the Virgins*, 1973), a throwback to gothic horror, seems to have been heavily influenced by the popular Hammer vampire movies of the '70s, particularly *Twins of Evil*. Several elements are cribbed from that film, from the pivotal plot device of one good twin and one evil twin down to a pulse-pounding main title theme which seems more like music for a Western than a horror movie. There is also some gratuitous lesbianism and much more nudity than in any of the Hammer horrors.

The Devil's Wedding Night stars Mark Damon in a dual role as twin brothers. You can tell them apart because the good twin has a shaggy, unkempt mop of hair and the evil one has slicked-back hair. Damon, a veteran of two classic horror movies (Roger Corman's *House of Usher* and Mario Bava's *Black Sabbath*), had been starring in Italian genre films for ten years at this point. The female lead in *The Devil's Wedding Night* is Rosalba Neri (aka Sara Bay) who also had a long career in Italian genre movies, in particular sword-and-sandal films. She had already starred in the 1971 Italian horror movie *Lady Frankenstein* in which she showed a willingness to shed her clothes to great effect. She shows that same willingness in *The Devil's Wedding Night*. The sequence in which she bathes nude in blood is a highlight.

12. Vampires Italian Style

Mark Damon as the evil twin Franz in *The Devil's Wedding Night* (1973).

The Plot: Studious Karl Schiller (Mark Damon) believes he has discovered the location of the legendary Ring of Nibelungen which grants great power to the wearer. He tells his wastrel brother Franz (also Damon) of his plans to go to Castle Dracula in Transylvania to find the ring. He is going to bring it back for the good of mankind, to keep it out of the clutches of power-hungry people. Power-hungry people like his brother Franz. Franz warns Karl that Transylvania is filled with vampires who are "alive without life, dead without death." Karl isn't worried because he has a magical Egyptian amulet which will protect him against all evil. Franz steals the amulet and heads off to Transylvania on his own. At a village inn, Franz is told by the innkeeper's daughter, Tanya (Francesca Romana Davila), that it will soon be the Night of the Virgin Moon and that five virgins will be called to Castle Dracula and never return. The next morning, Franz heads out for Castle Dracula but mistakenly leaves the Egyptian amulet at the inn. At the castle, Franz is welcomed by the current owner Countess de Vries (Rosalba Neri), who quickly takes him to her bed. After some prolonged love-making, she turns into a huge vampire bat and attacks him. Franz awakens the next day sealed in a coffin in the castle crypt.

    Having discovered his brother's perfidy, Karl appears at the castle where he is greeted by a puzzled Countess de Vries. After explaining to her that he and his brother are twins, he explores the castle and finds and rescues Franz. Together they plot to steal the Ring of Nibelungen from the countess. The countess tells Franz that she is really Countess Dracula and that he is the reincarnation of her husband Count Dracula. They will renew their wedding vows during a ceremonial blood sacrifice on the Night of the Virgin Moon. As the five virgins are being summoned to the castle by the power of the ring, Karl is attacked by Franz, who is now a vampire. Karl, who has regained the amulet from Tanya, defeats Franz and poses as his brother at the ceremony. The countess realizes the deception when she sees Karl's reflection in a mirror. Karl cuts off the hand of the countess, which deprives her of the ring's powers. She is destroyed by a bolt of lightning. There is a "twist" ending which had been used over and over again since Polanski's *The Fearless Vampire Killers* (1967). This is followed by a final shock shot which makes no sense whatsoever.

Chapter 13

¡Viva España!

Generalissimo Francisco Franco ruled Spain as a dictator from 1939 until his death in 1975. Spain under Franco was plagued by the oppression of artistic expression; the Spanish film industry suffered greatly. All films had to be produced solely in the Spanish language and content was heavily censored. Unlike the Motion Picture Association of America, the bureaucratic censorship of Spanish cinema was subject to caprice rather than rules.

In the early '70s, as Franco's life was coming to a close and his harsh grip on Spain loosened, Spanish directors embraced the horror genre and created some of the most over-the-top movies imaginable. They were obviously making up for lost time. Jess Franco led the pack but Amando de Ossorio, León Klimovsky and others were not far behind. A man who would go on to become Spain's greatest horror movie star appeared on the scene around this time in the unlikely person of a professional weightlifter named Jacinto Molina Álvarez aka Paul Naschy. More on Senor Naschy later.

The Horrible Sexy Vampire

One of the earliest Spanish vampire movies of the '70s is also one of the worst. Made in 1970 by director José Luis Madrid, its original title was *El vampiro de la autopista* (*The Vampire of the Highway*). The Spanish title makes no sense at all unless you know that the star of the film, Waldemar Wohlfahrt, was accused and acquitted of being a serial killer who picked up and murdered girls along a German highway in 1966. Wohlfahrt's other claim to fame, such as it is, was as a pop singer. His biggest hit was the 1967 German single "Du Brichst

The great Spanish horror star Paul Naschy in *Frankenstein's Bloody Terror* (1968).

Mein Herz Entzwei" ("You're Breaking My Heart in Two"). In 1968 it was released in Spain with the singer credited as Waldemar el Vampiro. Apparently this gave him sufficient notoriety to be cast as the lead in this movie ... and in a dual role, no less. As far as I can ascertain, this was his only film appearance. It's easy to understand why; he has no screen presence whatsoever. As the vampire, his performance may be horrible, but he is anything but sexy. However, most of the women in the movie are, and they get ample opportunity to show off their nude bodies, mostly in the bathtub or shower.

The Plot: A series of killings in Stuttgart has the police chief (Luis Induni) baffled. A local doctor suggests that they may be the work of Baron Winnegar (Wolf Wohlfahrt), a vampire who claims victims every 28 years. The police and the doctor go to the castle of the baron, and he promptly dispatches all of them. Count Oblensky (also Wohlfahrt), a descendant of the baron, is questioned by the new police commissioner (Barta Bari). Oblensky moves into the castle with his girlfriend (Patricia Loran) and proceeds to drink himself into an alcoholic stupor.

One evening Baron Winnegar appears to Oblensky and begs him to end his vampiric life. Oblensky tries to convince the commissioner that the murders are being committed by a vampire but he isn't believed. When the baron attempts to attack his girlfriend, Oblensky chases him with a cross to his coffin and stakes him.

Malenka

Amando de Ossorio was one of the great names in Spanish horror. He is most famous for his quartet of "Blind Dead" movies in which Knights Templar return as murderous zombies; his first horror movie was *Malenka* (*Malenka, la sobrina del vampiro*/*Malenka, the Vampire's Niece*). A Spanish/Italian co-production, it was filmed in Madrid and Rome and stars Anita Ekberg with a supporting cast of both Spanish and Italian players. Boris Karloff had recently completed *El coleccionista de cadáveres* (aka *Blind Man's Bluff*) in Spain and it was hoped that he would also appear in *Malenka*. But his health was deteriorating and he died shortly thereafter. One assume that he would have played the village doctor but some sources claim he was asked to play Count Walbrooke. That would certainly have made hash of the youthful immortality theme.

Made shortly after Roman Polanski's *The Fearless Vampire Killers*, *Malenka* is often called an imitation of that film. *Malenka is* sometimes played broadly, but it is more a horror film than a parody. The plot includes just about every vampire cliché in the book but de Ossorio somehow makes most of it work. *Malenka* premiered in Italy and Spain in the summer of 1969. In the U.S. it came out in 1973 under the title *Fangs of the Living Dead*, on a triple bill called "The Orgy of the Living Dead." The other two titles on this program were *Revenge of the Living Dead* (aka *Murder Clinic*) and *Curse of the Living Dead* (aka *Kill, Baby, Kill*).

The Plot: Sylvia Morel (Anita Ekberg) receives a letter from her uncle telling her of the death of her mother, from whom she has been estranged since childhood. Sylvia is now countess of Walbrooke and has inherited the family castle. Although her wedding to Dr. Piero Luciani (John Hamilton) is only two weeks away, she visits the castle where her uncle Count Walbrooke (Julian Ugarte) tells her the family history. Over a hundred years before, her aunt Malenka (also Ekberg in a black wig) was a brilliant biochemist dabbling in the supernatural in search of the key to youth and immortality. She succeeded in turning her husband into an immortal vampire but was burned at the stake by the villagers for witchcraft before she could do the same for herself. Count Walbrooke reveals that he is Malenka's husband and a vampire. He tells Sylvia that her family is cursed and that she must write a letter to her fiancée breaking off their engagement. Piero receives the letter and, unwilling to accept Sylvia's rejection, goes to the castle with his friend Max (Guy Roberts) to change Sylvia's mind. Piero and Max discover that the village is plagued by vampires and, with the local doctor (Carlos Casaravilla), they attempt to put an end to the Walbrooke curse. The climax occurs in the castle dungeon where Count Walbrooke confesses to Piero that the vampires were a hoax he concocted to drive Sylvia mad so he could inherit the castle. Piero drives a burning torch into Count Walbrooke and he disintegrates in typical vampire fashion, proving he was really a vampire after all. Or was he? A final scene that looks "tacked on" has Max turn into a vampire and chase one of the village girls.

Night of the Sorcerers

Amando de Ossorio may have incorporated all of the vampire clichés in *Malenka*, but there is none of the standard vampire lore to be found in his *Night of the Sorcerers*. In fact, the inclusion of the vampire element almost seems like an afterthought. *Night of the Sorcerers* (*La noche de los brujos*, 1973) is the oddest film in his career. In addition to vampires, it has voodoo and zombies. What it doesn't seem to have are the "Sorcerers" of the title. The very convincing location footage was not filmed in Africa but at the wild animal park Safari Madrid in Spain. In the U.S., *Sorcerers* went direct to TV: Avco Embassy made it part of one of their syndicated packages of movies and it captivated a generation of late-night movie vampire fans.

The Plot: In a prologue set in Bumbasa (no, not Mombasa), Africa, in 1910, a white woman is abducted by natives, whipped, raped and beheaded. The story resumes in modern times with a safari of five concerned with endangered wildlife: Professor Grant (Jack Taylor), big game hunter Rod Carter (Simón Andreu), Liz (Maria Kosti), Carol (Lorena Tower) and Tunika (Kali Hansa). They set up camp near the spit where the 1910 atrocity was committed. Tomunga (Jose Thelman), a local fur trader, warns them that at night they must not venture near the site where there are burial mounds and a voodoo altar. Of course, the very first night Liz decides she is going to take some pictures of the place by moonlight. Zombie natives rise from the burial mounds, tie Liz between two trees, whip her and cut off her head. All of this is overseen by the woman who was decapitated in the prologue: She has returned from the dead, intact, dressed in a fur bikini, and she is now a vampire. The next morning the rest of the group search for Liz in vain. That night Liz, who is now a vampire (and also dressed in a fur bikini), comes to the camp and lures Carol into the jungle. Liz and the other vampire woman drink Carol's blood and then she too is beheaded. The next night there are three bikini-clad vampire women running around. In the end, only Rod and Tunika are left alive. Rod throws his ammunition belt into the voodoo fire pit and the exploding ammo conveniently kills the vampire women and most of the zombies.

Frankenstein's Bloody Terror

Paul Naschy was a one-man horror industry in Spain, most famous for creating the character of Waldemar Daninsky, el Hombre Lobo. In addition to his wolf man, Naschy also portrayed a gallery of other monsters including a resurrected Egyptian mummy (*Vengeance of the Mummy,* 1973), Count Dracula (*Count Dracula's Great Love,* 1973), a murderous hunchback (*Hunchback of the Morgue,* 1973) and Dr. Jekyll and Mr. Hyde (*Dr. Jekyll vs. the Werewolf,* 1972).

Naschy only played a vampire once, but his wolf man character was pitted against vampires in several films. The first was *La marca del Hombre Lobo* (*The Mark of the Wolf Man*), directed by Enrique López Eguiluz. In 1968, the film was given a deluxe release in Spain: It was presented in 70mm 3D with stereophonic sound.

Enter American producer Sam Sherman, who co-founded Independent International Pictures with director Al Adamson in 1969. In 1971, Sherman was looking for a Frankenstein movie to release at the same time as Adamson's *Dracula vs. Frankenstein* to fulfill contractual distribution obligations with theater owners. Sherman had committed to 400 playdates but didn't have enough prints of *Dracula vs. Frankenstein* to go around. After viewing *Hell Creatures* (an English-language version of *La marcha del Hombre Lobo*), Sherman decided to buy the U.S. distribution rights and release it as a Frankenstein film. That it had nothing whatsoever to do with Frankenstein did not deter him.

The title was changed to *Frankenstein's Bloody Terror* and a voiceover prologue was added:

> Now the most frightening Frankenstein story of all as the ancient werewolf curse brands the family of monster makers as Wolfstein! Wolfstein ... an inhuman clan of blood-hungry wolf monsters!

Voila! Now Sam Sherman had the Frankenstein movie he wanted. In October 1971, *Frankenstein's Bloody Terror* premiered at Hollywood's Egyptian Theatre where it played a limited release in the 3D format. When 3D showings proved technically problematic, the film was briefly withdrawn and then released widely in standard 2D. In 1974, *Frankenstein's Bloody Terror* was reissued on a double bill with *Dracula vs. Frankenstein*.

The Plot: At a costume ball celebrating her 18th birthday, Countess Janice von Aarenberg (Dyanik Zurakowska) meets a mysterious man dressed as Satan. She is attracted to him although she is engaged to Rudolph Weissmann (Manuel Manzaneque). While shopping the next day, Janice meets him again, and he introduces himself as Waldemar Daninsky (Paul Naschy). Janice and Rudolph later encounter Waldemar while exploring the ruins of Castle Wolfstein. Waldemar tells them the strange history of Count Imre Wolfstein, who was a werewolf. That night, a gypsy couple takes shelter in Castle Wolfstein and decide to rob the graves of the Wolfstein family for their jewelry. The gypsy girl removes a silver jewel-studded dagger from the body of Count Imre and he returns to life. Turning into a werewolf, he kills them both. The werewolf then goes on a killing spree among the local villagers. The next night, the village men form a posse to hunt the werewolf. Among them are Rudolph and Waldemar. When the werewolf attacks Rudolph, Waldemar intervenes and kills the monster—but not before being bitten. Knowing he will become a werewolf, Waldemar asks Rudolph to chain him in the dungeon of Castle Wolfstein. Janice and Rudolph search the castle for information that may lead to a cure. Janice finds a 30-year-old letter from a Dr. Janos Mikhelov to Count Imre claiming he has found a cure for lycanthropy. Janice and Rudolph send for Dr. Mikhelov (Julián Ugarte), who arrives with his wife Wandessa (Aurora de Alba). Janice and Rudolph are amazed at how young the doctor looks until he explains that it was his father who corresponded with Count Imre. Actually Janos and Wandessa are vampires who quickly seduce Janice and Rudolph. Wandessa also brings Count Imre back to life yet again. In the meantime, the fathers of Janice and

Rudolph, concerned about their children, go to Castle Wolfstein. There they find Waldemar and Count Imre chained in the dungeon. As the horrified fathers watch, the men turn into werewolves and break their chains. In the battle which follows, Waldemar kills Count Imre and then reverts to his human state when the sun rises. Waldemar joins the fathers in their search for Rudolph and Janice. They find Rudolph at the coffin of Wandessa; Waldemar drives a stake through her heart. As night falls, Janos, with much cape-swirling, leads Janice into the forest. Waldemar turns into a werewolf and fights with Janos, who bursts into flames and disintegrates. Janice seizes her father's gun and fires several silver bullets into Waldemar, putting an end to his tormented life as a werewolf.

Assignment Terror

Europe has given the world some daffy horror movies and *Assignment Terror* (1970) is one of the daffiest. This Spanish/West German co-production was known in Spain as *Los monstruos del terror* (*The Monsters of Terror*) and in Germany as *Dracula jagt Frankenstein*, despite the fact that neither Dracula or Frankenstein appear. The screenplay, written by Paul Naschy (using his real name Jacinto Molina Álvarez), liberally borrows plot elements from the Universal "monster mash" movies of the '40, most conspicuously *Frankenstein Meets the Wolf Man* and *House of Frankenstein*. Naschy includes a mummy in his roster of monsters. (Kharis, Universal's resident mummy, was originally included in the *House of Frankenstein* script but later eliminated.)

The original script for *Assignment Terror*, titled *The Man Who Came from Ummo*, was far more elaborate than the final budget would allow, so some of Naschy's ideas were jettisoned during filming. One of these was the inclusion of the Golem, which is mentioned early in the film but not included in the monster lineup. Michael Rennie, in his last movie, stars in a part originally intended for Robert Taylor. It's a sad finale for Rennie, a fine actor who assayed many memorable roles during his long career.

Direction on the film is credited solely to Tulio Demicheli but, as funds ran out and filming repeatedly stopped and started, Hugo Fregonese and Eberhard Meichsner made significant directorial contributions. In the end, Spanish producer-director Antonio Isasi-Isasmendi came in and pulled the troubled production into some semblance of order.

The Plot: Unseen aliens from the planet Ummo resurrect brilliant scientist Dr. Odo Warnoff (Michael Rennie) and his assistant Maleva (Karin Dor). The aliens have come up with a clever plan to conquer Earth: Warnoff will bring back to life the monsters of legend and clone them into an army of creatures who will annihilate mankind. First up is a vampire. The skeleton of Count Janos de Mierhoff (Manuel de Blas) is on display in a traveling carnival. Warnoff sends his minions to kill the carnival owner and steal the skeleton. Warnoff removes the stake from the skeleton and, bingo, he has his vampire. Then the body of Waldemar Daninsky (Paul Naschy) is taken from his crypt and surgery is performed to remove the silver bullet from his heart, restoring him to his unwanted life. Now it is off to Egypt to bring back the scrawny living mummy Tao-Tet (Gene Reyes). Last on the monster shopping list is the Farancksalan monster (Ferdinando Murolo), looking suspiciously like Universal's Frankenstein Monster. With all his monsters now in place, Warnoff is ready to begin his cloning. Inspector Tobermann (Craig Hill) has been suspicious of the goings on at Castle Warnoff and when his girlfriend Ilsa (Patty Shepard) disappears, he goes to the castle to investigate. He is immediately taken prisoner and chained to a dungeon wall. Tobermann is set free by Waldemar in human form, and he stakes Count de Mierhoff before the vampire can make Ilsa his victim.

Tobermann and Ilsa are attacked by Tao-Tet but he is set on fire by Waldemar, who has now turned into a werewolf. As Tobermann and Ilsa flee, Waldemar breaks into the laboratory and kills the Farancksalan monster by pushing it into an electrical apparatus. One of Warnoff's female assistants has fallen in love with Waldemar and she shoots him with a silver bullet to put him out of his misery ... but not before he rips her throat out. With all the monsters dead and their grand plan thwarted, the aliens have no more need for Warnoff and Maleva, who are vaporized as the castle goes up in flames.

The Werewolf vs. the Vampire Woman

In 1971, Naschy's werewolf Waldemar Daninsky returned in another Spanish/West German production which is known by a variety of titles. In Spain it was *La noche de Walpurgis* (*The Night of Walpurgis*), in England, *Werewolf Shadow* and in the U.S., *The Werewolf vs. the Vampire Woman.* Given a far wider release than any previous Spanish horror movie, it went on to become a considerable success and helped establish both Paul Naschy and the Spanish movie industry as major forces in horror cinema. León Klimovsky directs what would be the first of many horror movies. Patty Shepard, who had appeared as the requisite damsel in distress in *Assignment Terror*, returns here in the pivotal role of the vampire woman.

The Plot: Students Elvira (Gaby Fuchs) and Genevieve (Bárbara Capell) are working on a thesis about 11th century Countess Wandessa Darvula de Nadasdy (Patty Shepard), whom legend says was a witch and a vampire. While searching for the countess' final resting place in a remote French forest, the women become lost and are invited to spend the night at the home of a man they meet, Waldemar Daninsky (Paul Naschy). The next day, Waldemar offers to help them search for the countess' tomb. They find the gravesite hidden in the forest but Elvira flees in fear before they open the coffin. Within is the desiccated body of the countess with a silver cross piecing her heart. Genevieve removes the cross but in doing so cuts her wrist and drips blood onto the corpse. That night, Countess Wandessa rises from her grave and turns Genevieve into a vampire. Together the two vampire women invade the local village in search of victims. When Elvira is threatened, Waldemar stakes Genevieve and, in werewolf form, rips out the throat of the countess and destroys her. For all his trouble, Waldemar gets another silver bullet in the heart.

Waldemar Daninsky reappeared in *Curse of the Devil* (*El returno de Walpurgis*, 1972) directed by Carlos Aured. In a prologue set in medieval times, Count Waldemar Daninsky executes the sorceress Elisabeth Bathory for practicing the Black Arts. Before she dies, she curses him and his family, a curse which eventually will cause his descendant to turn into a werewolf. In this film, Bathory is a witch and not a vampire.

Waldemar Daninsky would not have another actual confrontation with vampires until 1981 when he again meets Elisabeth Bathory in *The Night of the Werewolf* (*El retorno del hombre lobo*). In this film, Countess Bathory is both a sorceress and a vampire. Not only did Naschy star, but he wrote and directed as well. One of his most elaborate outings, it's marred only by plot elements which are a retread of material from *The Werewolf vs. the Vampire Woman* and *Curse of the Devil*. It's too bad that Nachy's most impressive production visually doesn't have a more original plotline, but there is plenty of werewolf and vampire action as compensation.

Vampire Films of the 1970s

Count Dracula's Great Love

The career of Paul Naschy had several parallels to that of Lon Chaney, Jr. Both made their marks in cinema history playing a tormented werewolf in a series films in addition to playing a number of other monster roles. And both of them played Count Dracula once, Chaney in *Son of Dracula* (1943) and Naschy in *Count Dracula's Great Love* (*El gran amor del conde Drácula,* 1973). Naschy, who always went to great lengths to stress the tragic aspects of his Waldemar Daninsky werewolf, herein goes to equally great lengths to stress the romantic angle as Count Dracula. With its period setting, *Count Dracula's Great Love* tries hard to emulate the look and feel of a Hammer film but Javier Aguirre's uninspired direction and the dreadful script by Aguirre, Naschy and Alberto Insua are about as far from Hammer as a movie can get. The last third of the picture makes no sense whatsoever, particularly when Dracula's dialogue is suddenly all delivered as voiceover.

Vic Winner is impaled on iron spikes in *Count Dracula's Great Love* (1973).

13. ¡Viva España!

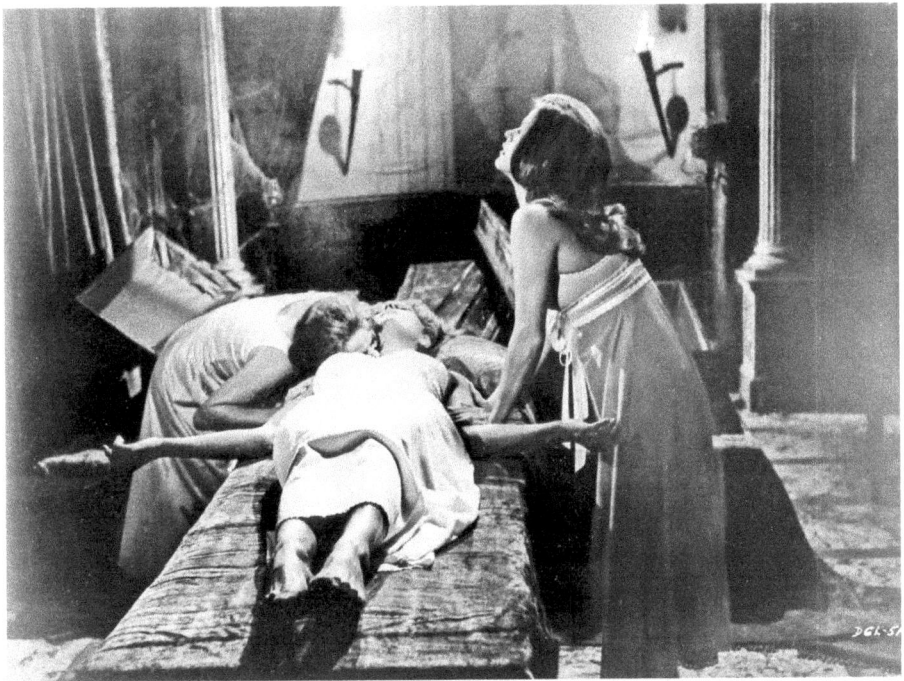

Vampire women feed on a victim in *Count Dracula's Great Love* (1973).

The Plot: Imre Polvi (Vic Winner) and his companions Karen (Haydée Politoff), Senta (Rossana Yanni), Elke (Mirta Miller) and Marlene (Ingrid Garbo) are traveling through Transylvania when their coach breaks down and the driver is killed. They seek refuge at a nearby castle, once the sanitarium of a Dr. Kargos. They are welcomed by Dr. Wendell Marlowe (Paul Naschy), who lives in the cobweb infested castle. Marlowe is actually Count Dracula. On their second night, Imre is attacked and bitten by a former male victim of Dracula. Imre, now a vampire, attacks Marlene and turns *her* into a vampire. Dracula needs the blood of a virgin who will give herself willingly to him in order to perform a ritual that will resurrect his daughter Radna, whose corpse lies mouldering in the basement. He sets his sights on Karen, who appears to be the only virgin in the bunch.

One by one, the other girls are turned into vampires and Dracula, still posing as the benevolent Dr. Marlowe, protects Karen from them. When Imre attacks Karen, Dracula throws him out a window and impales him on the spiked iron fence below. Suddenly Dracula drops all pretense and appears as his vampire self. He speaks in voiceover narration (is it some sort of vampire telepathy?) and imprisons Karen in a cell to await her participation in the ritual. Then Dracula has second thoughts about sacrificing Karen. A village girl is abducted for the rite instead but when her blood fails to restore Radna to life, Dracula has Elke and Senta unceremoniously dump Radna's coffin in the river. With no further use for the two vampire women, Dracula exposes them to the sunlight and they perish. Dracula approaches Karen, declares his love and asks her to join him in the world of the undead. When she refuses, Dracula drives a stake into his own heart and dies. As his body crumbles into dust, Karen repeatedly says, "Come back to me." Too late, dear. You should have made up your mind sooner.

The Curse of the Vampire

While *The Horrible Sexy Vampire* may have been one of the worst of the Spanish vampire films, the "distinction" of the absolute worst I award to *The Curse of the Vampire* (*La llamada del vampiro/The Call of the Vampire*, 1972). This film was directed by Jose Maria Elorrieta, whose only other contribution to vampire cinema was as the original director of the dreadful comedy *The Merry Vampires of Vogel.* There is so much wrong with *The Curse of the Vampire* that it's hard to decide where to begin. Terrible acting, muddled plot, murky photography and an awful, repetitive music score all come to mind. The movie is guilty of all these sins and more. It also features the most gratuitous, embarrassingly bad lesbian vampire love scene ever filmed. It is really the antithesis of erotic.

The Plot: In a brief prologue, the elderly Baron von Rysselbert (Antonio Escribano) is attacked by his vampire niece Margaret (Loretta Martin). She is quickly vanquished by a stake through the heart courtesy of the faithful housekeeper. After the credits, the story picks up at the funeral of the local doctor. A new doctor is hired, Dora Materlick (Diana Sorel), and she arrives in the small town with her nurse Erica (Beatriz Lacy, the daughter of the director). The baron has suffered a heart attack, and Dora and Erica are asked to stay in his castle to care for him. There they meet his eccentric son Karl (Nicholas Ney). Dora discovers that several of the townspeople are suffering from a strange form of anemia. She sends a telegram to her colleague Veronica (Inés Moreles), a specialist in blood diseases who joins the women at the castle. I should mention that this trio of medical experts are all sexy young chicks in mini-skirts. While Dora and Veronica fuss over the baron, Erica and Karl become more closely acquainted. In a flashback, we see that Karl was in love with his cousin Margaret who was attacked in some local ruins by a vampire man in a white robe. She quickly put the bite on Karl as well. Comes the full moon and Karl turns into a vampire and bites Erica. The first thing she does is go to the cellar of the castle to remove the stake from the heart of Margaret. Erica and Margaret go dancing and laughing off into the forest where they feast on a hapless young man taking a midnight ride on his bicycle. Margaret visits his widow in her bedroom, cuing the aforementioned lesbian love scene. Despite mounting evidence to the contrary, Dora and Veronica dismiss the notion of vampires although both admit something very odd is going on at Castle von Rysselbert. The incredibly confused climax has Dora taken captive by all the vampires, who chain and whip her in the castle dungeon. The next morning, an ambulance arrives and Veronica says that Dora has suffered a nervous breakdown and must be hospitalized. Could all this vampire nonsense merely have been in her mind? The ambulance drives off and we see that the driver is the vampire in the white robe who originally bit Margaret.

The Mystery of Cynthia Baird

One of the rarest of Spanish vampire films, *The Mystery of Cynthia Baird* (*El misterio de Cynthia Baird,* and also known as *El retorno de los vampiros*) stirred up much curiosity among genre fans ... until somebody finally saw it. As it turned out, it is a lamentable mess best left forgotten. It was written and directed in 1972 by José Maria Zabalza, who made Paul Naschy's *Fury of the Wolfman* earlier that same year. Rumor has it that Zabalza made *Cynthia Baird* in one day. I can believe it. The backers were not happy with the end result and briefly considered bringing in Amando de Ossorio to direct more scenes. In the end, they wisely decided to shelve the movie. It eventually surfaced on home video in 1985. Like the 1935 film *Mark of the Vampire, Cynthia Baird* is one of those "it's all a hoax" horror movies. The plot of this excruciatingly dull film involves a pair of duplicitous lovers (Susan Taff and Gullermo Mendez) who pose as vampires to steal money from a wealthy couple (Simón Andreu and Marta Monterrey). The story's only unusual aspect is that the Francisco

Goya painting "Saturn Devouring His Son" is the supposed cause of the vampirism.

The Dracula Saga

By the time he directed *The Dracula Saga* (*La saga de los Drácula*, 1973), Argentina-born León Klimovsky was already an established name in Spanish horror movies, having directed Paul Naschy's *The Werewolf vs. the Vampire Woman, Dr. Jekyll and the Werewolf* and *Vengeance of the Zombies*. Odd but interesting, *The Dracula Saga* is one of the better vampire movies to appear at the time from Spain but that's a rather low bar when you consider *The Curse of the Vampire* and *The Mystery of Cynthia Baird*. Nevertheless, *The Dracula Saga* tries and is largely successful at being something different. By this time, "clothed" and "unclothed" versions of Spanish horror films were a common occurrence with the more explicit scenes being shown in more liberal countries. *The Dracula Saga* was no exception to this rule. In this case, the nudity, for the most part, doesn't seem as gratuitous as in other films of this type and, when comparing the clothed and unclothed versions, the latter is far more effective. This is especially true in the scene in which Helga Liné seduces Tony Isbert.

The Plot: Berta (Tina Sáinz), the granddaughter of Count Dracula (Narciso Ibáñez Menta), has been raised in London, far from the Transylvanian family home. When she becomes pregnant, Berta and her husband Hans (Tony Isbert) decide to go to Castle Vlad so she can have the baby surrounded by her remaining family. They arrive at the castle, which appears to be deserted. Berta goes to the family crypt to see the grave of her grandmother. There she is upset to find coffins bearing the names of her grandfather and her cousins Xenia (Maria Kosti) and Irina (Christina Suriani). When night falls, the family appears, including Dracula's new wife Munia (Helga Liné). Disturbed by the events of the day, Berta retires. This gives Munia the opportunity to get naked with Hans. The two make love as Dracula, Xenia and Irina look on; Munia gives Hans the vampire's kiss. Later, Hans is seduced by the two cousins. As time passes, Berta becomes more mentally unstable. When Hans attempts to make love to her, she stabs him to death. It is revealed that Dracula's only son and heir is a badly deformed cyclopean boy named Valerio. Dracula is counting on Berta's baby to be normal and carry on the Dracula line. Berta's son is born dead. This

13. ¡Viva España!

sends her over the edge. She goes berserk with an axe and decapitates Dracula, Munia, Xenia and Irina in their coffins. She then returns to her bedroom and dies. That night, the infant boy comes to life and drinks his mother's blood. A voiceover narration tells us that the child grew to manhood and carried on the Dracula bloodline.

The Vampire's Night Orgy

In the year following *The Dracula Saga,* León Klimovsky directed six movies, one of them an opus titled *The Vampire's Night Orgy* (*La orgía nocturna de los vampiros*). Unlike his previous vampire movie, this one is set in modern times complete with a hilariously inappropriate background score which is apparently cobbled together from library elements. The only music credit given is "Musical Copyright Ediciones Phonorecord" and the soundtrack veritably screams "The '70s." Other than this major liability, *The Vampire's Night Orgy* is a

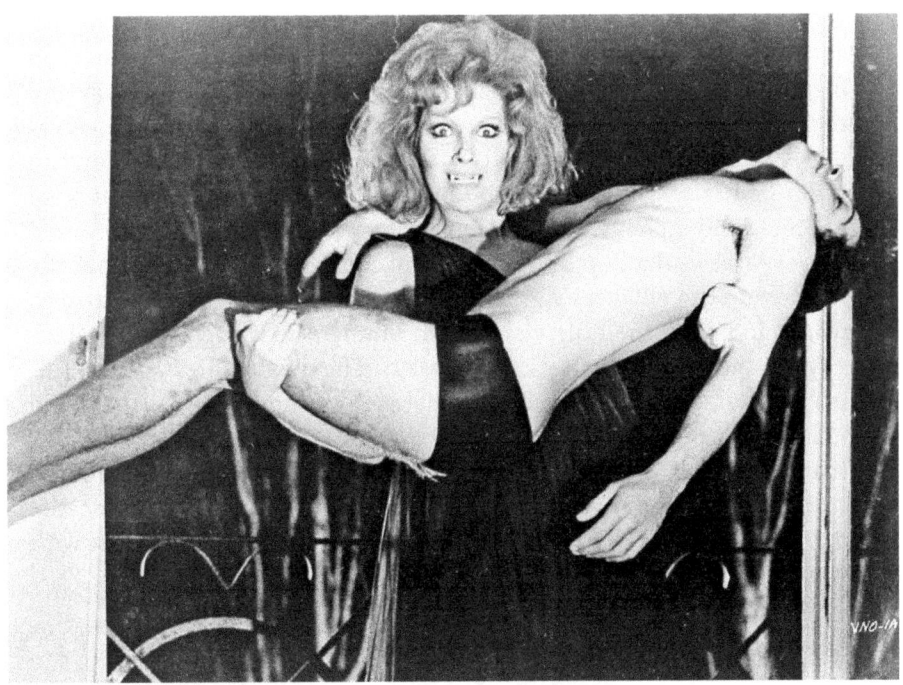

Vampire Helga Line and her scantily clad victim (David Aller) in *The Vampire's Night Orgy* (1974).

lively affair replete with all the wackiness which was part and parcel of Spanish horror movies.

The Plot: A busload of people are headed for the town of Bojoni to take up employment there. When the bus driver suffers a fatal heart attack, the passengers drive the bus to Tolnia, a nearby village which isn't on their map. They arrive at nightfall and the village seems to be deserted. At the local inn, also deserted, they avail themselves of the accommodations. The next morning they wake to find the inn filled with people and everything seemingly normal. The visitors attempt to leave on the bus but are dismayed to discover that it won't start. The local mayor, called the Major (José Guardiola), tells them that he will send to Bojoni for the part necessary to fix the bus but it will take several days. In the meantime, they are invited to stay as guests of the village. This hospitality includes a dinner roast made (unbeknownst to the visitors) from the leg of the blacksmith. A local countess (Helga Liné) invites some of the visitors to her mansion. There she shows them a portrait of her actor grandfather and says in one of the most absurdly stilted lines ever delivered: "It is from him that I inherited an undeniable inclination for the theater." The countess' theatrical inclination inspires her to ask one of her guests, Cesar (David Aller), to stay and recite Shakespeare to her.

The countess is so moved by Cesar's performance that they end up in bed (after all, it *is* Helga Liné!) and he gives a performance of another kind. Later, Cesar awakens to find his paramour has sprouted fangs. After biting him in the neck, the countess throws Cesar out the window to the villagers waiting below. Things rapidly go from bad to worse and soon the only visitors left among the living are Luis (Jack Taylor) and Alma (Dyanik Zurakowska). The next night, they flee Tolnia in a car, breaking through the barriers set up by the villagers and killing the countess, who tried to come along for a ride in the back seat. At Bojoni, Luis and Alma tell a skeptical police inspector their story. He takes them back to where they have told him Tolnia is located but the village has vanished completely. Sort of like Brigadoon with vampires.

The Strange Love of the Vampires

Despite León Klimovsky's previous successes, his final vampire entry *The Strange Love of the Vampires* (*El extrano amor de los vampiros*) aka *The Night of the Walking Dead*, had a very limited release. It debuted at the Stiges Film Festival in 1975 but did not get a Spanish theatrical release until two years later. I could find no indication of a U.S. theatrical or television release. The movie is heavily influenced by Roman Polanski's *The Fearless Vampire Killers,* minus the comedy. Many ideas and images are cribbed from the Polanski film and Carlos Ballesteros' vampire is made up to resemble Ferdy Mayne as Count von Krolock. There is also a nod to *The Vault of Horror* during a party scene in which reveling vampires string up a victim by his heels and fill their goblets with his blood. It's far more slow-moving than Klimovsky's other horror films; it takes about half the running time before the story really kicks in. Patience is necessary when watching this movie but it does have its rewards.

The Plot: Count Rudolph de Winberg (Carlos Ballesteros) is a vampire who falls in love with a terminally ill young woman, Catherine (Emma Cohen). She responds in kind but complications arise in the person of her father (Christino Almodovar), a rabid vampire hunter. Catherine's dilemma is that she can prolong her life indefinitely as a vampire but in doing so she goes against everything her father stands for. Once she makes her choice, the count must then decide if he is willing to consign the woman he loves to an undead existence.

Chapter 14

Jess Franco

During the first 20 years of Generalissimo Franco's dictatorship, Spain's cinematic output consisted mostly of comedies and dramas. Few were exported. It wasn't until 1962 that director Jesús Franco Manera (aka Jess Franco) took a chance and made what is generally considered to be Spain's first horror movie: *Girtos en las noche* (*Screams in the Night*), a Spanish/French co-production better known by its English title *The Awful Dr. Orloff*.

To circumvent Spain's heavy censorship, Franco made two versions; one for home consumption and the other for more liberal-minded venues. The film had its Spanish premiere in May 1962 and, even in its tamer form, it helped to bring about a relaxing of censorship in the Spanish film industry.

By the time he directed *Count Dracula* (1970), Franco had a huge and varied body of work behind him. Christopher Lee had already starred in three Franco films, *The Blood of Fu Manchu* (1968), *The Castle of Fu Manchu* (1969) and *The Bloody Judge* (1970). Both Franco and Lee had long-standing associations with Harry Alan Towers, the British producer of these movies. AIP's Louis "Deke" Heyward once discussed Towers with me and called him "a charming rogue and a scoundrel who should be known as the Father of Co-Productions." Towers may not have invented the co-production but he certainly fine-tuned it with regard to his own filmmaking, which involved multi-national partners for financing. As for being a scoundrel, in 1961 Towers fled the U.S. after being accused of operating a New York City-based vice ring. Nevertheless, he had a good working relationship with Lee, and the actor obviously felt that Towers and Franco would deliver the goods as far as a movie about Dracula was concerned.

14. Jess Franco

Count Dracula

Christopher Lee announced the forthcoming production of Jess Franco's version of *Dracula* to his fans in rapturous tones. Here, at last, would be a faithful representation of the story, unlike the Hammer Dracula films which by now Lee considered to be drivel. Lee was given free rein in his interpretation of Dracula in Franco's film and there is little doubt that this is what appealed to him about the project. In his autobiography, Lee wrote that *Count Dracula* "was a damn good try at doing the character as Stoker meant him to be. It was made with the deepest of bows to the actor manager who invented the character. In the whole vast Dracula industry, it was unique in that."

Whatever success *Count Dracula* has as a representation of Stoker's novel is solely due to Lee. He finally gets to play the part on his own terms and he obviously relishes this, intoning Stoker's prose as if it were the Old Testament Word of God. That the production overall falls below the level of the least of Hammer's Draculas has nothing to do with Lee's performance. Although Lee refers to Hammer's *Scars of Dracula* as "truly feeble" in his autobiography, that film is still light years ahead of *Count Dracula* in terms of style, atmosphere and pacing. *Count Dracula* features some potentially inspired casting in the persons of Klaus Kinski as Renfield and Herbert Lom as Van Helsing. But Kinski is given far too little to do and utters only one word of dialogue. The most exciting thing that happens to his Renfield is that he falls out of a window and breaks his arm. Lom's Van Helsing shares only one scene with Dracula and, since they never appear in the same frame together, I suspect the actors were filmed at different times.

The only real innovation in *Count Dracula* is that, as in the novel, Dracula first appears as an old man and gradually becomes more youthful as he drinks the blood of his victims. I'm certain that it was a detail Lee insisted on including. This plot device would not be used again until Gary Oldman's count sported a gray beehive hairdo at the beginning of Francis Ford Coppola's 1992 *Dracula* and a black, stylish, shoulder-length bob later in the movie.

The Plot: Jonathan Harker (Fred Williams), an English solicitor, comes to Castle Dracula to finalize the sale of a London property to Count Dracula (Christopher Lee). The first half-hour of the movie follows the book closely with Dracula's dialogue taken directly from the source. After Jonathan realizes that something very wrong is going on

Soledad Miranda as Lucy and Christopher Lee as the title character in *Count Dracula* (1970).

at Castle Dracula and escapes, there is a sudden cut to Jonathan in bed at Professor Van Helsing's mental institution in London. He tells Dr. Seward (Paul Muller) about his dire experience but Seward and Van Helsing (Herbert Lom) dismiss it as the ravings of a disturbed mind. Jonathan's fiancée Mina (Maria Rohm) arrives at the asylum with her friend Lucy (Soledad Miranda). Apparently to cut costs, most of the second half of the movie takes place in this setting, which unconvincingly substitutes Spanish locales for England. Dracula takes up residence in a nearby mansion and makes Lucy his victim. When Van Helsing tells the others that he has spent years studying the vampire, Jonathan asks why he didn't believe his story about Castle Dracula. The professor cryptically replies, "I cannot tell you. I dare not." Subject closed. Huh? When Lucy comes back as a vampire, she is quickly dispatched with a stake in the heart and Dracula turns his attentions to Mina. Dracula sends her a ticket to the opera (which looks more like

14. Jess Franco

Fred Williams as Jonathan Harker takes care of business in *Count Dracula* (1970).

a performance of the Gay Men's Chorus) and attacks Mina in her opera box. Van Helsing has a stroke and is confined to a wheelchair, thereby excluding him from the rest of the action. He tells Jonathan, Dr. Seward and the late Lucy's fiancée Quincey Morris (Jack Taylor) that they must go to Dracula's home and kill him. At the mansion, the three vampire hunters are confronted by Dracula's taxidermy collection in one of the most ridiculous and unconvincing scenes in the history of horror movies. Dracula has flown the coop, so Quincey and Jonathan take off for Transylvania in pursuit. At Castle Dracula they dispatch three vampire brides in their coffins with so much stake-hammering that it sounds like they are building a house. Dracula finally shows up in a crate which Quincey quickly sets on fire, making for a very rushed and tepid climax.

Franco's Lesbian Vampire Trilogy

After *Count Dracula*, Franco made a series of three vampire sex films. In many ways, they resemble the vampire movies of Jean Rollin with their emphasis on tits and torture. They are also heavily influenced by Hammer's *The Vampire Lovers* but with an even stronger content of lesbianism and nudity.

The first, *Vampyros lesbos* (1971), a Spanish/West German production filmed in Turkey, stars the beautiful Soledad Miranda as Countess Nadine Carody. Nadine becomes enamored of Linda Westinghouse (Ewa Stromberg) and lures her to the remote island where she lives in a residence that once belonged to Count Dracula. I recently read a *Vampyros Lesbos* review which called it "the *Citizen Kane* of lesbian vampire movies," which has to be hyperbole. The following year, Franco made *La Fille de Dracula (Daughter of Dracula)*, a French production filmed in Portugal. Luisa Karlstein (Britt Nicols) returns to the family castle, located on the cliffs near a remote seaside village. Her dying mother reveals to her that Count Dracula (Howard Vernon) is entombed in the Karlstein Castle crypt. For some unexplained reason, he can't leave the crypt and it is now up to Luisa to supply him with victims. Nude victims, of course, whom Luisa first seduces. This incoherent mess of a movie includes a host of disparate elements which never jell.

The third film in Franco's vampire sex trilogy, a 1973 French-Belgium co-production, was released in three different versions and is known by a variety of titles. Its original title was *La Comtesse noire (The Black Countess)* and this is the "straight" horror version. A longer, sexier cut is titled *Female Vampire* and a sexually explicit hardcore version is known at *The Bare Breasted Countess*. This time around we have Lina Romay as Countess Irina Karlstein, a vampire who needs sex instead of blood to maintain her immortality.

Dracula, Prisoner of Frankenstein

Between *Vampyros Lesbos* and *La Fille de Dracula*, Franco made a more conventional horror movie. Well, conventional for Franco. Like many of his films, *Dracula, Prisoner of Frankenstein* (1972), a Spanish-French production filmed in Spain and Portugal, is known by several titles including *Dracula vs. Frankenstein* and *The Screaming Dead*. In it, Howard Vernon makes his first appearance as Dracula, a part he reprised in Franco's *La Fille de Dracula* shortly thereafter. British actor Dennis Price is Dr. Frankenstein. Later the same year, Price played the role again in Franco's follow-up *The Rites of Frankenstein*, which has little connection to *Dracula, Prisoner of Frankenstein* other than sharing some of the same cast and characters. *Dracula, Prisoner of Frankenstein* seems to be Franco's tribute to Universal's *House of Frankenstein*, featuring not only Dracula but a very Universal-like Frankenstein Monster and a werewolf. One of the oddest things about this movie is that there is so little dialogue. It is more than a quarter of an hour into the picture before there is any dialogue at all, but considering the quality of the writing, perhaps this isn't a bad thing.

The Plot: Dracula (Howard Vernon) watches through a window as a young girl removes her Go-Go boots and then he kills her. The next morning, Dr. Jonathan Seward (Alberto Dalbés) examines her body and, after seeing the vampire's bite on her throat, drives a spike through her eyeball. He then goes to a nearby castle and drives a stake through Dracula's heart as he rests in his coffin. Not long after this, Dr. Ranier von Frankenstein (Dennis Price) and his manservant Morpho (Luis Barboo) move into Castle Dracula and set about resurrecting Frankenstein's Monster (Fernando Bilbao). With this task easily accomplished, Dr. Frankenstein has free time to explore the castle, and he discovers Dracula's remains in the cellar. The Monster abducts a cabaret singer and Frankenstein uses her blood to bring Dracula back to life. Dracula goes out and makes more vampires who will become an "Army of Shadows" under the control of Frankenstein. The doctor plans to use them in his insane plan to overrun the world with the living dead. Dr. Seward sets out for the castle to confront Frankenstein but is stopped by the Monster, who injures him badly. Gypsies find Seward in the forest and care for him. They ask him to repay them by destroying the evil in the castle. To this end, the gypsies also provide him with a werewolf ("Brandy") who will aid him. The werewolf goes to the castle where he fights with and is defeated by the Monster. One of the vampires attacks Frankenstein who, livid at their ingratitude, stakes them all in their coffins. Frankenstein attempts to hide the Monster but inadvertently destroys him instead. Seward and a band of torch-bearing gypsies arrive at the castle and discover the vampire skeletons in their coffins. Seward makes a typical end curtain speech about good overcoming evil.

CHAPTER 15

The Bottom of the Barrel with Al and Andy

The fact that a cult of fans revere the work of director Al Adamson is as strange to me as anything that appeared in his movies ... and that is mighty strange indeed. During the course of his checkered career, Adamson made three movies featuring Dracula, all of equal quality or lack thereof. The first, *Blood of Dracula's Castle* (1969), featured Alex D'Arcy as Dracula and Paula Raymond as his wife. The vampire couple resides happily in a desert castle in the American Southwest with their butler (John Carradine). When the real owners of the castle arrive to claim their property, trouble ensues for everybody. The proposed sequel *Dracula's Coffin* never materialized.

If many of Adamson's films have a patchwork quality about them, it is because they were often cobbled together from different projects that hadn't been completed. The two Dracula films he made in the '70s are prime examples of this haphazard mode of filmmaking but his next vampire outing was an even more extreme one.

Horror of the Blood Monsters

As previously stated, Adamson often made features by combining footage from a variety of his projects that hadn't quite jelled or that he felt could be improved upon. *Horror of the Blood Monsters* (1970) goes a step further because it started off as a movie that Adamson had nothing to do with in the first place. Somehow Adamson saw a 1965 black-and-white science fiction movie called *Tagani*, directed by Rolf Bayer in the Philippines. It appears to be a sort of Filipino version of *One Million B.C.* starring Cesar Ramirez and Alicia Vergel with "Winners of the Mr. Philippines Contest" as tribesmen. Adamson saw potential in the film so he bought the rights. Now he had to concoct a story which could utilize footage from this movie.

Adamson shot his new footage in color so the *Tagani* scenes would be tinted by a process called Spectrum X ("A New Dimension in Terror!") which recalls the less than terrifying Cinemagic of *The Angry Red Planet*. The new plot created by Adamson and Sue McNair involved a space flight to another planet populated by the tinted footage from *Tagani*. For the leader of the space exploration, Adamson once again called upon the increasingly feeble talents of John Carradine. This mishmash of a movie also incorporates stock footage from the original *One Million B.C.* Inserted at various points are meaningless scenes showing Robert Dix and Vicki Volante having some sort of futuristic sex. These were reportedly shot years apart from other scenes showing Dix and Volante in the space control center. When the movie was released to television, the title was changed to the more descriptive *Vampire Men of the Lost Planet*.

The Plot: A wave of vampire murders is spreading worldwide and a narrator tells us that the secret to destroying these bloodsuckers may lie in outer space. Cut to a space expedition led by the ever-cranky Dr. Rynning (John Carradine). A mishap in space forces the ship to land on the nearest planet where the atmosphere causes everything to appear in one color. While Dr. Rynning stays aboard the ship, his four fellow astronauts (Joey Benson, Bruce Powers, Fred Meyers and Britt Semand) go out to explore. The first thing they see are stock footage dinosaurs which causes one astronaut to remark, "All we need now is a Neanderthal Man or two to complete the picture." Cut immediately to footage of cavemen fighting from *Tagani*. For much of the film, the astronauts sit around on a hill smoking cigarettes and observing scenes from *Tagani*. They capture a cave girl named Malian (Jennifer Bishop) and perform a "minor" operation on her brain so she can communicate with them and enables her to explain the scenes from *Tagani*. The Tagani are a peaceful tribe continually beset upon by mutant tribes including men with snakes growing out of their shoulders, lobster men, bat men and, worst of all, blood-drinking vampire people. Eventually the Tagani defeat the vampire people, one of the astronauts is killed, and the rest of the crew fly back to Earth. No mention is ever made again of Earth's vampire plague.

Lurid poster art for *Vampire Men of the Lost Planet* (1970).

Dracula vs. Frankenstein

In typical Al Adamson fashion, *Dracula vs. Frankenstein* started out as something else entirely. Adamson and producer Sam Sherman had enjoyed some box office success with the motorcycle gang picture *Satan's Sadists* (1969) starring Russ Tamblyn. They wanted to bring Tamblyn back in a follow-up picture to be called *Satan's Bloody Freaks*.

15. The Bottom of the Barrel with Al and Andy

In the new film, a motorcycle gang would become involved with a mad doctor who is searching for the key to eternal life by draining the blood of young women. J. Carrol Naish was to play the doctor and Lon Chaney, Jr., would be his hulking, mute assistant. It would turn out to be the final movie for both actors.

In 1969, Adamson filmed some scenes with Tamblyn, Naish and Chaney for the film, which by then had been retitled *The Blood Seekers.* Leading lady Regina Carrol (Adamson's wife) often starred in her husband's pictures. The producer and director weren't happy with the way the production was headed so shooting was halted and it was back to the drawing board. Adamson and Sherman now decided they wanted to make a Frankenstein film. The script was rewritten and the mad doctor became a descendant of the original Dr. Frankenstein. Filming with Naish and John Bloom as Frankenstein's Monster was done in 1970 under the new title *Blood of Frankenstein.* Adamson and Sherman both felt that yet another element was needed to make it more exploitable so, since vampires were very much in vogue, they decided to include Dracula.

Reportedly Sherman wanted John Carradine as Dracula but Adamson had another person in mind: his stockbroker Roger Engel, a man with no acting experience. Adamson later said that he chose Engel because "he looked right." Right for what? Engel looks more like Sacha Baron Cohen as Borat than Count Dracula. Apparently his real name wasn't memorable enough for a new horror star so he was rechristened Zandor Vorkov by none other than *Famous Monsters of Filmland* editor Forrest J. Ackerman. FJA was repaid for his brilliant contribution with a cameo role in the picture and a technical consultant credit. New Dracula footage was filmed, including an ending in which Shelly Weiss substituted for an unavailable John Bloom as Frankenstein's Monster. This was edited together

Zandor Varkov (aka Roger Engel) as Dracula in *Dracula vs. Frankenstein* (1971).

with the previously filmed material into the mishmash that was released in December 1971 as *Dracula vs. Frankenstein*. What a Christmas present for moviegoers!

The Plot: Count Dracula (Zandor Vorkov) kills the Oakmoor Cemetery caretaker and steals the body of the Frankenstein Monster from its grave. Cut to an oceanside carnival where a woman is beheaded by an axe beneath a pier. Cut to Judith Fontaine's (Regina Carrol) awful Las Vegas musical number. Judith is summoned to Los Angeles by Police Sgt. Martin (Jim Davis) because her sister Joanie has gone missing. Back at the carnival, Dr. Durea's Creature Emporium is actually a cover for the experiments being conducted by the last of the Frankensteins (J. Carrol Naish). With the help of his moronic mute Groton (Lon Chaney, Jr.), Durea is using the blood of young women to create a formula which will turn freaks into normal humans. Dracula brings

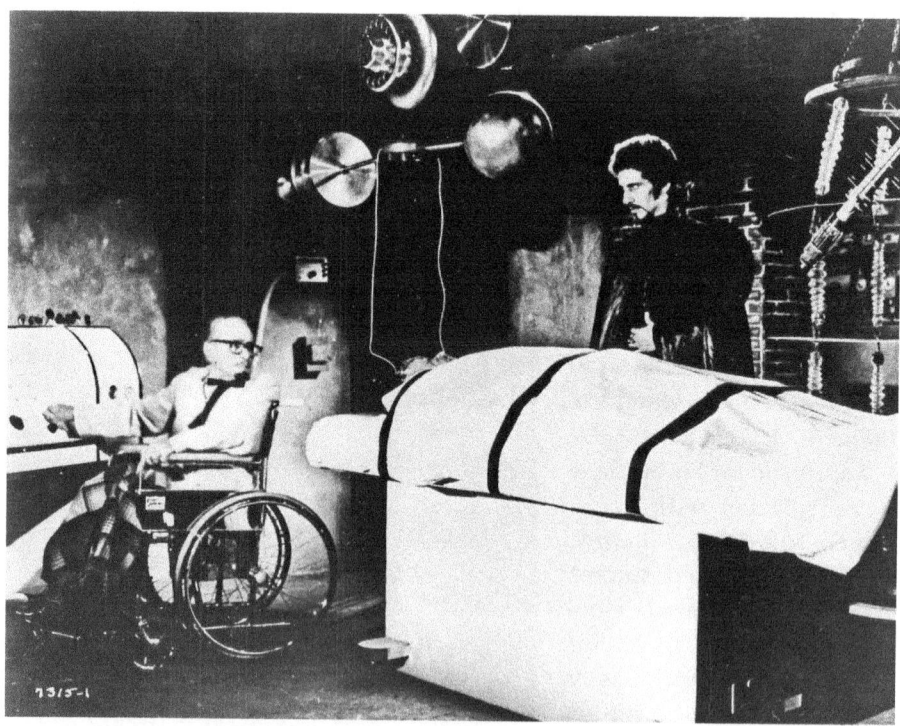

Dr. Frankenstein (J. Carrol Naish) and Dracula (Zandor Varkov) attempt to resurrect the Monster (John Bloom) in *Dracula vs. Frankenstein* (1971).

the Frankenstein Monster to Durea and tells him to revive the creature, which he does.

Despite the police telling her to leave the matter to them, Judith decides to go out on her own and search for Joanie. She ends up in a Sunset Strip club where a waiter slips LSD into her coffee. Judith awakens from her bad trip in the apartment of overaged hippie Mike Howard (Anthony Eisley), who agrees to help find her sister. The search leads to the Creature Emporium where they find the body of Joanie is being used in the doctor's mad experiments. In the ensuing fight, Durea is killed by one of his own diabolical devices, Groton is shot by the police and Judith is taken captive by Dracula. When Mike attempts to save her, Dracula kills him. Dracula and the Frankenstein Monster take Judith to a derelict church. The Monster, suddenly smitten by her beauty, prevents Dracula from killing Judith. He chases Dracula out into the woods where they fight. The vampire rips the arms and head off the Monster, which effectively destroys him. But then Dracula is unable to get back to the church before he is overtaken by the sunrise and is turned into a pile of dust (actually dirt and leaves). Judith leaves the church bewildered by what she has been through, as is the audience. In an alternate ending, Mark survives to set fire to the Monster with a flare and impale Dracula with the hood ornament of his car. One character in the film succinctly sums up the movie with a single line: "Man ... it's a real bummer."

Doctor Dracula

In 1977, Al Adamson acquired the rights to an unreleased 1974 movie, director Paul Aratow's *Lucifer's Women*. The plot had a hypnotist (Larry Hankin), who believes he is the reincarnation of Svengali, becoming involved with a Satanic cult in order to attain eternal life. After Adamson took the footage he needed from *Lucifer's Women*, he brought back Hankin and hired Geoffrey Land and John Carradine, among others, to film new scenes to create a movie called *Doctor Dracula*, which was released in 1978.

Doctor Dracula is a schizophrenic experience as it is clearly two different movies cobbled together with Hankin as the connecting thread. What *Lucifer's Women* and *Doctor Dracula* also have in common are some of the worst actress performances you are ever likely to see. It's easy to spot where scenes from one movie leave off and the others begin. Most of the scenes from *Lucifer's Women* take place at the Rendez-Vous Cocktail Lounge where the photography is usually grainy and out of focus. Surprisingly, the scenes shot by Adamson were far more professionally done. Geoffrey Land is a far better Dracula than Zandor Vorkov was in Adamson's previous Dracula film.

When compared to some of Adamson's other efforts, *Doctor Dracula* is a fairly coherent affair ... which really isn't saying very much at all.

The Plot: Dracula comes into a woman's bedroom and drains her of her blood. At a launch party for the new book *The Second Coming of Svengali,* author John Wainwright (Larry Hankin) is denounces as a fraud by psychiatrist Anatole Gregorio (Geoffrey Land). Also at the party is Elliot (Don Barry) who enlists Gregorio to help his daughter Stephanie (Susan McIver) get over the recent death of her mother.

Wainwright is the reincarnation of the hypnotist Svengali and a member of a Satanic cult, the Society of the Bleeding Rose, whose leader is Radcliff (John Carradine). The society wants Wainwright to bring nightclub dancer Trilby (Jane Brunel-Cohen) into the fold so they can sacrifice her and gain immortality for all the cult members. For some unexplained reason, Gregorio, who is really Dracula, is opposed to the cult and its beliefs. Wainwright-Svengali brings Trilby to the sacrificial mass but Dracula, masquerading as a cult member, kills her on the altar, robbing the cult of their chance at immortality. Svengali tries to bring Dracula under his hypnotic spell but dies in the attempt. As they leave the failed mass together, Stephanie realizes who Dracula really is and that he killed her mother (the woman in the first scene of the movie). She detonates a bomb hidden in her purse and kills them both. "Bomb" is the operative word here.

* * * * *

Vampire films of the '70s are all too often characterized by their terrible production values and poor acting but there are two from this period that make most of the others look good by comparison. These are *The Body Beneath* (1970) and *Blood* (1974), both directed by the maverick ultra-low-budget filmmaker Andy Milligan. Milligan's life, even more bizarre than most of his movies, has been chronicled in Jimmy McDonough's fine book *The Ghastly One: The Sex-Gore Netherworld of Filmmaker Andy Milligan.* I won't delve into his life here other than to say Andy was one strange, tormented dude. He made his first gore-fest horror movie, *The Ghastly Ones*, in 1968. The following year, he moved from New York to England and made *The Body Beneath*.

The Body Beneath

Although British gothic horror was all the rage at that time, Milligan chose to set *The Body Beneath* in modern times and disregard most of the typical trappings of vampire movies. It was filmed in 16mm and fans of Milligan generally consider it to be his most "polished" production. It may be polished for Milligan but it is still pretty rough around the edges as movies go. *The Body Beneath* was released in the U.S. in 1970 by Nova International Productions with another Milligan horror film, *Guru the Mad Monk* ("2 Staggering, Blood-Dripping Horror Hits in Color!").

The Plot: The Reverend Alexander Algernon Ford (Gavin Reed), who lives in London's Carfax Abbey, is one of the last in his family of vampires. Hoping to revitalize the anemic bloodline of his incestuous family, Ford abducts his distant relative Susan (Jackie Skarvellis) with the hope that she will give birth to a new batch of full-blooded vampires (are vampires born in litters like puppies?). Ford's plans are disrupted when Susan's boyfriend Richmond (Paul Donati) attempts to rescue her.

Milligan continued to make horror movies, including the deliriously titled *The Rats Are Coming! The Werewolves Are Here!*, and returned to New York in 1970. In 1971, he and Jim Moss co-directed *Dragula on Fire Island*. The film is apparently now lost. Little is known about it other than it starred Calvin Culver and Calvin Holt as Dracula's two homosexual sons. Cal Culver, using the screen name Casey Donovan, is credited with being the "first gay porn star" due to his part in Wakefield Poole's groundbreaking hardcore feature *Boys in the Sand* (1972), also filmed on Fire Island. In Culver's biography *Boy in the Sand: Casey Donovan, All-American Sex Star* by Roger Edmonson, Culver's friend Ted Wilkins says of *Dragula*, "It was a takeoff on *Dracula*, of course. It wasn't pornographic, but Cal may very well have appeared naked in it. I don't remember ever seeing the finished product." The book goes on the say that *Dragula* was "basically a home movie."

Blood

Milligan's next vampire film wasn't a home movie (although it was filmed at Milligan's Staten Island home) but if certainly looks like one.

If *The Body Beneath* represents Milligan at his most polished, *Blood* is definitely several steps backward. Imagine a period piece set in the 1890s and filmed in virtually unchanged modern locations with no budget whatsoever and you have *Blood*. Given the characters involved, one might think that *Blood* was Milligan's homage to the Universal horror films of the '30s and '40s but the movie is so bitter and nasty that it isn't a tribute to anything other than the director's own self-loathing persona.

The Plot: Dr. Lawrence Talbot (Alan Berendt) and his wife Regina (Hope Stansbury) move from Europe to claim the ancestral Talbot estate on Staten Island (huh?). Talbot is the son of Wolf Man Lawrence Talbot and Regina is Dracula's Daughter. Because of their unholy pedigree, they decide to change their name to Orlofsky. While waiting to take possession of the estate, the Orlofskys rent a small house (Milligan's). Here they experiment with raising a large man-eating plant. A serum extracted from its roots prevent Talbot from turning into a werewolf and also suppress Regina's lust for blood. The plot, however, is of secondary importance compared to the amount of footage devoted to the couple's continual arguing with each other. In fact, most of the movie is a constant barrage of hate-filled bickering. A representative line of dialogue: "I am brimming with hate for you." Oh yes, and Talbot briefly turns into a werewolf.

Chapter 16

Vampire Comedies

Movie vampires as comic foils date back to 1948 when Bela Lugosi as Dracula managed to keep his dignity against Abbott and Costello in *Abbott and Costello Meet Frankenstein.* Then they lost it in 1952 when Bela met Old Mother Riley (in *Mother Riley Meets the Vampire*). It was all downhill for poor Bela after that.

The combination of vampires and comedy in film seems to be a slippery slope. The only truly memorable one has been Roman Polanski's *The Fearless Vampire Killers* (aka *Dance of the Vampires,* 1967), and even that isn't without its problems. In the 1960s and '70s, the success of Hammer's horror films, their vampire movies in particular, made them prime targets for imitation or parody. Polanski's film is a lighthearted tribute to the Hammer vampire canon, specifically *The Brides of Dracula.* While Polanski had appropriated some of the content and style of Hammer vampire movies, other Continental European films used the actual people who had contributed to Hammer's great popularity. In the 1970s, Christopher Lee and Peter Cushing and director Freddie Francis were pressed into service for a trio of European vampire comedies, all with similar success ... or lack thereof. European comedy sensibilities and vampires were not a good mix in general and most of the following movies are sad proof of this.

The Vampire Happening

In 1971, wealthy Italian film producer Pier Caminnecci married Swedish actress Pia Degermark and wanted to showcase her in a movie. The end result was the West German production *The Vampire Happening* (*Gebissen wird nur nachts/Only Bitten at Night*), which shows

Ferdy Mayne as Count Von Krolock with Sharon Tate in *The Fearless Vampire Killers* (1967).

off Pia's nude body to great advantage but isn't much of a "showcase" for her acting talent. I suspect that Pia's acting wasn't all that important to Signore Caminnecci or he wouldn't have starred her in a movie called *The Vampire Happening* in the first place.

The August Rieger script is supposedly based on a 1836 French short story, "La Morte Amoureuse" ("Dead Woman in Love") by Theophile Gautier. Other than having a vampire woman named Clarimonde, there is only slight connection to the source. It seems to have been more important to connect *The Vampire Happening* to the popular vampire movies then being produced in England. To that end, Freddie Francis, veteran of several Hammer horrors including *Dracula Has Risen from the Grave*, was hired to direct. Ferdy Mayne (herein called Ferdie Mayne), Polanski's vampire Count von Krolock in *The Fearless Vampire Killers*, was cast as Count Dracula. He wasn't all that was directly borrowed from the Polanski film. *The Vampire Happening* shamelessly steals plot elements and gags from *The Fearless Vampire Killers* which only reinforces how much better the former film is in comparison to this sorry mess of a movie.

Francis tries hard to keep the story moving but, at 101 minutes, it's a losing proposition. For those who are thrilled by such things, *The Vampire Happening* is a real "breast fest." In fact, there are more jiggling jugs on view here than in the entire Hammer Karnstein trilogy combined. First and foremost are the boobs of Pia Degermark who, in a dual role, doffs her top every few minutes. Quite a comedown from *Elvira Madigan* for poor Pia, whose movie career was done in by this dud.

The Plot: American adult film star Betty Williams (Pia Degermark) comes to Transylvania to see the castle she has inherited from a recently deceased relative. Joseph (Yvor Murillo), the butler, tells her that she looks exactly like her great grandmother Baroness Clarimonde Catali (also Degermark), who was a witch and a vampire. The barebreasted portrait of Clarimonde which hangs in the castle confirms this. Fascinated by her family history, Betty removes the locks from Clarimonde's coffin, unknowingly setting free her vampire lookalike to prey on the priests at a nearby monastery. In the meantime, Betty falls for hirsute Jens Larsen (Thomas Hunter), a teacher at the local girls school. There is much juggling of wigs between blond Betty and brunette Clarimonde which creates endless confusion for the other characters and the viewer. These "comic" hijinks come to a head at a party honoring Count Dracula (Ferdy Mayne), which features more topless female vampires than you can imagine. There are few sorrier sights than seeing Dracula running to escape the sunlight with his pants around his ankles. Betty decides to stay in Transylvania with Jens while Clarimonde goes to Hollywood to continue Betty's film career. One hopes it turned out better than Pia Degermark's.

Dracula and Son

Christopher Lee has always been quite vocal about how important it is for him to maintain the integrity of the character of Dracula, something he claims he often found difficult in many of the Hammer productions. But he apparently had no problem playing the character for laughs. A year after playing Dracula for the first time, the future Sir Christopher signed on for a 1959 Italian comedy called *Uncle Was a*

Vampire. The Italian title *Tempi duri per i vampiri* (*Hard Times for Vampires*) sums it up. Lee plays a parody of Dracula, Baron Roderico da Frankurten, who turns his nephew Osvaldo (Renato Rascal) into a vampire. The film mainly consists of Osvaldo chasing girls around his castle, which has been converted into a hotel.

In 1969, Lee had a cameo as a vampire aboard a cruise ship in the Peter Sellers–Ringo Starr comedy *The Magic Christian*. Neither the movie nor Lee's part in it were anything to be particularly ashamed of but this could certainly not be said of Lee's next foray as a comic vampire.

Dracula and Son (*Dracula père et fils/Dracula Father and Son*) is a 1976 French comedy that Lee made in the wake of denouncing Hammer's disrespectful treatment of Dracula in *Dracula A.D. 1972* and *The Satanic Rites of Dracula*. "Never again!" he said often and loudly in sonorous tones. So then he made this unfunny film directed by Édouard Molinaro, which sometimes seems like a retread of *Uncle Was a Vampire*. And that was not a film I would think anybody would intentionally aspire to emulate. Lee later claimed that in the original script, his character was not called Dracula and this was added later in the dubbing process. (Pull the other leg, Christopher, it's got bells on it.) Lee's 1977 autobiography *Tall, Dark and Gruesome* doesn't bother to mention the film at all.

When *Dracula and Son* got a U.S. release in 1979, it was cut from 100 minutes to 78 and there was some major tampering with the dubbed dialogue. Fans of the film (and there are some) claim that this ruined it. Possibly, but I still can't imagine a longer length would do anything but prolong the torture of sitting through it.

The Plot: When Ferdinand (Bernard Menez) reaches manhood, his father Dracula (Christopher Lee) thinks it is time for them to escape the ever-angry Transylvanian villagers and leave their ancestral castle. Dracula heads for London where he becomes a horror movie star. Ferdinand goes to Paris, determined to overcome his vampiric tendencies and lead a normal life. Since he can't go out in the daylight, Ferdinand logically takes a job as a night watchman. He is able to resist his desire for human blood by drinking the blood of animals. He meets and falls in love with a girl named Nicole (Marie-Hélène Breillat), but when his father comes to Paris, Ferdinand must protect her from Daddy's vampire bite.

Tender Dracula

Christopher Lee wasn't the only Hammer alumnus involved with vampires and French farce. In 1974, 5wo years before *Dracula and Son*, Peter Cushing played his one and only vampire role in the French film *Tender Dracula, or Confessions of a Blood Drinker* (*Tendre Dracula*). Bernard Menez was the star of this one too. He appears to have been the kiss of death as far as French vampire comedies were concerned because *Tender Dracula* is worse than *Dracula and Son*... much worse. We can put most of the blame on director Pierre Grunstein, who provides lots of female nudity but little horror and even less laughs. Only Cushing livens up the proceedings to some degree. He certainly appears to be having a better time than any audience member forced to sit though this slow paced nightmare of a movie.

The Plot: Horror movie star MacGregor (Peter Cushing) announces to his producer (Julien Guiomar) that he is finished with horror and will now appear in romantic films. Fearful of losing his meal ticket, the producer sends underlings Boris (Stephane Shandor) and Alfred (Bernard Menez) to MacGregor's castle home to try and talk him out of this notion. Beautiful actresses Madeleine (Nathalie Courval) and Marie (Miou Miou) accompany them, to add a bit of persuasion. As the long weekend drags on, the four guests begin to suspect that MacGregor might really be a vampire. Yawn.

Lady Dracula

The Vampire Happening should have put an end to West German vampire comedies ... but it didn't. *Lady Dracula* was the brainchild of muscleman Brad Harris, the star of many sword-and-sandal films in the 1960s. Hoping to extend his career once the sword-and-sandal films petered out, Harris had been associate producer and star of the interesting British horror movie *The Mutations* (1973). He also penned the original story and stars in the far less interesting *Lady Dracula*. Filmed in West Germany by director Franz Josef Gottlieb in 1975, the movie was first screened at the Paris Festival of Fantastic Films in 1977 but did not get a German theatrical release until the following year. It's easy to understand why *Lady Dracula* had distribution problems as, even at a brief 75 minutes, it seems interminable. It also isn't very funny. The prologue is played totally straight and, other than a lame joke at the very end, so is the climax. The most interesting aspect of the movie is that it features Stephen Boyd as Count Dracula. It was his final film performance (lasting just seven minutes); he died of a heart attack shortly after completing the movie. He was only 45 years old. It was a tragic end to a notable career.

The Plot: In a prologue set in 1876, Count Dracula (Stephen Boyd) kidnaps a young girl, Barbara, and takes her to his castle where he kills her. The angry villagers and a priest storm the castle and stake Dracula in his coffin. In 1976, construction workers unearth the coffin of Countess Barbara von Weidenborn. The coffin is stolen and sold to an antiques dealer. Barbara, now a vampire herself, emerges from the coffin and kills the antiques dealer. After drinking his blood, she transforms into a beautiful woman (Evelyne Kraft). She gets a job in a mortuary where she can subsist on blood taken from the corpses. When a fire destroys the mortuary, Countess Barbara preys on living victims. Investigating the series of murders, the police commissioner (Brad Harris) meets Barbara and falls in love with her. He only discovers the secret of her true identity when it is too late.

The Merry Vampires of Vögel

Lest you think that the French and West Germans had a monopoly on terrible vampire comedies, I offer the Spanish film *The Merry Vampires of Vögel* (*Las alegres vampiras de Vögel*, 1975). If this isn't the worst vampire comedy discussed here, it is surely the silliest. I can't really judge the quality of the jokes as it was never dubbed into English but it certainly looks silly. A tourist bus breaks down in Vögel, Transylvania, and its passengers seek shelter at the nearby castle (sound familiar?). Infamous vampire Count Erik (Marques de Toro) welcomes his guests as potential new victims. There are a lot of girls in skimpy underwear but no nudity. There is also a werewolf (Gilberto Moreno) and a particularly goofy-looking vampire named Otto (José Maria Tasso). While watching it, I got the impression that I was better off not understanding the dialogue. The direction is credited to Julio Pérez Tabernero, who stepped in and finished the film when the original director, José Maria Elorrieta, died suddenly.

Vampira

During the '60s, director Clive Donner had a number of critical and popular successes including *What's New Pussycat?* His sole theatrical

16. Vampire Comedies 145

motion picture in the '70s was the British vampire spoof *Vampira*, which he made in 1974 for World Film Services Productions. I've wondered if *Playboy* supplied some of the financing as the film often seems like one big plug for the magazine. It's a curious blend of horror and Blaxploitation comedy written by Jeremy Lloyd, a former writer for *Rowan & Martin's Laugh-In*. With the combination of Donner, Lloyd and David Niven starring as Dracula, it wouldn't seem unreasonable to anticipate a rollicking good time. Sadly this is not always the case and much of *Vampira* falls rather flat. Still, there is some fun to be had and time has been far kinder to *Vampira* than it has to many of the other vampire comedies discussed here.

The best thing about the movie is the cast. Roger Ebert (*Chicago Sun Times*; December 15, 1975) was accurate when he summed up Niven's performance as a "combination of weary charm and seedy elegance." Teresa Graves, another *Laugh-In* alumnus, plays Countess Vampira with just the right touches of humor and glamour. Linda Hayden, Veronica Carlson and Luan Peters, all veterans of Hammer vampire movies, are also on hand. They seem to have been cast mostly for decoration, although Hayden does have a particularly delicious, but all too

Linda Hayden and David Niven in *Vampira* (1974).

Dracula (David Niven, right) and his hapless servant Maltravers (Peter Bayless) in *Vampira* (1974).

brief, bit of business at the beginning. Lovely Carlson, as one of the *Playboy* "Bunnies," fares the worst by being outfitted with a terrible, phony-looking wig and having her own voice dubbed over.

Vampira was picked up for distribution in the U.S. in 1975 by American International. They changed the title to *Old Dracula* with the hope of capturing some of the crowd who had flocked the previous year to see Mel Brooks' *Young Frankenstein.* American audiences and critics were mostly unimpressed. Richard Eder (*New York* Times; January 15, 1976) liked Niven but felt the movie might "quickly turn tedious" for viewers ... if there had been any.

The Plot: *Playboy* magazine sends publicity director Mark Williams (Nicky Henson) to Castle Dracula in Transylvania accompanied by a quartet of "Bunnies" to do a "Most Bitable Playmate of the Month" photo shoot. Castle Dracula is now a tourist attraction run by Count Dracula (David Niven) and his servant Maltravers (Peter Bayless). Dracula hopes that one of the "Bunnies" will have the right blood type to restore life to his beloved Countess Vampira, who has been lying dormant for the past 50 years. While the girls sleep, Dracula and Maltravers take some blood from each of them. When the blood is transfused into Vampira, she inexplicably turns black (and into Teresa Graves). Vampira is delighted with her new color but Dracula explains, "It's a small village and people might talk." The *Playboy* crew goes back to London and Dracula, Vampira and Maltravers follow, hoping they can discover which of the girls might have the element in her blood to turn Vampira white again.

In London, Dracula puts Williams under a hypnotic spell and instructs him to obtain the blood samples. In the meantime, Vampira is discovering the joys of the modern world. She goes to the cinema to see a blaxploitation movie (*Black Gunn* starring Jim Brown) and comes out of the theater a hip, jive-talkin' chick. Dracula is less than pleased and is now more desperate than ever to return Vampira to her former white self. In the end, all his efforts fail and a nip on the neck from Vampira turns Dracula black too. Actually, the worst thing about the movie is this final gag. Dracula looked pathetic with his pants down in *The Vampire Happening*, but the sight of David Niven in blackface is just about as bad.

Dracula in the Provinces

Italian director Lucio Fulci had a motion picture career which spanned decades and encompassed nearly every genre. His greatest fame was as the director of extremely gory horror films beginning with *Zombie 2* (1979). His film *Dracula in the Provinces* (*Il cav. Costante Nicosia demoniaco ovvero: Dracula in Briaza*, 1975) has very little to do with vampires and is basically a sex comedy with an emphasis on Italian machismo. It's definitely an anomaly in Fulci's career, made between his giallo and horror phases. From what I can tell, it had no U.S. release despite such familiar faces as Rossano Brazzi, Valentina Cortese and Sylva Koscina.

The Plot: Superstitious Costante Nicosia (Lando Buzzanca) is a wealthy businessman who mistreats his employees and his wife Mariu (Sylva Koscina). On a plane to Rumania to attend a business conference, he meets Count Dragalescu (John Steiner), who invites him to visit his castle in Bucharest. When the conference is cancelled, Constante decides to take the count up on his offer. At the castle, the count introduces Constante to his other guests, three young women and a gay man. That night the count throws a nude dinner party at which Constante gets drunk and passes out. He wakes up the next morning naked in bed with the count. He flees the castle and returns to Italy where he dreams that the count is a vampire attacking him in bed. When he visits his basketball team in the locker room and sees their bare butts in the shower, Constante swoons. Constante is now convinced he is a homosexual vampire. Far more concerned with his sexual leanings than his growing bloodlust, he hopes his doctor (Rossano Brazzi) and a medium (Ciccio Ingrassia) can cure him of his homosexuality. The moral of the story is, it's okay to be a vampire as long as you aren't a homosexual one. *Che schifo*!

Dracula Blows His Cool

Filmed in haste to capitalize on the success of AIP's *Love at First Bite* (see the chapter on American International), *Dracula Blows His Cool* (*Graf Dracula in Oberbayern*, 1979) also borrows ideas from *The Vampire Happening* and *Vampira*. As in *The Vampire Happening*, there are copious amounts of female nudity on display but the comedy is even worse than it was in that film. The comedy bits here, particularly one involving a giant silver phallus, are truly abysmal. If nothing else, *Dracula Blows His Cool* at least gives viewers a new appreciation for the jokes in *Vampira* and *Love at First Bite* which are hilarious by comparison. This West German production was the debut of Swiss director Carl Schenkel (using the pseudonym Carlo Ombra). Handsome Italian spaghetti Western star Gianni Garko (Johnny Garco in the U.S. version) plays the dual role of Dracula and his descendant. He makes a pretty decent-looking vampire so it's a pity he was wasted in this crummy movie.

The Plot: Erotic photographer Stan von Skrew (Gianni Garko) inherits his family's ancestral castle in Austria and takes his crew there for a photo shoot. While exploring the castle, a crew member, Chubby (Tobias Meister), discovers an underground crypt with two stone tombs. He brings the rest of the gang down to investigate but before they can open the tombs, they are driven away by a strange man. This is faithful servant Boris (Ralf Wolter), who has been keeping Count Stanislaus Dracula (also Garko) and his bride, Countess Olivia (Betty Verges), alive with blood stolen from the local hospital. Stan decides to turn the castle into a discotheque which is something the rural village obviously needs. His sexy models drive around the village naked in a Volkswagen convertible to drum up business. The publicity works and soon the castle is filled with people dancing to the song "Rock Me Dracula." Boris no longer needs to rob the hospital for blood as now Dracula and Olivia have a fresh supply of victims at hand. Stan eventually comes to realize that his lookalike great- grandfather is alive and a vampire. This gives him the idea to turn the castle into Hotel Dracula to capitalize on the hordes of tourists seeking a thrill. Dracula and Olivia prey on the guests until even they have had enough of the bloodletting. All these willing victims have become too much of a good thing. The movie ends with their coffins loaded on a coach and Boris driving them off to seek out less commercial endeavors.

Barry McKenzie Holds His Own

Leaving Europe and heading "Down Under" (in this case, way down under, quality-wise), we have a vulgar Australian comedy called *Barry McKenzie Holds His Own.* "Barry McKenzie" was a comic strip character created by Dame Edna Everage (aka Barry Humphries) for the British satirical magazine *Private Eye.* The fictitious McKenzie is an Australian bloke who travels to London where he continually shocks the gentry with his uncouth behavior. The character became so popular in Australia that a movie was made, *The Adventures of Barry McKenzie* (1972), in which singer-comedian Barry Croker played Barry McKenzie and Barry Humphries played his Aunt Edna. Funded by the Australian government, the $250,000 film went on to become the first Australian movie to make over a million dollars at the home box office. Its success led to a sequel two years later. Made for almost twice the budget of the first picture, *Barry McKenzie Holds His Own* still managed to make a million and a half dollars at the Australian box office. The most remarkable thing about the Barry McKenzie movies is that they were directed by Bruce Beresford, the man later responsible for *Breaker Morant* and the Academy Award-winning Best Picture *Driving Miss Daisy. Barrie McKenzie Holds His Own* was finally given a U.S. theatrical showing in New York in 1985, well after Bruce Beresford had established himself as a respected director. The two Barry McKenzie films were his first directorial efforts so I guess he can be forgiven.

The Plot: Barry McKenzie (Barry Croker) and his Aunt Edna (Barry Humphries) are flying home from their trip to London, chronicled in the previous movie. On the plane, the minions of the vampire Count Erich von Plasma (Donald Pleasence) somehow mistake Aunt Edna for the Queen of England. They kidnap her and take her to Transylvania where von Plasma intends to use her as a tourist attraction. In addition to being a vampire, the count is also the Transylvanian minister of tourism. Barry, his twin brother the Rev. Kevin (also Barry Coker) and several friends invade Transylvania to rescue Aunt Edna. In the end, Aunt Edna is safely returned home where Gough Whitlam, then the real-life prime minster of Australia, confers on her the title of Dame Edna Everage ... and the rest is female impersonator history.

CHAPTER 17

Vampire Porn

The softcore movie *Dracula—the Dirty Old Man* is an early example of vampire porn. Released in December 1969, it ended the decade with a groan rather than a bang. Vince Kelly stars as the vampire Alucard who enslaves Dr. Jekyll (Bill Whitton) and turns him into a Jackal-Man. There are also a lot of naked women but not much else. A year later, *Sex and the Single Vampire* starred porn legend John C. Holmes as Count Spatula. This is also a softcore film despite Holmes' participation, but there are rumors that a longer hardcore version existed. The plot has Count Spatula's nephew bringing a group of his friends to his uncle's house for an orgy. He doesn't know that his uncle is a vampire. Uncle Spatula observes the various naked couplings until he gets so excited that he must participate. Then he becomes so caught up in the sex that he fails to notice the rising sun and is reduced to a skeleton.

In 1971, Las Vegas filmmaker Ray Dennis Steckler, best known for his 1964 atrocity *The Incredibly Strange Creatures Who Stopped Living and Became Mixed-Up Zombies,* made two vampire porn films. On *The Mad Love Life of a Hot Vampire,* which didn't get released until 1975, Steckler directed using the pseudonym Sven Christian. Dracula (Jim Parker) is a Las Vegas pimp with a bevy of buxom vampire hookers who bite their male victims in a particularly vulnerable spot. Steckler's then-wife Carolyn Brandt plays Mrs. Dracula. The second film is *The Horny Vampire* with Jerry Delony as Count Talcum, who wanders the streets of Las Vegas cracking bad jokes and searching for loose women. Also in 1971 there was *Count Erotica—Vampire* directed by Antonio Teritoni and starring Antona Morell as a particularly unappealing vampire. This one is so bad that it actually makes the two Steckler films seem palatable. A sex scene featuring Count Erotica's bride and his imbecilic assistant Phallus is especially cringe-inducing.

Gerard Damiano's *Deep Throat* (1972) was the first of the hardcore sex films to reach a more mainstream audience and get widespread attention. It was instrumental in the creation of the genre which came to be known as "Porno Chic." Damiano followed up with *The Devil in Miss Jones*, which became one of the ten highest-grossing films of 1973. The new "Porno Chic" movies were shot with some style and actually had some okay acting and decent production values. They made the clunky porn films which preceded them look even worse than they already did. Moviegoers were now expecting quality, even in their adult entertainment.

Sexcula (1974) is notable for several reasons. The only XXX movie ever shot in Vancouver, British Columbia, it was partially funded by the Canadian Government film program. It had only one theatrical showing before being consigned to the vaults of obscurity by producer Clarence Frog (aka Clarence Neufeld). The plot involves Dr. Fellatingstein (Jamie Orlando), who has created a monster (John Alexander) to be her sex slave. The problem is, the monster has no interest in sex. Dr. Fellatingstein enlists the aid of her sexy vampire cousin, Countess Sexcula (Debbie Collins), with the hope that she can awaken sexual desire in the monster. For those who care, the movie was unearthed in 2013 for all to see on DVD.

Thankfully, *Gayracula* ("He'll suck you dry!") didn't show up until 1983 so I don't have to discuss it here other than to say that the catch line says it all.

Poorly photographed and filled with lame jokes, the majority of the vampire porn movies from the early '70s were so badly made that *Dracula Sucks* is a masterpiece by comparison. In fact, *Dracula Sucks* is far better from a technical standpoint than many of the "straight" vampire movies of the '70s. Perhaps this is because it was a movie conceived by its director with high hopes and lofty intentions.

Dracula Sucks

Director Phillip Marshak was a big fan of the Bela Lugosi 1931 *Dracula* and he had attempted, unsuccessfully, to get the rights from Universal to remake it. In 1978, he decided to try a different approach to filming the story. He gathered together an impressive cast of adult movie superstars and filmed a much more serious take on the vampire porn movie. The result was *Dracula Sucks*. With far better production values than the average adult film, Marshak hoped his movie would make a crossover to mainstream cinema audiences as Gerard Damiano's films had done. When his original 95-minute version failed to find the mass audience he hoped for, Marshak released two other versions of the film, each cut with specific audiences in mind. A toned-down version of *Dracula Sucks* for general audiences was released with a 76-minute running time. At the same time, a 74-minute version, *Lust at First Bite,* was released with far more explicit sex. A 108-minute version entitled *Dracula's Bride* is also reputed to have been prepared but it has yet to surface.

Dracula Sucks' eclectic cast features several of the most popular and prolific stars of the "Porn Chic" era. Jamie Gillis as Dracula and Annette Haven as Mina were major stars of the genre. Gillis would reprise his role as Dracula in the 1980 hardcore movie *Dracula Exotica*. Jonathan Harker was played by Paul Thomas, who began his movie career playing Peter (using his real name Philip Toubus) in the 1973 film version of the musical *Jesus Christ Superstar.* The following year he made the leap to performer and later director of nearly 400 hardcore porn films. John C. Holmes is also featured in a "standout" support role. In addition to these adult movie superstars, character actor Reggie Nalder (*Salem's Lot* and *Zoltan, the Hound of Dracula*) is Van Helsing. Richard Bulik as Renfield seems to be channeling Dwight Frye from the 1931 *Dracula* but he's even more over-the-top, if that's possible. In the hardcore version, Bulik is billed as "McGoogle Schlepper."

The differences between *Dracula Sucks* and *Lust at First Bite* are major. The *Dracula Sucks* sex scenes are far less explicit although the two sequences featuring John Holmes are the most hardcore of the lot. There are, however, no "money shots" in the film at all. Instead there are a lot of fangs and bloodletting. Huge chunks of dialogue are taken directly from the Hamilton Deane-John L. Balderston play *Dracula,* which was enjoying a successful Broadway revival at the time that *Dracula Sucks* was produced. *Lust at First Bite* rearranges the sequence of many of the scenes and cuts out several others, thereby removing most of the plot exposition. All of the shots showing fangs and excessive blood are eliminated. Several new sequences featuring explicit hardcore sex are added and Dracula is not destroyed at the end as he is in the original version. Incidentally, the 1979 George Hamilton comedy *Love*

Jamie Gillis is a bearded Dracula in *Dracula Sucks* (1979).

at First Bite was originally titled *Dracula Sucks Again* but the title was changed before release.

Dracula Sucks was filmed at Shea's Castle near Lancaster, California. The end credits read, "Filmed entirely on location in an authentic castle in the high desert of California." Apparently it was a popular hangout for vampires: It was used as a location for Al Adamson's *Blood of Dracula's Castle* and much later for the TV series *Buffy the Vampire Slayer*.

The Plot: Richard Renfield (Richard Bulik), who may be having a mental breakdown, is brought to Seward Sanitarium in the California desert. His first night there, he escapes and goes to the basement of nearby Carfax Abby where he removes a wooden stake from Dracula's heart, thus restoring him to life. Dracula (a curly haired, full bearded Jamie Gillis) wastes no time in making the women at Seward Sanitarium his victims. The first is Lucy Webster (Serena), who is attacked while seated on the toilet! Dracula now has his sights set on Mina (Annette Haven), fiancée of Jonathan Harker (Paul Thomas). Renfield tells Dracula, "Lucy is a slut, Harker is a homo, and Mina is a virgin." With all the strange goings-on, Dr. Seward (John Leslie) brings in Dr. Van Helsing (Reggie Nalder) to assess the situation. In the meantime, the maid (Irene Best) has been turned into a vampire by Dracula. She puts the bite on one of the sanitarium doctors (John C. Holmes) while they are having sex and turns *him* into a vampire. He in turn attacks nurse Betty Lawson (Seka) in a particularly nasty and bloody rape scene. Dracula dispatches Harker (after forcing him to perform oral sex) and then takes Mina to Carfax Abby where he makes love to her on top of his coffin. Seward and Van Helsing open the basement door and let the sunlight shine in on Dracula. Dracula, who is still on top of Mina, writhes in agony and perishes.

Chapter 18

Vampire Oddities

Vampire movies of the '70s showed a diversity unparalleled in the history of horror cinema. The ideas that filmmakers came up with were sometimes highly imaginative but often were just plain wacky. What other decade could have spawned a movie like *Deafula*? This 1975 production, filmed in Oregon and directed and written by Peter Wechsberg in "SignScope," features no spoken dialogue, only sign language.

Wechsberg also stars (under the name Peter Wolf) as a man who believes himself to be a vampire after he discovers that his mother was a victim of Dracula (Gary Holstrom). There is a voiceover narration for members of the audience without impaired hearing.

The eccentrically titled *She Was a Hippy Vampire* (1971) sounds like it might have some camp appeal until you discover it is merely a reissue of Jerry Warren's execrable *The Wild World of Bat Woman*. Originally released in 1966, this not a vampire movie at all. It's a superhero film which was made to capitalize on the popularity of the *Batman* TV series. Warren was sued by National Periodical Publications for copyright infringement so he shelved the picture and re-released it in 1971 under the new title after winning the lawsuit.

The French film *The Sadist with Red Teeth* (*Le Sadique aux dents rouges*, 1971) is an early entry in what I term the "delusional vampire" subgenre in which the main character suffers a mental breakdown and imagines himself to be a vampire. Novelty shop plastic fangs are usually involved. George Romero's *Martin* (1978) and *Vampire's Kiss* (1989) starring Nicolas Cage are better-known examples of this type of film. *The Sadist with Red Teeth* was directed by exploitation filmmaker Jean-Louis van Belle and stars Albert Simono as an artist who imagines he is a vampire after being involved in an automobile accident in which his best friend was killed. There is some comedy and nudity but all in all, it's a pretty grim and confused affair.

Guess What Happened to Count Dracula

You might think from the title that *Guess What Happened to Count Dracula* is a comedy. Nothing could be further from the truth. It's also not much of a horror film. This isn't the worst vampire movie of the '70s but it is one of the least interesting. As I watched, I kept waiting for it to "deliver the goods" but it just sort of lays there, not making much of an impression one way or the other. Considering when it was made, all of the exploitative elements of vampire movies at the time are missing. No nudity, no sex, no gore … no nothing. What it does have is colorful psychedelic lighting and a lot of bad acting. Des Roberts plays Dracula. Or is he Dracula's son? I was never clear on this. Whoever he is supposed to be, he doesn't seem to be sure of what type of film he is in. At times his performance seems as if it might veer towards tongue-in-cheek but then it doesn't. The movie pressbook states that Roberts "has made a specialty of playing Dracula, both on stage and in films" but the only other credit I can find for him is the blaxploitation biker movie *Black Angels*.

After a "premiere engagement" in September 1970 in Asheville, North Carolina (of all places), *Guess What Happened to Count Dracula* went into general release in the U.S. in February 1971. It was released in continental Europe the following May; that version featured nudity and sex scenes shot by director Mario d'Alcala. The European version played under a variety of titles including *Dracula the Sexual Vampire* and *The Orgy of the Vampires*.

The Plot: Count Dracula (Des Roberts) moves into a castle in the Hollywood Hills. Using the name Count Adrian, he opens a Sunset Strip nightclub called Dracula's Dungeon. At the club, he meets out-of-work actor Guy (John Landon) and his beautiful girlfriend Angelica (Claudia Barron). Dracula is drawn to Angelica and promises Guy stardom in exchange for his girlfriend. Guy accepts the offer. Later that night, Dracula bites Angelica while she sleeps. It turns out that there's another vampire in Hollywood, Imp (Frank Donato), and he doesn't like Dracula infringing on his territory. He challenges Dracula but is defeated in the ensuing fight for supremacy. In the meantime, Angelica isn't feeling at all well and goes to her doctor (Robert Branche), who

Ad art for *Guess What Happened to Count Dracula* (1971)

wisely gives her a book on vampires. After Dracula's second bite, Angelica craves raw meat and cannot bear the sunlight.

Guy comes to his senses and regrets his deal with Dracula. He and the doctor go to Dracula's castle to try and save Angelica from the third bite which will transform her into a vampire. They are already too late:

Angelica rips out Guy's throat with her fangs as the doctor flees in terror. Dracula and Angelica presumably live happily ever after in Hollywood.

Jonathan

Jonathan (1970) is the one film that eluded me for viewing when I was writing this book. It is only available on a German-language DVD with no English subs. Since I could not locate a copy of it in English, I had to rely on my recollections of the movie from when I first saw it circa 1973. This West German film, written and directed by Hans W. Geissendorfer, is more a political statement than a horror film with the vampires being a metaphor for fascism. The story revolves around a young man, Jonathan (Jürgen Jung), who leads a group of vampire hunters in an attempt to rid his town of the undead. Count Dracula (Paul Albert Brumm) and his military uniformed minions have taken over the government and reduced the remaining humans to the status of livestock.

My main impression of the movie at the time was that it looked great but was terribly pretentious. *New York Times* reviewer Roger Greenspun, who typically trashed vampire movies, responded to this pretension in a big way in his June 16, 1973, review: "The whole film is invested with a kind of solemnity that is sometimes terrifying (though never cheaply shocking) and sometimes silly, but that, on balance, makes it the most beautiful-looking vampire movie I have seen." To each his own.

Grave of the Vampire

One of the first films to capitalize on the idea of the modern vampire as portrayed in the Count Yorga movies was 1972's *Grave of the Vampire,* directed by John Hayes. The most interesting fact about this strange but effective film is that it was written by David Chase, reportedly based on his unpublished novel *The Still Life.* Two years later, Chase went on to become a story editor for the TV series *Kolchak: The Night Stalker.* He then produced the successful TV series *The Rockford Files* and *Northern Exposure.* Chase's greatest claim to fame, however, is as the creator of *The Sopranos.*

Filmed in Los Angeles on a budget of $50,000, *Grave of the Vampire* cost even less than the original Yorga film. Star Michael Pataki was a staple in vampire movies throughout the '70s and in this one he seemed to be channeling Robert Quarry, particularly during a séance sequence. For ruggedly handsome William Smith, his *Grave of the Vampire* role was be a departure from the biker flicks he was steadily appearing in at this time. In 2001, Smith played Count Dracula himself in the direct-to-video movie *The Erotic Rites of Countess Dracula.*

Producer Daniel Cady waxed enthusiastic about *Grave of the Vampire* at the time of its release: "Starting with a great property, we were sure we would come up with a good film at the very least. But thanks to a cast which outdistanced our every expectation, plus an outstanding labor by director John Hayes and fascinating cinematography throughout, it's all there." He wasn't far wrong and the movie quickly attained cult status.

The Plot: In 1940, frat boy Paul (Jay Scott) takes his girlfriend Leslie (Kitty Vallacher) to the local graveyard to propose marriage and get a little back seat action in his jalopy. As the two make love, the vampire Caleb Croft (Michael Pataki) rises from his grave. Croft tears the door off the car and rips out Paul's throat. He then drags Leslie into an open grave and rapes her.

The next day, a policeman visits Leslie in the hospital and shows her a photo of Croft. Her violent reaction indicates that this was her assailant despite the fact that Croft was a criminal who died three years earlier. Leslie is pregnant and her doctor urges her to abort the baby, but she decides to have it. When the baby is born, it is gray in color and refuses to drink milk. Leslie accidentally cuts herself and the baby greedily responds to the blood. She brings the child up feeding him her blood. The child grows into adult James Eastman (William Smith), who vengefully searches for the father who raped his mother. Thus far, James has managed to stave off his vampire tendencies by eating raw meat. James locates his father under the name of Adrian Lockwood, a professor who teaches night courses in metaphysics at a nearby university. James also discovers that Croft-Lockwood was originally a 17th century vampire named Charles Croydon whose wife Sarah was burned at the stake during the Salem witch trials. Professor Lockwood believes fellow teacher Anne Arthur (Lyn Peters) is the reincarnation of his wife. Further complicating the situation, James falls in love with Anne.

James confronts his father and during a violent fight manages to drive a wooden table leg into his heart. As Lockwood dies, his evil spirit goes into James and transforms him into a vampire.

The Brides Wore Blood

From what I had read prior to watching this movie, I was prepared to see the worst of the worst. It turns out this wasn't the case. There were worse movies that I suffered through when writing this book. That said, *The Brides Wore Blood* (1972) is by no stretch of the imagination a good movie. Made in 16mm in St. Augustine and Jacksonville, Florida, the movie has a definite "Amateur Night in Dixie" vibe and the 84-minute running time moves with all the speed of a glacier. The acting is uniformly dreadful and the story often makes no sense at all. Many of the plot elements are never explained or resolved. The one positive factor is that for a movie shot in 16mm, it looks surprisingly good. *The Brides Wore Blood* was produced, directed and written by Robert Favorite, who had made the intriguingly titled *Riverboat Mama* a few years before. His wife Dottie co-wrote the script, did the makeup and plays a small part. As far as I can ascertain, *The Brides Wore Blood* had only two public showings.

The premiere was held at the Fernandina Beach Municipal Auditorium in June 1972 and the second showing was at the University of South Florida in May 1975.

The Plot: A young man and his girlfriend discover the diary of Carlos De Lorca (Paul Everett), which chronicles his attempts to rid the family of the curse of vampirism. In flashbacks, we see Carlos go to psychic medium Madam Von Kirst (Billie Jensen), who tells him of a ceremony which can lift the vampire curse from his nephew Juan (Chuck Faulkner). To perform the ceremony, four young girls are needed. Carlos lures four women to Casa De Lorca (actually Flagler College in St. Augustine) but in the midst of the "conjuration," the boyfriend of one of the girls interrupts the ceremony and ruins it. Juan goes on a spree, killing one of the girls and turning another into a vampire. Juan then makes love to the remaining girl, Yvonne (Dolores Heiser), impregnating her. Now Uncle Carlos must contend with another vampire being born into the family. Enter Madam Von Kirst, who performs yet another ceremony to rid the unborn infant of the De Lorca curse. Uncle Carlos impales the vampire girl with a broken broom handle and Yvonne inadvertently exposes Juan to sunlight which destroys him. In the end, there is a shocking surprise for Uncle Carlos.

Ganja & Hess

I must confess that for many years *Ganja & Hess* (1973) was off my vampire radar. Given the title, I assumed it was a movie about marijuana. I may have even thought the title was *Ganja & Hemp*. Instead it is a blaxploitation vampire movie with art house aspirations. The film premiered at the 1973 Cannes Film Festival where it was reportedly very well received. It originally clocked in at 110 minutes. The producers were unhappy with director Bill Gunn's unconventional approach to horror and blaxploitation. It was pulled from distribution after only a week and cut down to 78 minutes, a running time thought to be more appropriate for the grindhouse circuit. Rightly displeased, Gunn demanded that his name be removed from the cut version. Lead actor Duane Jones' previous film was George Romero's *Night of the Living Dead* in which he played the ill-fated hero. As Hess he is ill-fated again.

Ganja & Hess is not your run-of-the-mill vampire movie and few of the conventions of the genre are present. The ones that *are* there ... immortality, blood-drinking, defeat by religious iconography ... are given a different spin by Gunn, making *Ganja & Hess* a unique and intriguing motion picture. Mabel King appears in a brief flashback as the Queen of Myrthia. She later played the wicked witch Evillene in the Broadway stage and movie versions of the musical *The Wiz*.

The Plot: The movie opens with a written prologue:

> Doctor Hess Green, Doctor of Anthropology, Doctor of Geology, while studying the ancient Black civilization of Myrthia was stabbed by a stranger three times ... one for God the Father, one for the Son, and one for the Holy Ghost ...
> stabbed with a dagger diseased from that ancient culture where upon he became addicted and could not die, nor could he be killed.

Dr. Hess Green (Duane Jones) has become addicted to blood and is a vampire. His story is divided into three parts.

Part One: "Victim"

Hess has hired a new research assistant, George Meda (played by writer-director Bill Gunn). Hess takes George to his home where he quickly learns that George is a neurotic and suicidal alcoholic. George attempts to murder Hess and then shoots himself in remorse. Hess finds George's body and drinks his blood.

Part Two: "Survival"

Hess survives by stealing blood from a medical facility. Later he is picked up by a prostitute. When her pimp stabs him, Hess kills the prostitute and the pimp in self-defense.

Part Three: "Letting Go"

George's wife Ganja (Marlene Clark) comes looking for her husband and Hess tells her that George has disappeared. The opportunistic Ganja decides to hang around awhile and soon she and Hess become romantically involved. One day, while Hess is out killing another prostitute, Ganja discovers George's body in the cellar. Instead of turning Hess over to the police, she marries him. Hess is so in love with Ganja that he wants to make her immortal like himself. He stabs her with the same dagger that turned him into a vampire. Hess brings a young man (Richard Harrow) home for dinner and Ganja seduces him and drinks his blood. The next day Ganja and Hess dispose of the body even though Ganja is sure the man is still alive. Hess goes to a church with the hope that he can be cleansed of the vampire curse. When this fails, he has Ganja destroy him with the shadow of the cross. Now alone, Ganja sees the young man whose blood she drank running toward the house. Ganja smiles, realizing that she will have a new companion.

Andy Warhol's Dracula

When director Paul Morrissey teamed with Andy Warhol, the avant-garde artist added movies to his list of artistic endeavors. Unlike other members of Warhol's creative company, known as "The Factory," Morrissey was a partner in the enterprise and not a Warhol employee. Morrissey started as a camera operator on Warhol's *My Hustler* (1965) and the next year graduated to director of *Chelsea Girls.* Warhol and Morrissey had their greatest mainstream successes with *Flesh* (1968), *Trash* (1970), *Women in Revolt* (1971) and *Heat* (1972). Although Warhol's name was always above the title, the creative force was mostly Morrissey. In *Holy Terror,* Bob Colacello's 1990 book on Warhol, he quotes Morrissey as saying, "Andy's idea of making a movie is going to the premiere." It's now well-known that Warhol took credit for everything that came out of "The Factory" but is this really unexpected or unfair? Without Warhol as the catalyst, would any of The Factory's projects even have seen the light of day? Warhol's cachet sold the product. But Morrissey feels that Warhol took far too much credit for the movies.

In 1973, following the box office success of *Heat*, Italian producer Carlo Ponti told Warhol he'd finance two back-to-back movies. They would have an $800,000 budget to work with and an eight-week shooting schedule at Cinecitta Studios in Rome. It was planned that both movies would be shot in 3D. As it turned out, the first film, *Frankenstein*, ate up so much of the budget that shooting the second feature, *Dracula*, in 3D wasn't possible with the remaining money. Italian director Antonio Margheriti was brought in by Ponti to serve as a second unit director on both films. Margheriti later claimed that he, not Morrissey, directed the movies, but German actor Udo Kier, the star of both films, has said that Morrissey was the sole director. The alliance of Ponti and Warhol turned out to be an unhappy one and both ended up suing the other regarding profits and screen credits.

Andy Warhol's Dracula (aka *Blood for Dracula*) features an eclectic cast. Kier stars as Dracula and Warhol superstar Joe Dallesandro, with his broad, incongruous New York accent, plays the hero Mario. Italian director Vittorio De Sica has a major supporting role and Roman Polanski is featured in a cameo. Kier was not Morrissey's first choice to play Dracula. Originally he had cast Srdjan Zelenovic in the part. Zelenovic had played Sacha, the male creation in *Frankenstein*. But Zelenovic's passport was stolen and complications with the police could not be resolved by the time *Dracula* shooting was scheduled to begin. Morrissey again employs the improvisational absurdist comic style he used in the Factory-based New York movies, including the obligatory Joe Dallesando nude butt shots. The end result is one of the most uniquely fascinating oddities in vampire cinema.

Andy Warhol's Frankenstein was released in the U.S. in March 1974 and made $7 million despite generally poor reviews and an X rating. Critics found it excessively gruesome but audiences flocked to see the 3D gore. *Andy Warhol's Dracula* was released the following November and got better reviews but made less money. Jay Cocks (*Time Magazine*, December 9, 1974) called the movie a "giddy and gruesome camp-out on the bones of Bram Stoker." Charles Michener (*Newsweek*, February 24, 1975) thought considered *Dracula* "far less bloody, considerably sexier and more consistently amusing" than *Frankenstein*.

The Plot: Count Dracula (Udo Kier) must reluctantly leave his family home in Romania. He can only survive on the blood of virgins and they have become scarce in his homeland. His domineering manservant Anton (Arno Juerging) reasons that virgins will be more

Paul Morrissey, Joe Dallesandro and Udo Kier (in coffin) on the set of *Andy Warhol's Dracula* (1974).

readily available in a country where the Catholic Church predominates, so the pair travel to Italy. At a country inn, the locals tell Anton about the aristocratic Di Fiores who have four young daughters. Actually, the Di Fiore family is hard up for money, most of their fortune having been gambled away by the father, the Marchese (Vittorio De Sica). The

Marchesa (Maxime McKendry) hopes that if one of her daughters can marry Count Dracula, their fortune will be restored. The Di Fiores invite Dracula to stay with them at their mansion where he is introduced to daughters Esmeralda (Milena Vukotic), Saphiria (Dominique Darel), Rubinia (Stefania Cassini) and Perla (Silvia Dionisio). Rubinia is an old maid and Perla is only 14, so Esmeralda and Saphiria are deemed the most likely candidates for marriage. Since the girls have been "raised according to the Holy Mother Church," it is assumed they are all virgins. The problem is that Esmeralda and Saphiria are both regularly "serviced" by their hunky Communist manifesto-spouting handyman, Mario (Joe Dallesandro). When Dracula samples their blood, he becomes violently ill and vomits it back up. ("The blood of these whores is killing me!") Mario finally realizes that Dracula is a vampire and that virginal Perla is likely to be his next victim. To save Perla, he deflowers her. The climax is one of the bloodiest in any vampire movie: The Marchesa is stabbed by Anton but before she dies she shoots him in the head. Mario pursues Dracula with an axe and chops off all of his limbs before driving the wooden axe handle into his heart. In despair, Rubinia, who has become a vampire, impales herself on the stake protruding from Dracula's body.

Son of Dracula

In the early '70s, Beatles drummer Ringo Starr had aspirations as a film actor and producer. He decided to make a vampire spoof called *Count Downe* and hired Jennifer Jayne and her husband Art Fairbank (writing together as Jay Fairbank) to provide a script. At first Ringo planned to make the film a straight comedy but then he decided to make it a comedy-musical as well. He asked his friend, singer Harry Nilsson, to come on board and play the lead. Most of the music would be taken from Nilsson's previous albums *Nilsson Schmilsson* and *Son of Schmilsson*. Only one new song, "Daybreak," was written by Nilsson specifically for the film, which was now titled *Son of Dracula*.

Horror movie veteran Freddie Francis was brought on as director and the cast included Hammer alumni Suzanna Leigh, Dennis Price, Freddie Jones and Skip Martin. Ringo cast himself in the part of Merlin the Magician. Other famous musicians appearing in the film are Keith Moon, Peter Frampton, John Bonham and Leon Russell.

Filming was completed in late 1972 but Ringo was unhappy with the result. He hired writers Graham Chapman, Douglas Adams and Bernard McKenna to fashion a new script that would then be dubbed over the existing dialogue. Ringo eventually abandoned the idea of redubbing the dialogue and, after a brief theatrical release in 1974, *Son of Dracula* vanished into limbo during a kerfuffle involving the Beatles' company Apple. The soundtrack album received a far wider release than the movie ever did.

The Plot: The film opens with a prologue set in Dracula's Transylvanian castle during the 1800s where an unknown person stakes Dracula (Dan Meaden) in his coffin. Dracula's pregnant human wife is overlooked and thus spared. A hundred years later, Count Downe (Harry Nilsson), the son of Dracula, reluctantly goes to London to be crowned King of the Netherworld. His guardian Merlin the Magician (Ringo Starr) is there to assist him along with Baron Frankenstein (Freddie Jones). Count Downe wanders the streets of London and jams with a band in a Soho nightclub. He also meets a beautiful girl named Amber (Suzanna Leigh) which makes him decide he wants to become human. Frankenstein offers to perform the "humanizing" operation but Merlin discovers that it was Frankenstein who killed Dracula and now wants to kill his son as well. Merlin deals with Frankenstein. Count Downe goes to Dr. Van Helsing (Dennis Price), who agrees to humanize him with the help of a blood transfusion from Amber. Although most of the music in the film is randomly inserted and does little to further the plot, the use of Nilsson's version of Badfinger's song "Without You" during the transfusion scene is very effective. The operation is a success and Count Downe can now join Amber in the sunlight.

Chosen Survivors

Chosen Survivors (1974), a U.S.–Mexican co-production, reflects the anti-government, anti-nuclear sentiments of the era. It's a post-apocalyptic story with some vampire bats thrown in for good measure. One of the characters, a former Congresswoman, says, "In Washington, major secrets are kept from people every day," and this statement is the core of the plot. The premise is interesting but the execution often isn't. *Chosen Survivors* has the murky look of the made-for-TV movies of the time and the special effects are simply awful. The cast certainly deserves praise for what they must have endured making this movie. All those bats! Yikes! The next time Tippi Hedren complains about having had birds hurled at her during the making of *The Birds*, somebody should make her watch this movie. That would shut her up! The film has one of my favorite odd movie credits: "Vampire Bat Consultants and Trainers: Dr. G. Clay Mitchell and William Lopez Forment C."

The Plot: Ten people are drugged by the military and taken to a underground facility in the Mexican desert. Here they discover that they are part of a government plan to preserve groups of "chosen survivors" from an impending nuclear holocaust which will make the surface world uninhabitable. The ten are joined by Major Gordon Ellis (Richard Jaeckel), a computer expert there to make sure everything runs properly. This eclectic bunch includes scientists, an athlete and a politician. The "fly in the ointment" is industrialist tycoon Raymond Couzins (Jackie Cooper). The computer that chose him for inclusion desperately needs reprogramming: He's a drunk, a bigot and a rapist. He also complains a lot. Just the sort of person one would want to be cooped up with in an underground bunker. Shaggy-haired and mustachioed Stephen Mayes (Alex Cord) wears shades underground and is the cynical voice of the '70s ("People don't even have time for people!"). While the group tries to get used to their new glass and stainless steel accommodations, they are treated to satellite footage of the destruction of the world above. The first night in their new home, the most neurotic person in the group is attacked in her room by bats. And not just any bats. These are vampire bats. Major Ellis clicks on his keyboard and the response is that everything is secure. But the bats keep getting in somehow. When one of the bat attacks claims the life of scientist Luis Cabral (Pedro Armendariz, Jr.), Peter Macomber (Bradford Dillman) confesses that he is really a government official and that this is all a military experiment; there has been no nuclear holocaust. The system which is supposed to allow them to exit in case of emergency fails. Their only hope of rescue is for former athlete Woody Russo (Lincoln Kilpatrick) to climb the 1758-foot shaft to the surface and push a button which will open the door and alert the military.

In Search of Dracula

The best-selling book *In Search of Dracula* is sometimes credited with the '70s surge of interest in vampires in general and Dracula in particular, but vampire mania was already well underway by the time

18. Vampire Oddities

the book came out in January 1972. It is possible that the authors recognized a popular trend and decided to capitalize on it. *In Search of Dracula* was co-written by Romanian historian Radu Florescu and his American colleague Raymond McNally, professors of history at Boston College. The major doctrine put forth in their book was that Bram Stoker's fictional character Dracula was based on the 15th century historical personage Vlad III, prince of Wallachia, a fierce nobleman warrior who later became known as Vlad Tepes and Vlad the Impaler. Florescu and McNally's research and conclusions were so thorough and convincing that Vlad Tepes has been an unwavering element of the Dracula mythology ever since the book was published. Florescu and McNally continued to mine the vampire treasure trove with their books *Dracula: A Biography of Vlad the Impaler* (1974), *The Essential Dracula* (1980) and *Dracula, Prince of Many Faces* (1989). On his own, McNally wrote *A Clutch of Vampires* (1976) and *Dracula Was a Woman* (1983), which is about Elisabeth Bathory.

A documentary film based on *In Search of Dracula* was released in 1975. It was originally conceived as a 60-minute television program but was later padded to feature length when a theatrical release seemed a viable option. Produced by a Swedish company with additional financial participation from France and the U.S., it presents the premise of the book in cinematic terms. The Swedish title is *Vem var Dracula?* (*Who Was Dracula?*). The movie was produced and directed by Calvin Floyd from a script by his wife Yvonne. Christopher Lee does triple duty: He narrates the film, appears in scenes as Dracula (looking much like he did in the Jess Franco version) and also shows up in Wallachian drag as Vlad Tepes. His contribution enhances the effectiveness of the film; it wouldn't be much of a movie without him.

In Search of Dracula is divided into three parts. The first could be called "Everything You Always Wanted to Know About Vampires": It deals with the various origins and legends which comprise the vampire mythology. The second part is the bloody history of Vlad Tepes. The third and least rewarding section deals with the vampire as presented in literature and motion pictures. While the first two-thirds of *In Search of Dracula* are fascinating and packed with interesting information, the last part seems padded. After going off on a tangent about the origins of *Frankenstein*, the movie returns to the vampire subject with lengthy footage from two silent movies. The first of these deals with a "vamp" of the non-supernatural female variety and the second is from one of Bela Lugosi's early films. Both are scored with silly "silent movie music" which makes the clips even more unbearable. After this unwelcome departure, things get back on track with scenes from Murnau's *Nosferatu*. Then Lee gives a quick rundown of other vampire movies, accompanied by a few stills and posters, and ending with a description of Hammer's contribution to the genre.

One truly cheesy aspect of *In Search of Dracula* is the arbitrary inclusion of scenes from *Scars of Dracula*. The movie opens with Dracula's resurrection from *Scars of Dracula* and includes several other scenes randomly inserted during the rest of the film. It would have been more effective if these scenes had been used at the end to illustrate Lee's narration about the Hammer Dracula films, particularly since the use of actual movie clips is so sparse.

The music score is credited to director Calvin Floyd, but James Bernard's wonderful *Scars of Dracula* score is liberally sprinkled throughout. Neither Hammer Films nor James Bernard are acknowledged in the credits.

Satan's Black Wedding

This obscure vampire outing was made in 1975 by Nick Philips (real name: Nick Millard), who had previously filmed porn movies with titles such as *Nympho, The Slut* and *Pornografi*. For some reason, Nick decided he needed a change of pace so he made two quickie horror movies back to back, *Satan's Black Wedding* and *Criminally Insane*. Shot in San Francisco and Monterey, California, on a very low budget, *Satan's Black Wedding* runs a brief 61 minutes but manages to seem much longer. It was originally called *Brother of the Vampire*; when movies about Satan came into vogue, it was retitled to capitalize on that trend. A ruined church figures heavily in the plot but apparently no appropriate location could be found so we never actually see it. What we do see are gallons of fake blood and vampires with so many phony dime store fangs that it makes their mouths look like bear traps. Even the vampire women in the Count Yorga films have more convincing fangs, and those are pretty bad. Nick Millard later incorporated footage from *Satan's Black Wedding* into his 1987 films *Doctor Bloodbath* and *Cemetery Sisters*.

The Plot: Mark Gray (Greg Braddock) comes to Monterey to attend the funeral of his sister Nina (Lisa Milano), who has apparently committed suicide by slashing her wrists. Mark discovers a manuscript that Nina had written chronicling the history of a nearby church, the site of Satanic worship in the previous century. When Mark's aunt and her housekeeper are murdered, Mark and Nina's friend Joan (Zarrah Whiting) are convinced that there was more to Nina's death than suicide. Their investigation eventually leads them to the desanctified church Nina wrote about. There Mark is confronted by Father Daken (Ray Myles), a 150-year-old vampire. Daken tells Mark that he must marry his sister Nina, who is now a vampire, and together they will conceive a deformed offspring that will be the Son of Satan. Mark flees in his car but it crashes. The last shot shows Father Daken performing a marriage ceremony between Mark, who is covered in blood, and the vampire Nina.

Ken Russell's Dracula

In 1976, director Ken Russell wrote a *Dracula* script inspired by Leonard Wolf's 1975 book *The Annotated Dracula*. The character, as conceived by Russell, was a patron of the arts or, as Russell wrote in his autobiography, "a philanthropist with a taste for the blood of genius." Producer Michael Nolin worked with Russell to develop the screenplay and Martin Poll, producer of several high-profile films (including *The Lion in Winter*), attempted to secure financing. Likely backers pulled out when several other Dracula projects were announced and the Russell film, which would probably been the most interesting of all, was never made. Actors under consideration included Peter O'Toole or Mick Fleetwood (of Fleetwood Mac) as Dracula, Oliver Reed as Renfield (just imagine!), Peter Ustinov as Van Helsing, Sarah Miles as Mina, Mia Farrow as Lucy, Michael York or Alan Bates as Jonathan Harker, and James Coburn as Quincey Morris. The unproduced script was published in 2012 with an introduction by Ken Russell biographer Paul Sutton.

Martin

In 1978, ten years after directing the landmark horror film *Night of the Living Dead,* George Romero made another Pittsburgh-based horror movie, *Martin.* Martin Mathias (John Amplas) is a mentally disturbed young man who believes himself to be a vampire. His old

Mittel European uncle, Tateh Cuda (Lincoln Maazel), also believes his nephew is a Nosferatu. He invites Martin to live with him and unhappy cousin Christina (Christine Forrest) so he can keep an eye on his nephew's actions. Ambiguous, unpleasant and disturbing, *Martin* is one of those "love it or hate it" movies. But it is undeniably a film you will not forget once you've seen it. Romero's original cut ran a whopping 165 minutes and it was cut to 95 for the U.S. theatrical release. A completely different cut of the movie, retitled *Wampyr,* was made for Italian audiences. Most of the psychological aspects of the story are eliminated in this version, which results in Martin appearing to be a real vampire.

Zoltan, the Hound of Dracula

I know it sounds ridiculous, given the absurd sounding premise of *Zoltan, the Hound of Dracula* (1978), but it isn't really all that bad. In fact, it is considerably better than many of the other vampire movies made during the '70s. There seems to have been a "thing" for nasty dogs in movies at this time: They were featured in big-budget horror movies (*The Mephisto Waltz,* 1971, and *The Omen,* 1976), low-budget horror movies (*Dogs,* 1976, and *The Pack,* 1977) and TV horror movies (*Devil Dog: The Hound of Hell,* 1978). With all of these badass bow-wows running around, it was inevitable that at least one would turn out to be a vampire.

Zoltan, the Hound of Dracula was directed by Albert Band (real name: Alfredo Antonini), a "jack of all trades" in the movie business. During his career he was an actor, writer, producer and director. In 1983, Band and his son Charles founded Empire Pictures, a company which specialized in low-budget horror movies.

Makeup artist Stan Winston, whose first brush with vampires was *The Bat People,* this time around had to work his magic on humans and canines alike. Another alumnus from *The Bat People* was star Michael Pataki, who appeared in five vampire movies during the '70s, beginning with *The Return of Count Yorga.* In *Zoltan,* Pataki gets to play both Count Dracula and his descendant Michael Drake. It was filmed entirely in Hollywood (it says so at the end) so there are a number of recognizable locations. The Eastern European tomb of the Draculas is actually the remains of the old Los Angeles Zoo in Griffith Park. The remote camping location where most of the story takes place was filmed at Lake Hollywood Reservoir. And then there is the Port of Los

18. Vampire Oddities

Veidt Smit (Reggie Nalder) in the tomb of the Draculas in *Zoltan, the Hound of Dracula* (1978).

Angeles, familiar U.S. entry point for '70s vampires. I wonder if Count Yorga and Blacula were on the same freighter with Zoltan.

The film was produced independently by Vic Productions. Crown International picked it up for distribution in the U.S. and changed the title to *Dracula's Dog*, robbing the film of any chance it might have had of being taken seriously. But then the "twist" at the end would probably have done that too. It's a real "what were they thinking?" moment and proves that there are few things less frightening than a vampire puppy. Woof!

The Plot: Eastern European soldiers on maneuvers unearth the tomb of the Dracula family and inadvertently release both Dracula's dog Zoltan and his half-vampire servant Veidt Smit (Reggie Nalder). In a flashback, Zoltan is shown attempting to protect his human mistress from Dracula. Dracula turns into a bat and bites Zoltan instead, turning the dog into a vampire. Now freed from their graves, Smit and Zoltan seek out the last of the Dracula family. This is Michael Drake (Michael Pataki) who, as a child, was sent to live in the U.S. to escape his evil heritage. Ignorant of his past, Michael resides in Los Angeles with his wife and children. Smit takes a ship to the port of Los Angeles where a crate containing Zoltan is unloaded. Michael and his family have recently set out on a vacation camping trip. Smit and Zoltan track the family to their camping spot and proceed to terrorize them, turning the family dogs into vampires too. Inspector Branco (Jose Ferrer), a vampire hunter, has come from Europe in pursuit of Veidt Smit and shows up just as the Drake family is packing to go home. After Michael learns the truth about his lineage, he convinces his wife and children to go on without him and he stays to battle the vampire dogs with Branco.

Nocturna

First off, who the hell was Nai Bonet? Well, she was a Vietnamese belly dancer who, after some minor belly-dancing film roles, decided she wanted to be a star. So she formed Nai Bonet Enterprises Ltd. (very limited) and starred herself in *Nocturna* (1979), a disco vampire movie. *Nocturna* gives the term "vanity piece" new meaning. Not only does Bonet star in the film but she was executive producer and wrote the story as well. She also provided work for her family members Laura, Dolores and Pete Bonet, who are listed in the crew credits. Nai was pretty enough (characters in the film call her "beautiful" in breathless tones) but she was a really terrible actress. Not just bad. Terrible. But since this is a Nai Bonet Enterprises Ltd. production, the camera is focused on Nai the majority of the time. Endlessly in some cases. A nude bathing scene goes on forever and it is followed by a disco dance scene which goes on even longer. If you are a fan of Nai Bonet (and there must be someone out there), this is the movie for you.

Perhaps suspecting that even her stellar presence might not be enough to attract a large audience, Nai made sure that *Nocturna* would be a movie that had everything: horror, comedy, romance, music, dancing, drugs and sex. It covers all the bases. That these many elements add up to absolutely nothing is an achievement of sorts. The only good thing I can say about this movie is that it opens with a catchy, pounding disco song called "Love Is Just a Heartbeat Away" sung by the wonderful Gloria Gaynor.

Nocturna also features two aging stars who actually get billing over Nai Bonet: John Carradine as Count Dracula and Yvonne DeCarlo as Jugulia Vein (the name alone should indicate the level of the comedy in *Nocturna*). We first see poor Carradine as Dracula in his coffin without his false teeth. He takes his fanged dentures out of a glass of water and puts them in his mouth. This is a comedy highlight. For her leading man, Nai picked Anthony Hamilton in what has to be one of the most embarrassing film debuts ever. Born in England and brought up on an Australian sheep farm, Hamilton is a tragic Hollywood footnote. Impossibly handsome, he was a trained classical dancer who appeared with the Australian Ballet before seeking greener pastures as a model. Although he is "introduced" in *Nocturna* as Tony Hamilton, a bigger, buffer version of him was also introduced five years later as Anthony Hamilton in a TV remake of *Samson and Delilah*. Anthony was under serious consideration to play James Bond in *The Living Daylights* but producer Albert R. Broccoli reportedly decided to pass on him because of his openly homosexual lifestyle. Hamilton died of pneumonia in 1995 at age 42, a victim of the AIDS epidemic.

Nai Bonet as the title character in *Nocturna* (1979).

The Plot: Castle Dracula has been turned into Hotel Transylvania, which is run by Dracula's granddaughter Nocturna (Nai Bonet). Nocturna falls in love with Jimmy (Tony Hamilton), a musician who plays in the band at the hotel's discotheque. After making love with Jimmy, Nocturna can see her reflection for the first time and feels that she has a chance at real happiness as a human being. She tells Dracula (John Carradine) that she wants to go to New York with Jimmy and try to live a normal life. He protests but she goes anyway. Afraid that Jimmy will discover she is a vampire, Nocturna stays with an old family friend, Jugulia Vein (Yvonne DeCarlo). Jugulia introduces her to the Blood Suckers of America (B.S.A.), a group that wants to promote Vampire Power. After this dreadfully unfunny scene, Nocturna walks interminably through sleazy areas of New York City (to a disco beat) until she arrives at the Juicy Hickey whorehouse. While she watches four naked vampire hookers drain a customer of blood, Jimmy cools his heels waiting for her at the Star Ship disco. Nocturna finally shows up with apologies and she and Jimmy clear the dance floor with their fantastic display of dancing. Jimmy takes Nocturna back to his crummy apartment and teaches her how to get stoned on grass. Under the influence, she confesses to Jimmy that she is a vampire. He's so stoned that it doesn't matter.

Dracula has come to New York with his henchman Theodore (Theodore Gottlieb). He sends Theodore to Jimmy's apartment to kill him and bring back Nocturna but she bares her fangs and drives Theodore away. Then she and Jimmy go back to the disco for more dancing. Dracula shows up at the disco but is repulsed when Jimmy brandishes a large illuminated cross taken from the disco's marquee. Dracula turns into a bat (with the help of some especially bad animation) and flies back to Transylvania. Nocturna, transformed by love into a real human, watches her first sunrise with Jimmy at her side. Cue disco song over end credits.

CHAPTER 19

Dan Curtis
Dark Shadows *and Other Vampires*

TV producer Dan Curtis originally pitched the idea of *Dark Shadows* to the ABC television network as a daytime soap opera with no supernatural elements. When the show premiered on June 27, 1966, it was a gothic mystery which took its inspiration from Charlotte Bronte's *Jane Eyre* but with a contemporary setting. During the first year, the storyline continued in this vein with only modest ratings success. If the series were to continue, Curtis realized it would need to move in a different direction.

Episode 211 of *Dark Shadows* (April 18, 1967) introduced Jonathan Frid as the vampire Barnabas Collins. This was the turning point for the series and afterward the ratings began to climb. The ratings reached an apex between March 1969 and November 1969 when the series adopted a flashback storyline set in 1897 which showed how Barnabas became a vampire due to the curse of the jealous witch Angelique (Lara Parker). After this story arc ended, the show began to decline in popularity and the ratings fell drastically throughout 1970. *Dark Shadows* ended its original run on April 2, 1971, after 1225 episodes.

In 1987, NBC wanted to revive *Dark Shadows* as a prime-time TV series. After several years in gestation, the new *Dark Shadows* finally appeared as a four-hour mini-series in January 1991. Ben Cross now played Barnabas Collins and the debut of the show had a huge audience. But the ratings for the subsequent series failed to live up to expectations and the show was cancelled after 12 episodes. This was due more to poor scheduling by the network than a lack of quality in the series.

For fans of the original show, the less said about the 2012 comedy movie remake, the better. Tim Burton directed and Johnny Depp starred as Barnabas. Jonathan Frid had a cameo. Frid died in April 2012, a month before the movie was released. The film got mixed reviews but was a box office hit, particularly in Europe.

House of Dark Shadows

As early as 1968, Dan Curtis had wanted to do a movie based on *Dark Shadows* and, with the show reaching a high point in popularity in 1969, MGM agreed to finance his production. Rather than being a continuation of the TV series, the plot of the movie cobbles together various characters and elements from the show into a one-off story focusing on Barnabas Collins. The movie does rely heavily on audience familiarity with the characters and situations. Because of this, there is little or no character or background development provided. Nevertheless, it is a good introduction to the world of *Dark Shadows*, albeit a far more bloody one than the TV series could ever have been.

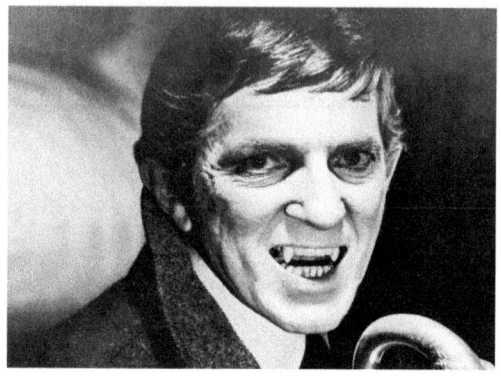

Jonathan Frid as Barnabas Collins in *House of Dark Shadows* (1970).

House of Dark Shadows was released in September 1970 and managed to get some respectable reviews. Foremost among these must be the overly effusive one written by Frederick S. Clarke for *Cinefantastique* (January 1971). He lays it on pretty thick when he says, "The viewer leaves *House of Dark Shadows* with the affirmative sense that the horror film can also be a work of art, and that Dan Curtis is certainly one of the finest talents working in the genre." Really? I think the movie has way too much plot and far too many characters crammed into its 97-minute running time.

The Plot: Demented handyman Willie Loomis (John Karlen) searches the Eagle Hill Cemetery for a treasure he believes to be hidden there. Instead he finds a coffin sealed with chains in the Collins family mausoleum. Willie unwisely removes the chains and sets free the vampire Barnabas Collins (Jonathan Frid). Barnabas shows up at Collinwood Mansion posing as a cousin recently arrived from England. He is shocked to see that governess Maggie Evans (Kathryn Leigh Scott)

19. Dan Curtis

Vampire Thayer David attacks Roger Davis in *House of Dark Shadows* (1970) (courtesy Photofest).

is the image of his lost love Josette DuPres from 180 years before. When a number of bloodless corpses are discovered, Professor T. Eliot Stokes (Thayer David) and Dr. Julia Hoffman (Grayson Hall) conclude that a vampire is on the loose at Collinwood. Noticing that Barnabas casts no reflection in a mirror, Julia goes to him with the theory that she can turn him back into a "normal human being" by isolating the vampire cell in his bloodstream. Eager to have a life with Maggie, Barnabas accepts. Julia succeeds in creating a serum which suppresses Barnabas' vampiric tendencies but in the process she falls in love with him. Consumed with jealously over Maggie, Julia switches the serum which causes Barnabas to look like the 200-year-old man he is. Draining blood from Maggie causes him to regain his more youthful appearance. Barnabas is finally staked through the heart by a dying Willie, but not before most of the main characters have also met bloody ends.

House of Dark Shadows was a big success and a sequel, to be called *Curse of Barnabas Collins,* was quickly planned. When Jonathan Frid declined to participate, the story was rewritten as a ghost story centered around the character of Quentin Collins (David Selby). The resulting film, *Night of Dark Shadows* (1971), eliminated the vampire aspect of the story entirely. Apparently vampires were what audiences wanted to see and *Night* did considerably less well at the box office than its predecessor.

The Night Stalker

Dark Shadows may have ended in 1971 but Dan Curtis was not finished with vampires. Shortly after the gothic soap opera's cancellation, Curtis purchased the rights to an unpublished Jeff Rice novel, *The Kolchak Papers*, which he then turned over to Richard Matheson to fashion into a script. The end result was the TV movie *The Night Stalker*. It was directed by John Llewellyn Moxey, whose previous experience directing horror was the excellent British film *The City of the Dead* (aka *Horror Hotel,* 1960). Darren McGavin stars as Las Vegas reporter Carl Kolchak, who discovers that a vampire is responsible for a series of murders. The supporting cast included some of Hollywood's finest character actors: Ralph Meeker, Kent Smith, Charles McGraw, Claude Akins, Simon Oakland and Elisha Cook, Jr.

The Plot: A number of young women are found murdered in Las Vegas, their bodies drained of blood. Investigative news reporter Carl Kolchak (Darren McGavin), always on the lookout for a sensational story, begins to do some sleuthing on his own. He comes to the conclusion that the murders may have been committed by a vampire. The D.A. (Kent Smith) and police officials refuse to consider the idea until a man with superhuman strength raids the local hospital blood supply, killing several people in the process. Kolchak's friend, FBI agent Bernie Jenks (Ralph Meeker), identifies the killer as Janos Skorzeny (Barry Atwater), a mysterious personage who has left a trail of death wherever he has appeared over the years in various guises. The police now begin to believe that Kolchak may be on to something but ignore his theory that they must seek out Janos in the daylight when he is helpless and drive a stake through his heart. They want to capture him alive and bring him to trial. When Kolchak discovers the house where Janos is residing, he goes there alone to dispatch the vampire ... unwisely ignoring his own advice to wait until daylight. Kolchak confronts Janos, who quickly gets the best of him. The sudden intervention of Bernie Jenks allows Kolchak to overpower Janos and drive a stake through his heart. The police and D.A. decide to bury the story and Kolchak is fired from his job and forced to leave town.

When *The Night Stalker* aired as an ABC Movie of the Week in January 1972, it got the highest ratings of any made-for-TV movie up to that time. A year later, the follow-up movie *The Night Strangler,* also proved to be a ratings winner. A third movie, *The Night Killers,* was planned but ABC requested that the Kolchak character be developed into a TV series instead. Curtis thought this was a bad idea and declined to be involved with the series. In *Kolchak: The Night Stalker* (1974–75), Kolchak (still McGavin) was pitted against a variety of supernatural beings, including a particularly nasty female vampire. The series lasted 20 episodes. In 2005, a reboot of the series, starring Stuart Townsend as Carl Kolchak, ran only six weeks on ABC before being cancelled.

Dracula

The success of *Dark Shadows* made Curtis TV's "go to" guy for horror subjects. *Trilogy of Terror* (1975) starring Karen Black is arguably the most famous of his TV horror movies. He also produced TV adaptations of a number of classic horror stories: *The Strange Case of Dr. Jekyll and Mr. Hyde* (1968); *Frankenstein,* which was featured on the ABC anthology series *The Wide World of Mystery* in 1973; *The Picture of Dorian Gray* (1973) and the best-known of the lot, *Dracula* (1974).

To play *Dracula,* Curtis hired Jack Palance, who had previously starred in his TV *Jekyll and Hyde.* Taking advantage of a larger budget than afforded most of his productions, Curtis shot some location footage in Yugoslavia before moving on to England for the bulk of the filming. This allowed him to utilize a fine cast of British supporting players. Curtis' *Dracula* is a fairly faithful adaptation of the novel with two major differences. This is the first film which adds the element of a female character being the reincarnation of Dracula's long-lost love. By Curtis' own admission, the concept is a retread of the *Dark Shadows* plot line in which Maggie Evans is the reincarnation of Barnabas' former love Josette DuPres. (This plot device has been retained for many subsequent movie versions of the Dracula story and even shows up in the epilogue of 2014's *Dracula Untold.*) The other change is that Jonathan Harker becomes a vampire and never returns to England.

Curtis' *Dracula* debuted on CBS in February 1974. (Later that year, a bloodier version was released by EMI Film Distributors to British cinemas.) The *Los Angeles Times* called it "the definitive Count Dracula" at the time of its original showing, but I find it to be a rather middling version of the story. Palance plays most of his part with a pained expression, as if his collar has been fastened too tightly. He does manage to throw two major hissy fits, however, and they are quite impressive.

The Plot: In 1897, British solicitor Jonathan Harker (Murray Brown) arrives in Bistriz, Hungary, where the local innkeeper gives him a letter from Count Dracula (Jack Palance). Harker is instructed to take a coach to Borgo Pass where he will be met and transported to Castle Dracula. At the castle, Dracula takes notice of Harker's photo showing his friend Lucy Westenra. Harker, who has come to sell Dracula real estate in England, tells him about Carfax Estate, which the count quickly agrees to purchase. Dracula then takes off for England, leaving Harker locked in his castle with three vampire women.

Five weeks later, Dracula arrives in Whitby, England. A short time later, Mina Murray (Penelope Horner) visits her friend Lucy (Fiona Lewis), who has been suffering from an unknown malady. Lucy's fiancé Arthur Holmwood (Simon Ward) has brought in his family friend, Dr. Van Helsing (Nigel Davenport), to make a diagnosis. Van Helsing realizes that she is the victim of a vampire. Dracula has set his sights on Lucy because she is the image of the woman he loved and lost hundreds of years before. Dracula turns Lucy into a vampire and Van Helsing eventually destroys her (first hissy fit from Dracula).

Jack Palance in the title role in Dan Curtis' TV *Dracula* (1973).

Arthur and Van Helsing go to Carfax Estate (good

old Oakley Court) and find nine boxes of earth that Dracula has hidden there. They set the boxes on fire (this prompts Dracula's second hissy fit). Dracula flees back to Castle Dracula with Arthur and Van Helsing in pursuit. At the castle, they stake the three vampire women and then kill Harker, who has himself become a vampire. Dracula is confronted in his library and, in a scene reminiscent of *Horror of Dracula*, Van Helsing rips down the drapes and exposes him to sunlight. Then he drives a lance through his heart for good measure. The camera dollies in on a closeup of a painting of Vlad Tepes and the film ends with this epilogue:

> In the 15th Century in the area known as Transylvania, there lived a nobleman so fierce in battle that his troops gave him the name *Dracula* which means "devil." Soldier, statesman, alchemist and warrior, so powerful a man was he that it was claimed he succeeded in overcoming even physical death. To this day it has yet to be disproven.

Curtis' last vampire offering *Dead of Night,* a horror trilogy, aired on NBC in March 1977. The segment "No Such Thing as a Vampire" stars Patrick Macnee as a doctor whose wife (Anjanette Comer) may be the victim of a vampire. The script was adapted by Richard Matheson from his short story in the anthology book *Shock II*.

Chapter 20

More Television Vampires

During the 1970s, Dan Curtis didn't have a monopoly on television vampires. The small screen yielded a number of other impressive takes on the undead.

Count Dracula

The 1977 British Broadcasting Corporation production *Count Dracula* is certainly the most faithful of all screen adaptations of Bram Stoker's novel. It was presented on British television in its 160-minute entirety in December 1977. In March 1978 it was shown in the U.S. in three parts on the PBS series *Great Performances*. Many critics were impressed by Phillip Saville's direction and the cast, but some found the performance of Louis Jourdan as Dracula to be wanting. Jeffrey Frentzen, writing in the Summer 1978 issue of *Cinefantastique*, thought Jourdan was "the major disappointment" but that the rest of the performances were "uniformly good." Nancy Banks-Smith (*The Guardian*) also found fault with Jourdan, saying that he "emphasized the lover at the expense of the demon." His performance has always been the one controversial element in this production. I find the casting of Jourdan to be spot on, with his somewhat gone-to-seed European charm an asset rather than a liability.

The script incorporates most of Stoker's novel, including much of the dialogue. Other than some unimpressive special effects, it is an all-around handsome production considering the limitations of being made on videotape rather than shot on film. The fine supporting cast includes Frank Finlay as Van Helsing, Susan Penhaligon as Lucy and Judi Bowker as Mina. One odd deviation from the novel is that herein

Lucy and Mina are sisters. Also, and a bit more understandably, Lucy's suitors Arthur Holmwood and Quincey Morris are merged into one character, Quincey Holmwood. For a plot synopsis, one need only read the original novel.

Curse of Dracula

A real television oddity, the NBC series *Cliffhangers* premiered in February 1979. It was created by writer-producer Kenneth Johnson, who had previous successes with *The Bionic Woman* and *The Incredible Hulk*. The series was based on the serials which aired in installments in movie theaters in days gone by. The 60-minute show consisted of three 20-minute segments, each with a different theme. These were "Stop Susan Williams," "The Secret Empire" and "Curse of Dracula." Johnson's luck didn't hold out with *Cliffhangers* which was cancelled after ten episodes. Only the storyline of "Curse of Dracula" was wrapped up in the final episode.

"Curse of Dracula" features Michael Nouri as Count Dracula who, circa 1979, is teaching night classes in European history at a San Francisco college. Hot on his heels is Kurt Van Helsing (Stephen Johnson), the grandson of Dracula's old foe, who is aided in his pursuit by Mary Gibbons (Carol Baxter). Mary attends one of Dracula's classes and becomes infatuated with him. Dracula, who once loved Mary's mother, now wants Mary to join him as his immortal consort. In the end, Mary and Kurt locate Dracula's coffin in the basement of a museum. Mary cannot bring herself to kill the count so Kurt uses a crossbow to shoot an arrow through Dracula's heart.

NBC announced a possible Dracula spin-off series starring Nouri for the 1979–1980 TV season. An hour-long recap of the "Curse of Dracula" segments was shown in March 1979 as a sort of pilot episode. When *Cliffhangers'* ratings were less than impressive, the project was cancelled. The "Curse of Dracula" episodes were later edited into two TV movies, *The World of Dracula* and *The Loves of Dracula*.

Vampire

On October 7, 1979, a few days after Werner Herzog's *Nosferatu the Vampyre* opened in the U.S., ABC televised *Vampire*, a TV movie made by Mary Tyler Moore's production company MTM Enterprises.

TV Guide advertisement for *Cliffhangers*.

It was directed by E.W. Swackhamer, veteran of such sitcoms as *Bewitched, The Flying Nun* and *I Dream of Jeannie*; the script was written by Steven Bochco, who went on to create the successful TV series *L.A. Law, Hill Street Blues*, etc., and Michael Kozoll, a veteran of the *Kolchak: The Night Stalker* series. The fine cast includes Jason Miller, who had scored a great success in *The Exorcist* in 1973, E.G. Marshall, Richard Lynch and Jessica Walter. Joe Spinell played a small role.

Vampire was intended to be the pilot film for a proposed series, so it has an open ending. Apart from a long out-of-print VHS tape,

Vampire is unavailable and has been mostly forgotten. This is a pity as it is quite good and Lynch makes a wonderful vampire. The one drawback is that there are no fangs on view at all.

The Plot: In San Francisco, a new church is being built, the construction unearthing the grave of Anton Voytek (Richard Lynch), a 700-year-old vampire. The architects of the new church are John Rawlins (Jason Miller) and his wife Leslie (Kathryn Harrold). At a social gathering, John and Leslie's friend Nicole (Jessica Walter) introduces them to her new boyfriend Anton Voytek, who hires John to excavate his former home and thereby regain the riches he had accumulated there. John recognizes some of the valuable items as stolen goods and reports Voytek to the police. Voytek takes his revenge by turning Leslie into a vampire. Vowing to destroy Voytek, John is joined in his mission by retired police detective Harry Kilcoyne (E.G. Marshall), who had encountered Voytek 40 years before. John and Harry manage to thwart Voytek's present plans, but the vampire escapes into the night.

'Salem's Lot

When Stephen King wrote his novel *'Salem's Lot*, his admitted inspiration was *Dracula*. His idea was to bring Dracula into modern America. But vampires weren't his only agenda. When he was working on this book, originally titled *Second Coming*, the Watergate scandal had broken and exposure of corruption in the federal government was coming to light. King incorporated into his novel the idea of how easily corruption can run rampant and destroy from within. The complacency of people to recognize and resist underlying evil, be it governmental or vampiric, became a major theme in the story. King later referred to *'Salem's Lot* as "a peculiar combination of *Peyton Place* and *Dracula*," a very apt description. In *Peyton Place*, sex is perceived by the townspeople as a corrupting influence and a failure to recognize and openly deal with it ruins the lives of many of the characters living in that small New England town. The people of *'Salem's Lot* react much the same way to vampirism.

'Salem's Lot, King's second published novel following *Carrie*, came out in October 1975 and became a bestseller, another step toward establishing King's place as the preeminent writer of modern horror fiction. Warner Bros. quickly bought the rights to the novel with plans to adapt it into a feature film. The complexity of the plot and multitude

of characters defeated the attempts of several screenwriters. The project was eventually turned over to the Warner Bros. television division to develop into a TV mini-series. Paul Monash, producer of the movie version of King's *Carrie*, was hired to write the script. Monash had the advantage of having written for the *Peyton Place* TV series so he was no stranger to small towns with myriad characters. Tobe Hooper, director of the groundbreaking horror movie *The Texas Chain Saw Massacre* (1974), was hired to direct.

The CBS mini-series was filmed in Ferndale, California, in July and August 1979 and it ran in two installments in November 1979. It ran 183 minutes. A 112-minute version, with some alternate scenes featuring stronger violence, was released theatrically in Europe and shown on U.S. cable television. Richard Korbitz, who produced *Salem's Lot*, hoped to follow up with a TV series in which main characters Ben Mears and Mark Petrie returned as vampire hunters. This never came to fruition.

The main difference between the novel and the mini-series is in the representation of the character of the chief vampire, Kurt Barlow. In the novel, he is presented as a rather urbane gentleman, much like Dracula. In the TV version, Reggie Nalder is made up to look like an even more horrifying version of Max Schreck's Nosferatu. There is no trace of humanity in this blue-skinned, growling monster, one of the most frightening-looking vampires in all of filmdom. At the time, Stephen King said, "CBS worried about a few things in the screenplay. Some things were left out because of time, some because it's television." In his 1981 book *Danse Macabre*, he wrote that he felt that with the mini-series, he had been "fairly treated."

The Plot: Writer Ben Mears (David Soul) returns to Salem's Lot, Maine, the small town where he had spent part of his childhood. He has come back to write a novel about the sinister Marsten House which overlooks the town and is responsible for his own childhood trauma. Ben wants to rent the house but is surprised to learn that the decaying mansion has recently been bought by antiques dealer Richard Straker (James Mason). Straker is actually the servant of Kurt Barlow (Reggie Nalder), a vampire, and has come to Salem's Lot to pave the way for his master's arrival. Shortly after a large crate is delivered to the Marsten House, a series of mysterious deaths begin to plague the town. Ben becomes convinced that these deaths are the work of a vampire. When the townspeople fail to acknowledge the danger, Ben's main ally becomes Mark Petrie (Lance Kerwin), a young boy whose parents were murdered by Barlow. To destroy the vampire, they must brave the terrors of the Marsten House and locate his resting place.

In 2004, the TNT network aired a new *Salem's Lot* mini-series, directed by Mikael Salomon and starred Rob Lowe. The story is updated to take place in the 21st century. In this version, Rutger Hauer plays a Kurt Barlow far closer to the concept in the novel. The 2004 mini-series adheres more closely to the book but genre fans seem to prefer the 1979 version. Perhaps nostalgia plays a big part in this preference. Both TV adaptations stress some elements in the novel and eliminate others, but each can stand on its own as faithful to the spirit of the book and as good, frightening entertainment.

CHAPTER 21

Full Circle

As the '70s drew to a close, the proliferation of vampire movies continued. The excellent BBC version of Stoker's original had shown on American television in 1978, while 1979 boasted *Love at First Bite*, which is covered in the chapter on American International; a remake of the movie that started it all, *Nosferatu*; and a re-imagining of the 1931 version of *Dracula*. Those last two films were a fitting climax to a decade of vampires.

Dracula

A few months before the BBC *Count Dracula* debuted on British television, a major revival of the Hamilton Deane–John L. Balderston play *Dracula* opened on Broadway in October 1977, just in time for Halloween. The sets and costumes were designed by famed illustrator Edward Gorey and the leading role made a star of Frank Langella. The play had a very successful run (925 performances) although reviews were mixed. Walter Kerr thought Langella was "a superb Dracula." *New York Times* critic Richard Eder opined that the play was "visually stunning—it also tends to be bloodless." Eder found Langella "beautiful and sensual" as Dracula but also felt "he notably lacks terror." After a year, Raul Julia replaced Langella on Broadway and Jeremy Brett went on to play Dracula in the U.S. touring company.

Film producer Walter Mirisch saw *Dracula* on Broadway and approached Universal with the idea of remaking one of their most famous properties with Langella as the star. The studio agreed and offered the job of directing to John Badham, who had just had a phenomenal success with *Saturday Night Fever*. Badham agreed after he

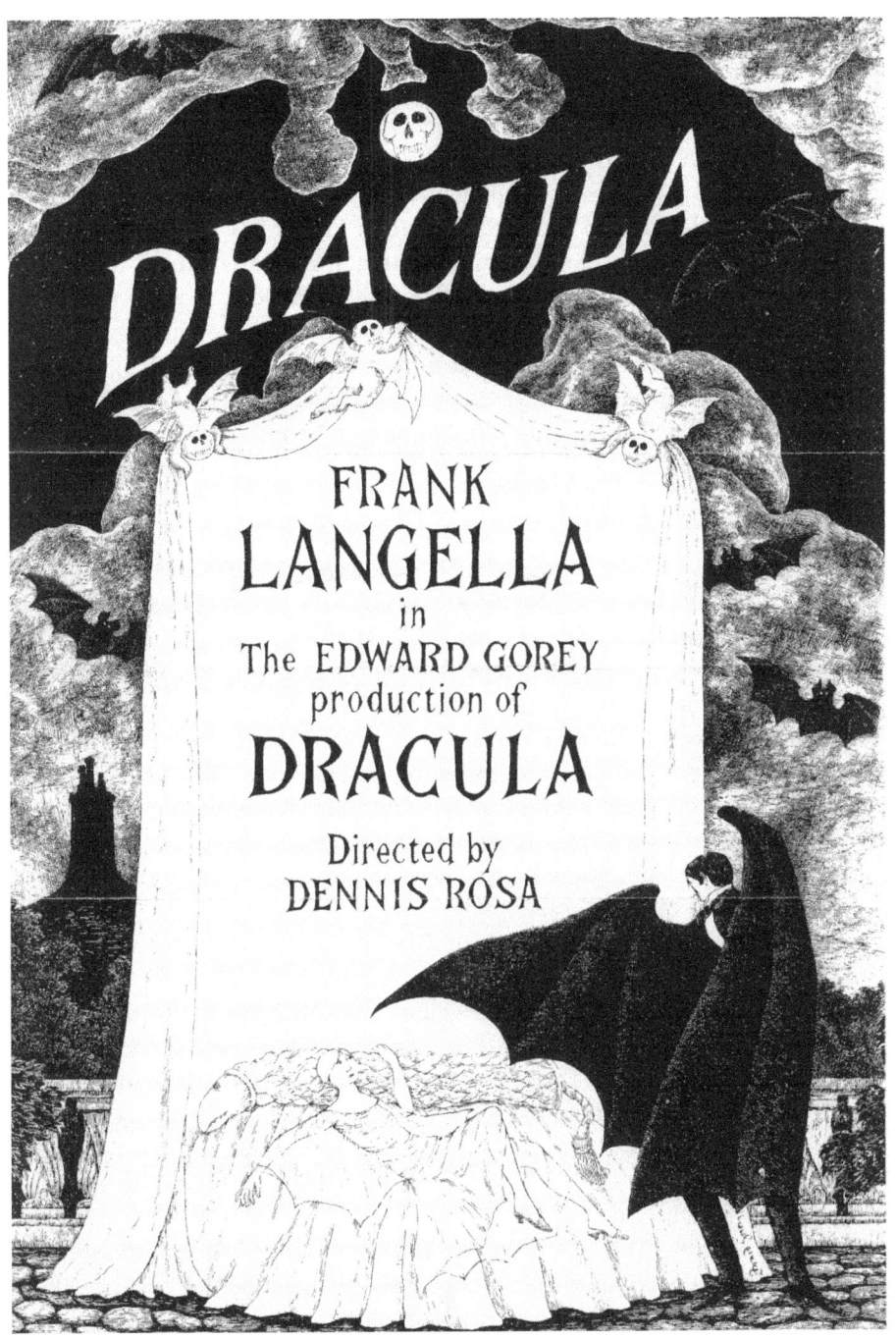

Original playbill for the 1977 Broadway production of *Dracula*.

saw Langella on stage but he didn't want to do a straightforward adaptation of the play. Badham and screenwriter W.D. Richter put elements from the play and the novel into a script which retains a lot of the romantic elements from the play but also includes far more horror.

It was decided to shoot the movie in England with a four-month shooting schedule and a $12 million budget. Badham wanted to shoot in black and white but Universal rejected that idea. To the movie's detriment, Badham finally got his way with the home video versions of *Dracula* where he was allowed to reduce the color drastically.

Released in July 1979, the new *Dracula* was widely considered to be the "Cadillac" of Dracula films. It definitely had the biggest budget of any Dracula film to date. Like the Broadway play, the movie received mixed reviews. Janet Maslin (*New York Times*, July 13, 1979) wrote that it had "style to spare" and praised John Williams' "ravishing score" but her overall impression was that it was "overwrought." Roger Ebert (*Chicago Sun Times*, July 20, 1979) called it "a triumph of performance, art direction and mood over materials." He also praised Williams' score as "soaringly ominous." Richard Schickel (*Time*, July 23, 1979) titled his lukewarm review "Stuffy Nonsense" but he also found it to be "lushly scored." Schickel's review begins with the statement "This is the expensive Dracula that the gang at Hammer Films must have dreamed of making back in the '50s and '60s." True, perhaps, but the makers of this *Dracula* have never acknowledged the debt they obviously owed to Hammer, who had been the first to exploit the sexuality of Dracula in movies.

The greatest achievement of *Dracula* is that it preserves Frank Langella's mesmerizing Broadway performance for all time. The film also served to introduce the marvelous Kate Nelligan to a wider audience. As the willful Lucy (the Mina and Lucy roles are reversed as in all adaptations of the Deane-Balderston play), she often manages to steal scenes from Langella. The same cannot be said of Laurence Olivier, who gives a dreadfully hammy performance as Van Helsing complete with a phony "Mittel European" accent (although he is supposed to be Dutch).

As a whole, *Dracula* is quite good but there are several missteps. One scene in particular seems to be have been added just for the sake of shock value. The vampire Mina, looking decayed and hideous, is staked by her father, Van Helsing, in the mines beneath the cemetery. Mina's body is later seen on a bier in the cemetery looking perfectly

Frank Langella as the count in the 1979 *Dracula*.

normal and obviously not having been staked. Van Helsing then proceeds to remove her heart with a scalpel. The first scene is effective but it makes the second one seem redundant and out of continuity. Dr. Seward's insane asylum is like something out of a Ken Russell movie and the character of Renfield is apparently included only for the sake of grossing out the audience (he eats cockroaches instead of flies).

194 Vampire Films of the 1970s

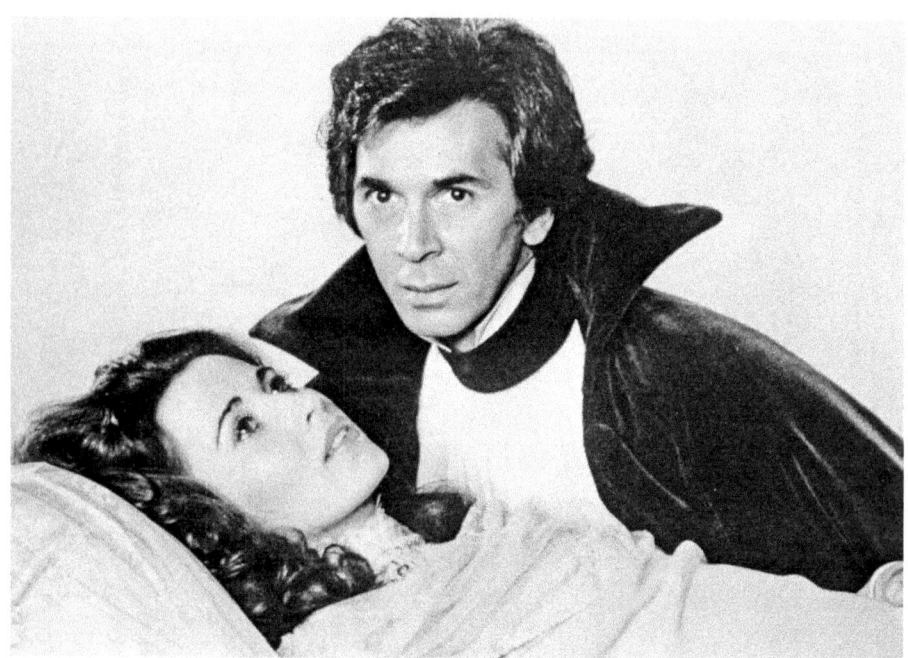

Dracula (Frank Langella) and Lucy (Kate Nelligan) in the 1979 *Dracula*.

Dracula made over $20 million at the U.S. box office but was considered a failure by Universal who had hoped for a real blockbuster. It was felt that *Love at First Bite*, released several months earlier, had ruined audiences' ability to take Dracula seriously. Possibly, but maybe by this time, moviegoers were just getting tired of vampires.

The Plot: During a violent storm, the ship *Demeter* runs aground at Whitby, England. The crew are either dead or missing but the sole passenger, Count Dracula (Frank Langella), is found alive by Mina Van Helsing (Jan Francis). Dracula has recently purchased Carfax Abbey in Whitby for his home. Mina is staying with her friend Lucy (Kate Nelligan), whose father Dr. Seward (Donald Pleasence) runs the nearby insane asylum. Lucy's fiancé Jonathan Harker (Trevor Eve) is a solicitor who had arranged the sale of Carfax to Dracula by mail. Seward invites Dracula to dinner, where Lucy flirts with him to the annoyance of Harker. The evening is marred by the sudden illness of Mina. Later that night, Dracula visits Mina in her bedroom and drinks her blood. The next morning Mina cannot breathe and, despite the efforts of Dr. Seward, she dies. Seward notifies Mina's father, Professor Van Helsing

(Laurence Olivier), who immediately comes to Whitby. Van Helsing suspects that his daughter may have been the victim of a vampire, a theory which proves correct when her coffin is opened and found to be empty. Van Helsing encounters his daughter, who is now a vampire, in the mine shaft below the cemetery and drives a stake through her heart. In the meantime, Lucy's attraction to Dracula has become irresistible and she readily gives herself to him. Dracula responds in kind and decides to make her his vampire bride. All efforts to protect Lucy fail and Dracula eventually abducts her. Van Helsing and Harker finally catch up with them cuddling in a crate in the hold of a ship bound for Dracula's Romanian homeland. When Van Helsing attempts to kill Dracula, the vampire grabs the wooden stake and impales the professor instead. With a last dying effort, Van Helsing hurls a hook into Dracula's back and Harker hoists the vampire up the ship's mast into the sunlight. Dracula is presumably killed by the sun but a final shot shows Lucy smiling mysteriously as she watches a bat-like form float away in the sky.

In my opinion, this ambiguous ending tarnishes the film and seems an obvious device created in anticipation of a sequel. This is now denied by the filmmakers but you can bet that if *Dracula* had been a huge success, a sequel would have been forthcoming. Photos of Dracula reduced by the sun's rays to a skeleton hanging from the mast of the ship were published prior to the film's release but these shots were eliminated to create the ending as it now stands.

Nosferatu the Vampyre

The last vampire movie theatrically released in America in 1979 brought vampire cinema full circle as it was a remake of the first vampire movie, F.W. Murnau's 1922 *Nosferatu: A Symphony of Horror*. German director Werner Herzog considered *Nosferatu* to be "the very best and most important film ever made in Germany." His idea was to directly remake it as a homage and not make just another version of Stoker's novel. In the silent *Nosferatu*, the names of Stoker's *Dracula* characters had been changed in a vain attempt to avoid copyright restrictions; Herzog chose to go back to the names used in the novel. He wanted to film in Wismar, the North German port city which was the original location used by Murnau. When permission to film there was denied him, he decided to film in Delft, in the Netherlands, instead.

The scenes showing Dracula's castle were shot in Czechoslovakia. Klaus Kinski plays Count Dracula in makeup replicating the look of Max Schreck in the Murnau original.

Herzog says that he filmed English-language (*Nosferatu the Vampyre*) and German-language (*Nosferatu: phantom der nacht*) versions of *Nosferatu* at the behest of 20th Century–Fox, who would be releasing the film. I first saw the movie in London where it was shown in English. A few months later I saw it at one of the art house cinemas in San Diego where it was shown in German with English subtitles. I asked the theater manager about this and he said Fox was only offering it in German in an attempt to attract the art house theater crowd who would not generally patronize a horror film. This same strategy was used a few years later for the U.S. release of Fassbender's *Querelle.* Crafty.

Nosferatu the Vampyre was fairly successful worldwide, making a profit on its relatively meager $2.5 million budget. It was much more of a success critically. Vincent Canby (*New York Times,* October 1, 1979) thought it was "a kind of charming diversion" in Herzog's filmography.

Klaus Kinski as the undread count in *Nosferatu the Vampyre* (1979).

21. Full Circle

He added, "It's funny without being silly, eerie without being foolish, and uncommonly beautiful in a way that has nothing to do with mere prettiness." Vampire hater Roger Ebert (*Chicago Sun Times,* October 5, 1979) gave it four stars and said, "There are movies for people who like to yuk it up and make barfing sounds while Christopher Lee lets the blood dribble down his chin, but they're not the audience for *Nosferatu.*" In 2011 Ebert included it in his list of "Great Movies." Kevin Thomas (*Los Angeles Times,* October 12, 1979) found it to be "a film of astonishing beauty and daring." ... [It's] "a dazzling, bravura work for cineastes and is not for audiences expecting *Love at First Bite* or even the new *Dracula.*" The Fox art house ploy had worked beautifully. I wonder what "cineastes" would have thought of the English-language version? All aspirations toward art aside, Roland Topor is terrible in any language as Renfield and even Herzog could not resist using that clichéd '70s vampire "zinger" in his final scene.

The Plot: Jonathan Harker (Bruno Ganz) is sent by his employer Mr. Renfield (Roland Topor) to Transylvania to finalize the sale of a home in the city of Wismar to Count Dracula (Klaus Kinski). Dracula, a strange-looking creature, soon attacks Harker and drinks his blood. Harker realizes that Dracula is a vampire who is going to Wismar in search of new victims. As he attempts to escape from Castle Dracula, a ship bearing several coffins arrives in Wismar. Crew-wise, only the dead body of the captain is aboard. Not long after, Harker is delivered home; he is ill and does not recognize his wife Lucy (Isabelle Adjani) or his surroundings. Meanwhile a plague sweeps Wismar with most of the population perishing. Lucy reads Harker's diary and realizes that Count Dracula who is causing the deaths. She attempts to convince Dr. Van Helsing (Walter Landengast) to help her hunt down the vampire but to no avail. Lucy realizes she must sacrifice herself by keeping the vampire with her past sunrise. That night Dracula comes to Lucy and she welcomes him. Dracula is killed by the sun but Lucy dies too. In the final scene, a fanged Jonathan Harker rides off into the sunset.

With the end of the '70s, the continual release of vampire movies all but dried up. Perhaps Badham's *Dracula* and Herzog's *Nosferatu the Vampyre* were too tough an act to follow ... or maybe the genre had simply played itself out. The three most notable vampire movies from the '80s were *The Hunger* (1983), *Fright Night* (1985) and *The Lost Boys* (1987), all big-budget, major studio releases. Of the few lower budgeted vampire movies released during that decade, *Near Dark* (1987) was the most original and impressive with its "trailer trash" bloodsuckers.

Werewolves briefly supplanted the vampire as Hollywood's supernatural creature of choice. *An American Werewolf in London, The Howling* and *Wolfen* were all released in 1981, but werewolves didn't have the staying power of their bloodsucking brethren. The sexual element which helped make vampire movies so popular wasn't part of the werewolf lore and variations on the theme of lycanthropy weren't as readily applied. There would be no *Black Werewolf* or *Wolf Man's Dog*.

Appendix: Vampires in Print

Movies and television weren't the only entertainment media to exploit the undead in the '70s. Two of the great works of modern vampire fiction appeared during that decade. The 1975 novel *'Salem's Lot* made good the promise of *Carrie* that Stephen King would be a major force in horror fiction. The following year, Anne Rice's *Interview with a Vampire* began "The Vampire Chronicles" which introduced the enduring character of vampire Lestat de Lioncourt. This series has had 11 entries to date. Fred Saberhagen's 1975 novel *The Dracula Tape* made less popular impact but it does offer the novelty of Stoker's original story being told from the point of view of Dracula himself. Saberhagen's 1978 follow-up novel *The Holmes-Dracula File* features two of literature's most famous characters joining forces to fight evil. Saberhagen wrote ten novels in his Dracula series prior to his death in 2007.

During the '70s, the comic book industry also embraced the renewed interest in vampires. Warren Publishing was one of the first to take advantage of the potential of a vampire comic book character with Vampirella, a creation of *Famous Monsters of Filmland* editor Forrest J. Ackerman. The sexy vampire from the planet Drakulon was introduced in the black-and-white magazine *Vampirella* which debuted in September 1969. The popular magazine had an original run of 112 issues which ended in March 1983.

Back in 1954, in response to publisher William Gaines' comic books *Tales from the Crypt, Vault of Horror* and horror comics from other publishers, the Comics Code Authority put a ban on vampires, werewolves, zombies and the like. In 1969, *Vampirella* could circumvent these restrictions because it was a magazine, not a comic book, aimed at a more mature audience and thereby not subject to CCA restrictions. In March 1969, Gold Key Comics, which did not subscribe to the Comic Code, began a series based on the *Dark Shadows* TV series. It ran through February 1976 and totaled 35 issues.

In January 1971, the CCA guidelines were revised and now vampires and other monsters were once again allowed to appear in comic books "when handled in the classic tradition," whatever that meant. Monster comics quickly began to flood the market. Marvel Comics introduced Morbius, the Living Vampire, in *The Amazing Spider-Man* #101 in October 1971. Originally presented as a villain, Morbius proved popular in the Marvel Universe and became a more heroic figure as time went on. He appeared in two publications at the same time: Curtis Magazines, a Marvel subsidiary, put out the black-and-white magazine *Vampire Tales* which ran 11 issues from August 1973 to June 1975, and nine had stories featuring Morbius. Morbius was also the main attraction in 11 issues of Marvel's *Adventure Into Fear* comics, beginning in February 1974 and ending in December 1975.

The Tomb of Dracula, the most successful of all Marvel's monster comics, premiered in April 1972 and ended in August 1979 after 70 issues. During this time, Curtis published the black-and-white magazine *Dracula Lives!* which ran 13 issues between June 1973 and July 1975. In *The Tomb of Dracula*, the arch-vampire vacillates between being a villain and a hero, sometimes joining forces with his enemies to battle even greater forces of evil. The popular vampire-hunting character Blade, introduced in issue #10, also made appearances in *Vampire Tales* #8 and *Adventure Into Fear* #24. In 1975, Blade was given a magazine of his own, Curtis' *Marvel Preview Presents Blade the Vampire-Slayer.* When the comic book series *The Tomb of Dracula* ended, Curtis published a black-and-white magazine version beginning in October 1979. In addition to comic stories, the first issue also featured articles on the upcoming films *Dracula* and *Love at First Bite.* The magazine ended in September 1980 after only six issues.

In September 1976, the ninth issue of the *Marvel Classics Comics* series was a 52-page adaptation of Bram Stoker's *Dracula.* This outstanding comic, written by Naunerle Farr and illustrated by Nestor Redondo, had originally been published by Pendulum Press in 1973. Seeing its striking cover, one might surmise that it was part of the *Tomb of Dracula* series, not surprising as it was drawn by Gil Kane who had done many *Tomb of Dracula* covers. Marvel's answer to *Classics Illus-*

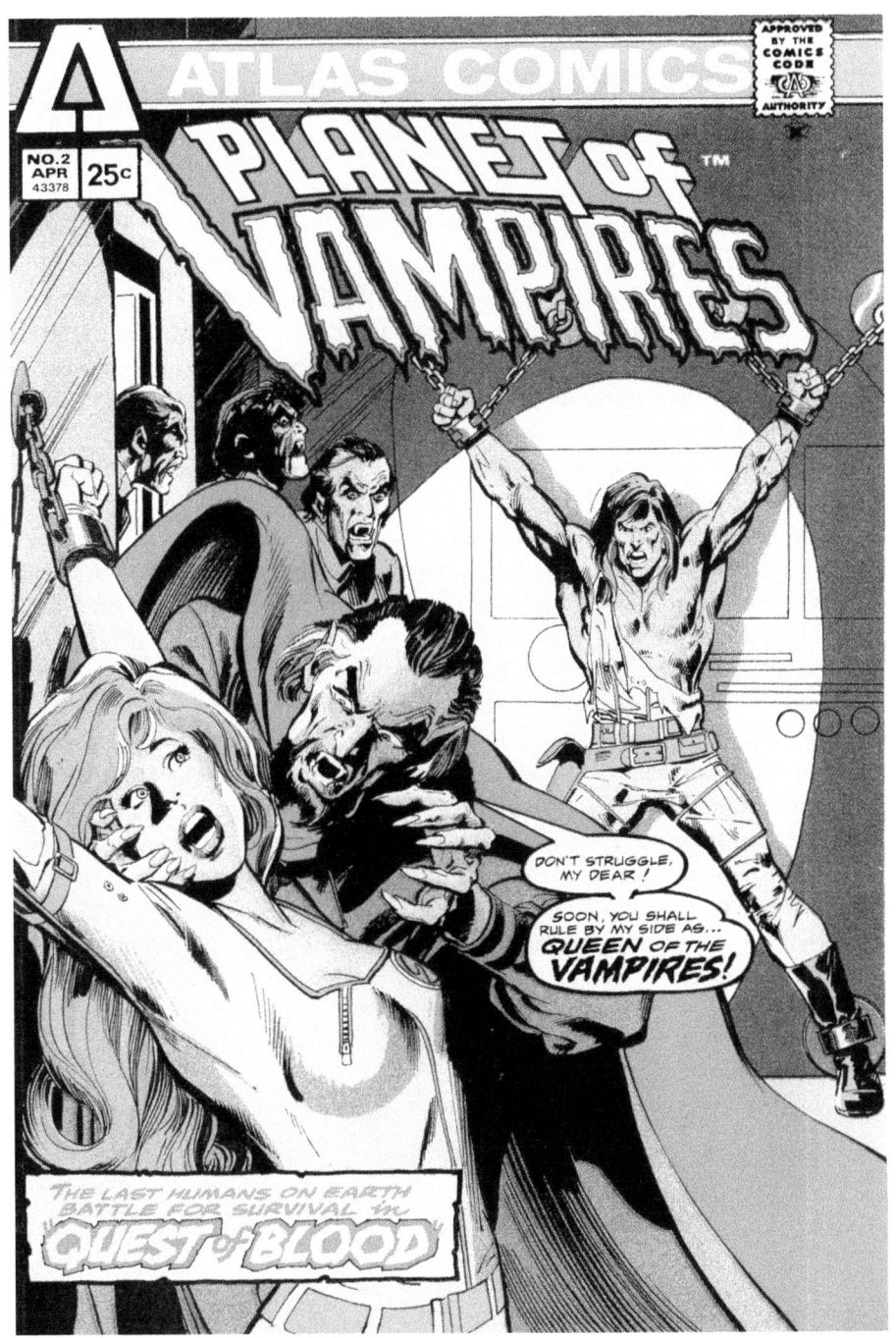

Issue 2 of Atlas Comics' short-lived series *Planet of Vampires* (1975).

trated, the Marvel Classics Comics series ran for 36 issues from 1976 to 1978.

Although Marvel totally embraced the monster comic boom of the '70s and utilized continuing characters such as Morbius, Dracula, the Werewolf and Frankenstein's Monster, their chief rival DC opted for horror anthology comics without continuing supernatural characters. It wasn't until *House of Mystery* #290 (March 1981) that DC introduced their vampire character Andrew Bennett in the continuing story series "I ... Vampire!" which appeared in 24 issues. The "I ... Vampire!" stories were generally quite good but by the time they appeared, the subject was already becoming overly familiar.

The short-lived Atlas Comics line published the three-issue series *Planet of Vampires* (February–July 1975). The continuing story was more science fiction than supernatural although the cover of the second issue would lead one to believe otherwise as it shows a very Dracula-like vampire attacking a woman. Nothing like this appears inside the comic. Atlas put out another vampire comic in June 1975, *Fright #1: Featuring the Son of Dracula*, written by Gary Friedrich and illustrated by Frank Thorne. An editorial column in the book acknowledges the present trend in vampires: "Dracula. It is a sinister word that has passed into common usage. Yet it has not outworn its insidious appeal. Witness the continuing proliferation of interest in the cloaked nightstalker, most recently evidenced by Andy Warhol's *Dracula*, a cinematic bloodbath." *Son of Dracula* didn't make it beyond the first issue as Atlas Comics went out of business a few months after it was released. This is a real pity as it was one of the most well-written and finely drawn of all the vampire comics.

Filmography

Andy Warhol's Dracula (aka *Blood for Dracula*)
"He couldn't live without a virgin's blood.... So a virgin had to die!"
Italy: Compagnia Cinematografica Champion Production (1974) USA: Bryanston (1974)
PRODUCERS: Andy Warhol, Andrew Braunsberg, Jean Yanne DIRECTOR/WRITER: Paul Morrissey MUSIC: Claudio Gizzi CAST: Udo Kier, Joe Dallesandro, Arno Juerging, Vittorio De Sica, Maxime McKendry

Assignment Terror
(*Los monstruos del terror*/*Monsters of Terror*) "The Ultimate in Horror!"
Spain/West Germany
Eichberg Film, Producciones Jaime Prades (1970) USA: American International Television
PRODUCER: Jaime Prades DIRECTOR: Tulio Demicheli WRITER: Jacinto Molina Álvarez MUSIC: Franco Salina CAST: Paul Naschy, Michael Rennie, Karin Dor, Patty Shepard, Craig Hill

Barry McKenzie Holds His Own
"Hard on the heels of evil ... soft on the lips of sheilahs!" Australia: Reg Grundy Productions Ltd. (1974)
USA: Satori (1985)
PRODUCERS: Bruce Beresford, Drummond Challis DIRECTOR: Bruce Beresford WRITERS: Bruce Beresford, Barry Humphries MUSIC: Peter Best CAST: Barry Crocker, Barry Humphries, Donald Pleasence, Nancy Blair, Dick Bentley

The Bat People (aka *It Lives by Night*)
"No matter how hard you pray ... or how loud you scream it's no use!"
USA: A Lou Shaw Production; American International (1974)
PRODUCER/WRITER: Lou Shaw DIRECTOR: Jerry Jameson MUSIC: Artie Kane CAST: Stewart Moss, Marianne McAndrew, Michael Pataki, Paul Carr, Robert Burke

Blacula

"The most horrifying film of the decade."—Count Dracula Society
USA: American International (1972)
PRODUCER: Joseph T. Marr DIRECTOR: William Crain WRITERS: Joan Torres, Raymond Koenig MUSIC: Gene Page CAST: William Marshall, Denise Nichols, Vonetta McGee, Gordon Pinsent, Thalmus Rasulala

Blood

"Sickening horror to haunt your nightmares!" USA: Damiano Film Productions Inc. (1974) PRODUCER: Walter Kent DIRECTOR/WRITER: Andy Milligan CAST: Allan Berendt, Hope Stansbury, Patricia Gaul, Pamela Adams, Michael Fischetti

William Marshall as the title character in *Blacula* (1972).

The Blood Drinkers

(*Kulay dugo ang gabi*; *Blood Is the Color of the Night*)
"Blood Drinkers begin where Dracula, Frankenstein, and the Wolf Man left off!" Philippines: A Cirio H. Santiago Production (1964)
USA: Hemisphere Pictures (1966); The Vampire People (1971)
PRODUCER: Cirio H. Santiago DIRECTOR: Gerardo de Leon WRITER: Cesar Amigo CAST: Ronald Remy, Amalia Fuentes, Mary Walter, Eva Montez, Eddie Fernandez

The Blood Spattered Bride

(*La novia ensangrentada*; *The Bloody Bride*)
"See why she had to kill every man on his wedding night!" Spain: Morgana Films (1972)
USA: Europix International (1974)
PRODUCER: Jaime Fernandez-Cid DIRECTOR/WRITER: Vicente Aranda MUSIC: Antonio Perez Olea CAST: Simón Andreu, Alexandra Bastedo, Maribel Martin, Rosa M. Rodriguez, Dean Selmier

Bloodsuckers (aka *Incense for the Damned*)

"A distorted world comes to life—forbidden secrets sensationally revealed! It's Way Out!" England: A Lucinda Production (1970)
USA: Chevron Pictures (1971)
PRODUCER: Graham Harris DIRECTOR: Robert Hartford-Davis WRITER: Julian More MUSIC: Bobby Richards CAST: Patrick Mower, Patrick Macnee, Peter Cushing, Alexander Davion, Imogen Hassall

The Body Beneath
"Sexually rampant ghouls, depraved souls ... and blood-red roses!"
England: Cinemedia Films (1969)
USA: Nova International Productions Ltd. (1970) PRODUCER: Graham Steane
DIRECTOR/WRITER: Andy Milligan CAST: Gavin Reed, Jackie Skarvellis, Susan Heard, Emma Ross, Berwick Kaler

The Brides Wore Blood
"Sometimes death is the easy way out"
USA: A Robert R. Favorite Production (1972)
PRODUCER/DIRECTOR: Robert R. Favorite WRITERS: Robert R. Favorite, Dottie Favorite, Liz Blanda, Tom Rahner, Bob Smith MUSIC: Lee Peters CAST: Dolores Heiser, Chuck Faulkner, Paul Everett, Ben Robinson, Jan Sherman

Captain Kronos Vampire Hunter
"The only man alive feared by the walking dead"
England:Hammer Films (1973)
USA: Paramount (1974)
PRODUCERS: Albert Fennell, Brian Clemens
DIRECTOR/WRITER: Brian Clemens MUSIC: Laurie Johnson CAST: Horst Janson, Caroline Munro, John Carson, Shane Briant, John Cater

Horst Janson as *Captain Kronos Vampire Hunter* (1973).

Chosen Survivors
"1,758 feet underground, a perfect world programmed for man's survival, except for..."
USA/Mexico: An Alpine Production in association with Churubusco Studios Metro Media Producers Corporation (1974)
PRODUCERS: Leon Benson, Charles Fries DIRECTOR: Sutton Roley WRITERS: H.B. Cross, Joe Reb

Moffly, MUSIC: Fred Karlin CAST: Jackie Cooper, Richard Jaeckel, Alex Cord, Diana Muldaur, Pedro Armendariz, Jr.

Count Dracula (El Conde Dracula)
"The moon is full ... the tomb is empty ... and terror lurks!" Spain/West Germany: Korona Film; Towers of London (1970)
USA: Warner (1972)
PRODUCERS: Arturo Marcos, Harry Alan Towers DIRECTOR: Jess Franco WRITER: Augusto Finocchi MUSIC: Bruno Nicolai CAST: Christopher Lee, Herbert Lom, Maria Rohm, Soledad Miranda, Klaus Kinski

Count Dracula
England: British Broadcasting Corporation (1977) USA-PBS TV (1978)
PRODUCER: Morris Barry DIRECTOR: Philip Saville WRITER: Gerald Savory MUSIC: Kenyon Emrys-Roberts CAST: Louis Jourdan, Susan Penhaligon, Judi Bowker, Frank Finlay, Bosco Hogan

Count Dracula's Great Love
(*El gran amor del conde Drácula*)
"She's the kind of girl you can sink your teeth into." Spain: Janus Films (1973)
USA: International Amusement Corp. (1974)
PRODUCER: Francisco Lara Polop DIRECTOR: Javier Aguirre WRITERS: Javier Aguirre, Alberto Insura, Jacinto Molina Álvarez MUSIC: Carmelo Barnaola CAST: Paul Naschy, Rossana Yanni, Haydée Politoff, Álvaro De Luna, Vic Winner

Count Erotica—Vampire
USA: Lobo Films (1971)
PRODUCER: Hans Klepper DIRECTOR: Antonio Teritoni WRITER: Ivan Canter CAST: Antona Morell, Joy Winters, Phil Craig, Anna Busch, Robin Tate

Count Yorga—Vampire
"A tale of unspeakable cravings.... The most terrifying experience of your life!" USA: American International (1970)
PRODUCER: Michael Macready DIRECTOR/WRITER: Bob Kelljan MUSIC: Bill Marx CAST: Robert Quarry, Roger Perry, Donna Anders, Judith Lang, Michael Murphy

Countess Dracula
"Blood. The more she drinks the prettier she gets. The prettier she gets, the thirstier she gets." England: Hammer Films (1971)
USA: 20th Century–Fox (1972)
PRODUCER: Alexander Paal DIRECTOR: Peter Sasdy WRITER: Jeremy Paul MUSIC: Harry Robinson CAST: Ingrid Pitt, Sandor Eles, Nigel Green, Leslie-Anne Down, Maurice Denham

Curse of Dracula
USA: Universal Television; NBC-TV (1979)
PRODUCER: Kenneth Johnson DIRECTORS: Kenneth Johnson, Richard Milton, Jeffrey Hayden, Sutton Roley WRITERS: Kenneth Johnson, Myla Lichtman MUSIC: Joe Harnell, Charles Cassey, Les Baxter, Ira Hearshen CAST: Michael Nouri, Stephen Johnson, Antoinette Stella, Mark Montgomery, Carol Baxter

The Curse of the Vampire
(*La llamada del vampiro; The Call of the Vampire*) Spain: Arco/Lacy/Sesena Films (1972)
PRODUCER: Riccardo Vazquez DIRECTOR: José Maria Elorrieta WRITERS: José Maria Elorrieta, Enrique Gonzalez Macho CAST: Nicholas Ney, Diana Sorel, Inés Moreles, Loretta Martin, Beatriz Lacy

Curse of the Vampires
(*Ibulong mo sa hangin; Whisper to the Wind*) "Creatures of evil ... draining the blood of the innocent!" Philippines: AM Productions (1966) USA: Hemisphere Entertainment (1971)
PRODUCER: Amalia Muhlach DIRECTOR: Gerardo de Leon WRITERS: Ben Feleo, Pierre Salas MUSIC: Tito Arevalo CAST: Amalia Fuentes, Romeo Vasquez, Eddie Garcia, Mary Walter, Johnny Monteiro

Daughters of Darkness
(*Les Lèvres rouges; The Red Lips*)
"They are waiting for you—They thrive on BLOOD!"
Belgium: Cine Vog/Roxy/Maya/Showking Production (1971) USA: Maron Films (1971)
PRODUCERS: Paul Collet, Henry Lange DIRECTOR: Harry Kumel WRITERS: Harry Kumel, Pierre Drouot MUSIC: Francois de Roubaix CAST: Delphine Seyrig, John Karlen, Danielle Ouimet, Andrea Rau, Georges Jamin

Deafula
"It began as a quiet country weekend ... it ended as a nightmare journey!"
USA: Signscope/Holstrom Production (1975)
PRODUCER: Gary Holstrom DIRECTOR/WRITER: Peter Wechsberg (Peter Wolf) MUSIC: Jerry Gregorius CAST: Peter Wechsberg, James Randall, Lee Darel, Katherine Wilson, Gary Holstrom

The Deathmaster
"Eyes like hot coals ... fangs like razors! An adventure in ultimate terror!"
USA: A World Entertainment Production; American International (1972)
PRODUCERS: Fred Sadoff, Robert Quarry DIRECTOR: Ray Danton WRITER: R.L. Grove MUSIC: Bill Marx CAST: Robert Quarry, Bill Ewing, John Fiedler, Brenda Dickson, Bob Pickett

The Devil's Wedding Night

(*Il plenilunio delle vergini; Full Moon of the Virgins*) "Satan is coming!"
Italy: A Virginia Cinematografica Production (1973) USA: Dimension Pictures (1973)
PRODUCER: Ralph Zucker DIRECTOR: Paul Solvay (Luigi Batzella) WRITER: Alan Harris MUSIC: Vasil Kojucharov CAST: Mark Damon, Sara Bay (Rosalba Neri), Esmeralda Barros, Xiro Papas, Carlo Gentili

Doctor Dracula

"He leads the way to the torment of the UNDEAD"
USA: A Rafael Film Associates Production; Independent International Pictures (1978)
PRODUCER: Lou Sorkin DIRECTORS: Paul Aratow, Al Adamson WRITERS: Paul Aratow, Cecil Brown, Gary Reathman, Samuel Sherman CAST: Geoffrey Land, John Carradine, Donald Berry, Larry Hankin, Susie McIver

Dracula

"The newest, scariest telling of the classic throat-clutcher" USA/England: A Dan Curtis Production; CBS TV (1973) PRODUCER/DIRECTOR: Dan Curtis WRITER: Richard Matheson MUSIC: Robert Cobert CAST: Jack Palance, Simon Ward, Nigel Davenport, Fiona Lewis, Penelope Horner

Dracula

"Throughout history he has filled the hearts of men with terror, and the hearts of women with desire."
USA/England: A Mirisch Corporation Production; Universal Pictures (1979) PRODUCER: Walter Mirisch DIRECTOR: John Badham WRITER: W.D. Richter MUSIC: John Williams CAST: Frank Langella, Kate Nelligan, Laurence Olivier, Donald Pleasence, Trevor Eve

Dracula A.D. 1972

"The Count is back, with an eye for London's hotpants ... and a taste for everything!" England: Hammer Films (1972) USA: Warner Bros. (1972)
PRODUCER: Josephine Douglas DIRECTOR: Alan Gibson WRITER: Don Houghton MUSIC: Mike Vickers CAST: Christopher Lee, Peter Cushing, Stephanie Beacham, Christopher Neame, Caroline Munro

Dracula and Son

(*Dracula père et fils; Dracula Father and Son*) "Like father like son, it's in the BLOOD" France: Gaumont Productions (1976)
USA: Quartet Films (1979)
PRODUCER: Alain Poiré DIRECTOR: Édouard Molinaro WRITERS: Alain Godard, Édouard Molinaro, Jean-Marie Poiré MUSIC: Vladimir Cosma CAST: Christopher Lee, Bernard Menez, Catherine Breillat, Claude Génia, Maria-Hélène Breillat

Dracula Blows His Cool
(*Graf Dracula in Oberbayern*; *Count Dracula in Upper Bavaria*)
"It's love at first bite"
West Germany: Lisa-Barthonia Film Productions of Munich (1979) USA: Martin Films Release (1983)
PRODUCER: Karl Spiehs DIRECTOR: Carlo Ombra (Carl Schenkel) WRITERS: Grunbach & Rosenthal MUSIC: Gerhard Heinz CAST: Gianni Garko, Betty Vergès, Bea Fiedler, Giacomo Rizzo, Linda Grondier

Dracula in the Provinces
(*Il cav. Costante Nicosia demoniaco ovvero: Dracula in Brizia*)
Italy: Coralta Cinematografica/Titanus (1975)
PRODUCER: Alfonso Donati DIRECTOR: Lucio Fulci WRITERS: Mario Amendola, Pupi Avanti, Bruno Corbucci MUSIC: Franco Bixio, Fabio Frizzi CAST: Lando Buzzanca, Rossano Brazzi, Sylva Koscina, Miora Orfei, John Steiner

Dracula, Prisoner of Frankenstein
(*Dracula contra Frankenstein: Dracula Against Frankenstein*)
Spain/France: Comptoir Francais/Fénix Cooperative Cinemtográfica (1972)
PRODUCER: Arturo Marcos DIRECTOR: Jess Franco WRITERS: Paul D'Ales, Jess Franco MUSIC: Bruno Nicolai CAST: Dennis Price, Howard Vernon, Mary Francis, Alberto Dalbés, Fernando Bilbao

The Dracula Saga
(*La saga de los Drácula*)
Spain: Profilmes Production (1973)
USA: International Amusements Corp. (1975)
PRODUCER: Jose Antonio Perez Giner DIRECTOR: León Klimovsky WRITER: Lazarus Kaplan MUSIC: Antonio Ramirez Angel, Daniel White CAST: Narciso Ibáñez Menta, Tony Isbert, Helga Liné, Tina Sáinz, Henry Gregor

Dracula Sucks
"This time the Count is not just going for the throat" USA: First International Pictures (1979)
PRODUCER: Darryl Marshak DIRECTOR: Philip Marshak WRITERS: Darryl Marshak, David Kern MUSIC: Lionel Thomas CAST: Jamie Gillis, Annette Haven, Serena, Reggie Nalder, John Holmes

Dracula vs. Frankenstein
"The Kings of Horror battle to the DEATH!" USA: Independent International Pictures (1971)
PRODUCERS: Al Adamson, Samual Sherman, John Van Horn DIRECTOR: Al Adamson WRITERS: William Pugsley, Samuel Sherman MUSIC: William Lava CAST: J. Carrol Naish, Lon Chaney, Jr., Anthony Eisley, Regina Carrol, Russ Tamblyn

Evil of Dracula (aka *The Bloodthirsty Roses*)
Japan: A Toho Company Ltd. Production (1974)
PRODUCER: Fumio Tanaka DIRECTOR: Michio Yamamoto WRITERS: Ei Ogawa, Masaru Takesue MUSIC: Riichirô Manabe CAST: Toshio Kurosawa, Mariko Mochizuki, Shin Kishida, Kunie Tanaka, Katshuhiko Sasaki

Fascination
France: Comex Productions, Films ABC (1979)
PRODUCER: Joe de Lara DIRECTOR/WRITER: Jean Rollin MUSIC: Philippe D'Aram CAST: Franka Mai, Brigitte Lahaie, Fanny Magier, Sophie Noel, Alain Plumey

Frankenstein's Bloody Terror
(*La marca del Hombre Lobo; The Mark of the Wolf Man*)
"Now—more HORROR, more SCREAMS, more FRIGHT than you'd ever dare to dream!" Spain: Maxper Producciones Cinematograficas (1968)
USA: Independent International Pictures (1971)
PRODUCER: Maximiliano Pérez Flores DIRECTOR: Enrique López Eguiluz WRITER: Jacinto Molina Álvarez MUSIC: Angel Arteaga CAST: Paul Naschy, Dyanik Zurakowska, Manuel Manzaneque, Aurora de Alba, Julián Ugarte

Ganja & Hess
"Bad blood runs between them"
USA: Kelly/Jordan Enterprises (1973)
PRODUCER: Chiz Schultz DIRECTOR/WRITER: Bill Gunn MUSIC: Sam Waymon CAST: Duane Jones, Marlene Clark, Bill Gunn, Sam Waymon, Leonard Jackson

Grave of the Vampire
"Father and son related by BLOOD ... everyone's BLOOD!"
USA: A Millenium Production; An Entertainment Pyramid Release (1972)
PRODUCER: Daniel Cady DIRECTOR: John Hayes WRITER: David Chase MUSIC: Jaime Mendoza-Nava CAST: Michael Pataki, William Smith, Lyn Peters, Diane Holden, Eric Mason

Guess What Happened to Count Dracula
"TRIP ... into a nightmare of evil!"
USA: Merrick International Films (1971)
PRODUCERS: Leo Rivers, Laurence Merrick DIRECTOR/WRITER: Laurence Merrick MUSIC: Des Roberts CAST: Des Roberts, Claudia Barron, John Landon, Frank Donato, Robert Branche

Hannah, Queen of the Vampires
(*La tomba de la isla maldita; The Tomb of the Damned Island*) "Have you ever done it the Transylvanian way?"

Spain/USA: Orita Films/ Coast Industries Inc. (1973) USA: Atlas Films (as *Crypt of the Living Dead*, 1973)
PRODUCER: Lou Shaw DIRECTORS: Julio Salvador, Ray Danton WRITERS: Ricardo Ferrer, Lou Shaw MUSIC: Phillip Lambro CAST: Teresa Gimpera, Andrew Prine, Mark Damon, Patty Sheppard, John Alderman

The Horrible Sexy Vampire
(*El vampiro de la autopista*; *Vampire of the Highway*) "His lust for blood meant death!"
Spain: A Cinefilms/Fida Cinematografica Production (1970) USA: A Peppercorn/Wormser Release (1970)
PRODUCER: Al Peppard DIRECTOR/WRITER: José Luis Madrid MUSIC: Ángel Arteaga CAST: Wal Davis, Barta Barri, Anastasio Campoy, Susan Caravasal, Kurt Estaban

Horror of the Blood Monsters
"You'll SCREAM yourself into a state of SHOCK!" USA: Independent International (1970)
PRODUCER/DIRECTOR: Al Adamson WRITER: Sue McNair MUSIC: Mike Velarde CAST: John Carradine, Robert Dix, Vicki Volante, Jennifer Bishop, Bruce Powers

House of Dark Shadows
"Barnabas Collins, vampire, takes a bride in a bizarre act of unnatural lust." USA: MGM (1970)
PRODUCER/DIRECTOR: Dan Curtis WRITERS: Sam Hall, Gordon Russell MUSIC: Robert Cobert CAST: Jonathan Frid, Kathryn Leigh Scott, Nancy Barrett, John Karlan, Grayson Hall

The House That Dripped Blood
"Terror waits for you in every room." England: Amicus Films (1971) USA: Cinerama Releasing (1971)
PRODUCERS: Max J. Rosenberg, Milton Subotsky DIRECTOR: Peter Duffell WRITER: Robert Bloch MUSIC: Michael Dress CAST: Ingrid Pitt, Jon Pertwee, Peter Cushing, Christopher Lee, Nyree Dawn Porter

Immoral Tales
(*Contes immoraux*)
"You don't have to go to a museum to see an X-rated Picasso." France: Argos Films (1972)
USA: New Line Cinema (1976)
PRODUCER: Anatole Dauman DIRECTOR/WRITER: Walerian Borowczyk MUSIC: Maurice Leroux CAST: Paloma Picasso, Lise Danvers, Fabrice Luchini, Charlotte Alexandra, Pascale Christophe

In Search of Dracula
(*Vem var Dracula?*; *Who Was Dracula?*)

Ingrid Pitt in *The House That Dripped Blood* (1971).

"Believe The Unbelievable! A truth ten thousand times stranger and more terrifying than any fiction! There really was a Dracula!"
Sweden: An Aspekt/SFP Production (1975) USA: Independent International Pictures (1975)
PRODUCER/DIRECTOR: Calvin Floyd WRITER: Yvonne Floyd MUSIC: Calvin Floyd (and James Bernard, uncredited) CAST: Christopher Lee

Jonathan

"Vampires are still with us." Germany: Iduna Films (1970) USA: New Yorker Films (1973)
PRODUCER: Helmut Haffner DIRECTOR/WRITER: Hans Geissendorfer MUSIC: Roland Kovac CAST Jurgen Jung, Hans Dieter Jendreyko, Hertha von Walther, Paul Albert Krumm, Ilona Grubel

Lady Dracula

Germany: IFV Productions (1975)
DIRECTOR: Franz Josef Gottlieb WRITERS: Redis Read, Bradford Harris MUSIC: Horst Jankowski CAST: Brad Harris, Evelyne Kraft, Theo Lingen, Christine Buchegger, Walter Giller

Lake of Dracula (aka *The Bloodthirsty Eyes*)
"Dracula's victims rise to become slaves!" Japan: A Toho Company Ltd. Production (1971)
PRODUCER: Fumio Tanaka DIRECTOR: Michio Yamamoto WRITERS: Ei Ogawa, Masaru Takesue MUSIC: Riichirô Manabe CAST: Midori Fujita, Sanae Emi, Shin Kishida, Tadao Futami, Tatsuo Matsushita

Legacy of Dracula (aka *The Bloodthirsty Doll*)
Japan: A Toho Company Ltd. Production (1970)
PRODUCERS: Fumio and Tomoyuki Tanaka DIRECTOR: Michio Yamamoto WRITERS: Ei Ogawa, Hiroshi Nagano MUSIC: Riichirô Manabe CAST: Kayo Matsuo, Akira Nakao, Atsuo Nakamura, Yôko Minakaze, Yukiko Kobayashi

The Legend of Blood Castle
(*Ceremonia sangrienta*; *Blood Ceremony*)
"DEPRAVED! She bathed in virgin blood to stay eternally young!" Spain/Italy: Luis Films, Rome/X Films, Madrid (1973)
USA: Film Ventures International (as *The Female Butcher*, 1974)
PRODUCER: José Maria González Sinde DIRECTOR: Jorge Grau WRITERS: Jorge Grau, Juan Tébar, Sandro Continenza MUSIC: Carlo Savina CAST: Lucia Bosé, Ewa Aulin, Espartaco Santoni, Silvano Tranquilli, Ana Farra

The Legend of the 7 Golden Vampires
"HAMMER HORROR! DRAGON THRILLS! The First Kung Fu Horror Spectacular!" England/Hong Kong: A Hammer/Shaw Production (1974)
USA: Dynamite Entertainment (as *The Seven Brothers Meet Dracula*, 1979)
PRODUCERS: Don Houghton, Vee King Shaw DIRECTOR: Roy Ward Baker WRITER: Don Houghton MUSIC: James Bernard CAST: Peter Cushing, Julie Ege, David Chiang, John Forbes-Robertson, Robin Stewart

Lemora
"Run little girl ... innocence is in peril tonight!"
USA: Blackfern Productions (1973); Media Cinema Group (1975)
PRODUCER: Robert Fern DIRECTOR: Richard Blackburn WRITERS: Richard Blackburn, Robert Fern MUSIC: Dan Neufeld CAST: Cheryl Smith, William Whitton, Lesley Taplin, Parker West, Maxine Ballantyne

Let's Scare Jessica to Death
"Something is after Jessica. Something very cold, very wet ... and very dead." USA: Paramount (1971)
PRODUCER: Charles B. Moss Jr. DIRECTOR: John Hancock WRITERS:

Ralph Rose, Norman Jonas MUSIC: Orville Stoeber CAST: Zohra Lampert, Barton Heyman, Mariclare Costello, Kevin O'Connor, Gretchen Corbett

Lips of Blood
(*Lèvres de sang*)
France: Nordia Films (1975)
PRODUCER: Lionel Wallmann DIRECTOR: Jean Rollin WRITERS: Jean-Loup Philippe, Jean Rollin MUSIC: Didier William Lepauw CAST: Jean-Loup Philippe, Annie Briand, Natalie Perrey, Catherine and Marie-Pierre Castel

Love at First Bite
"DRACULA... Your favorite pain in the neck is about to bite your funny

Arte Johnson as Renfield and George Hamilton as Dracula in *Love at First Bite* (1979).

bone." USA: A Melvin Simon/George Hamilton/Robert Kaufman Production; American International (1979)
PRODUCERS: Joel Freeman, Melvin Simon DIRECTOR: Stan Dragoti WRITER: Robert Kaufman MUSIC: Charles Bernstein CAST: George Hamilton, Susan Saint James, Richard Benjamin, Arte Johnson, Dick Shawn

Lust for a Vampire
"DEVILS IN FEMALE BODIES ... whose embrace is the kiss of death for man or woman!" England: Hammer Films (1970)
USA: American Continental (1971)
PRODUCERS: Harry Fine, Michael Style DIRECTOR: Jimmy Sangster WRITER: Tudor Gates MUSIC: Harry Robinson CAST: Yutte Stensgaard, Ralph Bates, Barbara Jefford, Suzanna Leigh, Michael Johnson

The Mad Love Life of a Hot Vampire
USA (1971)
DIRECTOR/WRITER: Sven Christian (Ray Dennis Steckler) CAST: Jim Parker, Carolyn Brandt, Rock Heinrich, Greta Smith, Fritz King

Malenka
(*Malenka, la sobrina del vampiro*; *Malenka, the Vampire's Niece*) "Can you survive this ORGY of the LIVING DEAD?"
Spain/Italy: Cobra Films/ Felix Cinematografica (1969)
USA: Europix International (as *Fangs of the Living Dead*, 1973)
PRODUCER: Aubrey Ambert, Rosanna Yanni DIRECTOR/WRITER: Amando de Ossorio MUSIC: Carlo Savina CAST: Anita Ekberg, John Hamilton, Diana Lorys, Rosanna Yanni, Guy Roberts

Martin
"He could be the boy next door."
USA: Laurel Production; Libra Films International (1978)
PRODUCER: Richard Rubinstein DIRECTOR/WRITER: George A. Romero MUSIC: Donald Rubinstein CAST: John Amplas, Lincoln Maazel, Christine Forrest, Tom Savini, James Roy

Mary, Mary, Bloody Mary
"She's a beauty! She's a beast! She's Bloody Mary!"
USA/Mexico: Translor/Proa Films-Cinema Management Inc. (1975) USA: Black Lion Release (1975)
PRODUCERS: Henri Bollinger, Robert Yamin DIRECTOR: Juan López Moctezuma WRITER: Malcolm Marmorstein MUSIC: Tom Bahler CAST: Cristina Ferrare, David Young, John Carradine, Helena Rojo, Arthur Hansel

The Merry Vampires of Vögel
(*Las alegres vampiras de Vögel*) Spain: Titanic Films (1975)

PRODUCER/DIRECTOR: Julio Pérez Tabernero WRITERS: Antonio Baylos, Julio Pérez Tabernero MUSIC: Alfonso Santisteban CAST: German Cobos, Ágata Lys, Maria José Cantudo, José Maria Tasso, Maria Vidal

The Mystery of Cynthia Baird
(*El misterio de Cynthia Baird*) Spain: Nueva Films (1972)
DIRECTOR/WRITER: José Maria Zabalza MUSIC: Ana Satrova CAST: Simón Andreu, Susan Taff, Guillermo Mendez, Maria Salerno

Night of the Devils
(*La notte dei diavoli*) "Creatures of the living dead!"
Italy: Filmes Cinematografica (1972)
PRODUCERS: Eduardo Manzanos, Luigi Mariani DIRECTOR: Giorgio Ferroni WRITERS: Romano Migliorini, Gianbattista Mussetto MUSIC: Giorgio Gaslini CAST: Gianni Garko, Agostina Belli, Mark Roberts, Teresa Gimpera, Bill Vanders

Night of the Sorcerers
(*La noche de los brujos*) Spain: Hesperia Films (1974)
USA: Avco Embassy Television (1976)
PRODUCERS: Luis Laso, Ricardo Muñoz Suay DIRECTOR/WRITER: Amando de Ossrio MUSIC: Fernando Garcia Morcillo CAST: Simón Andreu, Kali Hansa, Maria Kosti, Lorena Tower, Joseph Thelman

The Night Stalker
USA: A Dan Curtis Production; ABC-TV (1972)
PRODUCER: Dan Curtis DIRECTOR: John Llewellyn Moxey WRITER: Richard Matheson MUSIC: Robert Cobert CAST: Darren McGavin, Carol Lynley, Barry Atwater, Ralph Meeker, Simon Oakland

Nocturna
"From Transylvania to Manhattan.... She'll get under your skin!"
USA: A Nai Bonet Enterprises Ltd. Production; Compass International (1979)
PRODUCERS: Nai Bonet, Vernon Becker DIRECTOR: Harry Tampa WRITERS: Nai Bonet, Harry Tampa MUSIC: Norman Bergen, Reid Whitelaw CAST: Nai Bonet, Anthony Hamilton, John Carradine, Yvonne De Carlo, Brother Theodore

Nosferatu the Vampyre
(*Nosferatu: phantom der nacht*; *Nosferatu: Phantom of the Night*) "A tale of seduction in the dark night of the soul."
Germany: Werner Herzog Filmproduktion/Gaumont/ZDF (1979) USA: 20th Century–Fox (1979)
PRODUCER/DIRECTOR/WRITER: Werner Herzog MUSIC: Popol Vuh CAST: Klaus Kinski, Isabelle Adjani, Bruno Ganz, Roland Topor, Walter Ladengast

The Nude Vampire
(*La Vampire nue*)
"Let terror join his mind to yours and know the touch of shuddering uncontrollable fear!" France: Les Filmes ABC (1970)
USA: Boxoffice International Pictures (1973)
PRODUCER: Jean Lavie DIRECTOR: Jean Rollin WRITERS: Jean Rollin, Serge Moati MUSIC: Yvon Serault CAST: Christine Francois, Oliver Martin, Maurice Lemaître, Catherine and Marie-Pierre Castel

The Omega Man
"The last man alive ... is not alone!"
USA: Walter Seltzer Productions; Warner Bros. (1971)
PRODUCER: Walter Seltzer DIRECTOR: Boris Sagal WRITERS: John and Joyce Corrington MUSIC: Rob Grainer CAST: Charlton Heston, Anthony Zerbe, Rosalind Cash, Paul Koslo, Eric Laneuville

Requiem for a Vampire
(*Les Vierges et vampires; Virgins and Vampires*) "Two young girls ... trapped with no escape!" France: Les Films ABC (1971)
USA: Boxoffice International (as **Caged Virgins**, 1973) PRODUCER: Sam Selsky DIRECTOR/WRITER: Jean Rollin MUSIC: Pierre Raph CAST: Marie-Pierre Castel, Mireille Dargent, Philippe Gasté, Michel Delesalle, Louise Dhour

The Return of Count Yorga

"A terrifying tale of unearthly hungers!"
USA: A Michael Macready–Bob Kelljan Production; American International (1971)
PRODUCER: Michael Macready DIRECTOR: Bob Kelljan WRITERS: Bob Kelljan, Yvonne Wilder MUSIC: Bill Marx CAST: Robert Quarry, Mariette Hartley, Roger Perry, Yvonne Wilder, Walter Brooke

The Sadist with Red Teeth
(*Le Sadique aux dents rouges*) "Un film de sex horreur"
Belgium: Cinevision Production (1971)
PRODUCER: Charles Van der Haeghen DIRECTOR/WRITER: Jean-Louis van Belle MUSIC: Raymond Legrand CAST: Daniel Moosmann, Jane Clayton, Albert Simono

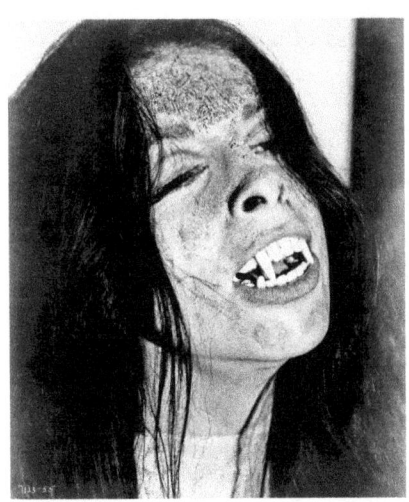

A particularly toothsome lady vampire from *The Return of Count Yorga* (1971).

'Salem's Lot
"The Ultimate in Terror!"
USA: Warner Bros. Television; CBS-TV (1979)
PRODUCER: Richard Kobritz DIRECTOR: Tobe Hooper WRITER: Paul Monash MUSIC: Harry Sukman CAST: David Soul, James Mason, Lance Kerwin, Bonnie Bedelia, Lew Ayres

Santo and Blue Demon vs. Dracula and the Wolf Man
(*Santo y Blue Demon vs. Drácula y el Hombre Lobo*) Mexio: Cinematográfica Calderon (1973)
PRODUCER: Guillermo Calderón Stell DIRECTOR: Miguel Delgado WRITER: Alfredo Salazar MUSIC: Gustavo Carrión CAST: Santo, Blue Demon, Aldo Monti, Agustin Martínez Solores, María Eugenia San Martín

Santo and the Vengeance of the Vampire Women
(*La venganza de las mujeres vampiro*) Mexico: Cinematográfica Flama (1970)
PRODUCER: Jorge García Besné DIRECTOR: Federico Curiel WRITERS: Fernando Osés, Jorge García Besné MUSIC: Gustavo Carrión CAST: Santo, Norma Lazareno, Gina Romand, Aldo Monti, Alfonso Munguía

Satan's Black Wedding
"A blood marriage of ghouls"
USA: I.R.M.I. Films Corporation (1975)
PRODUCER: Tamara Brown (Frances Millard) DIRECTOR/WRITER: Philip Miller (Nick Millard) MUSIC: Ronald Stein CAST: Greg Braddock, Ray Myles, Zarrah Whiting, Barrett Cooper, Lisa Milano

The Satanic Rites of Dracula
"Evil begets evil on the Sabbath of the Undead!" England: Hammer Films (1973)
USA: Dynamite Entertainment (as *Count Dracula and His Vampire Bride*, 1978) PRODUCER: Roy Skeggs DIRECTOR: Alan Gibson WRITER: Don Houghton MUSIC: John Cacavas CAST: Christopher Lee, Peter Cushing, Joanna Lumley, Michael Coles, Freddie Jones

Scars of Dracula
"Hammer's NEW super thriller!" England: Hammer Films (1970) USA: American Continental (1971)
PRODUCER: Aida Young DIRECTOR: Roy Ward Baker WRITER: John Elder MUSIC: James Bernard CAST: Christopher Lee, Jenny Hanley, Dennis Waterman, Christopher Matthews, Patrick Troughton

Scream, Blacula, Scream
"The Black Prince of Shadows stalks the earth again!" USA: American International (1973)

PRODUCER: Joseph Naar DIRECTOR: Bob Kelljan WRITERS: Joan Torres, Raymond Koenig, Maurice Jules MUSIC: Bill Marx CAST: William Marshall, Don Mitchell, Pam Grier, Richard Lawson, Michael Conrad

Sex and the Single Vampire
USA (1970)
PRODUCER: Wolfgang Klutzman DIRECTOR: Modunk Phreezer WRITER: F.N. Spelling MUSIC: Sigfried von Wanghunt CAST: John Holmes, John Dullahan, Jesse Moreno, Sanday Dempsey, L.G. Allard

Sexcula
"She'll suck more than your blood"
USA: Frog Productions (1974)
PRODUCER: Clarence Frog (Clarence Neufeld) DIRECTOR: Bob Hollowich (John Holbrook) WRITER: David Hurry MUSIC: John Holbrook, Keith Woods CAST: Debbie Collins, Jamie Orlando, John Alexander, Tim Lowery, David Hurry

Anoushka Hempel puts the bite on Christopher Matthews in *Scars of Dracula* (1970).

The Shiver of the Vampires
(*Le Frisson des vampires*) France: Les Films ABC (1971)
USA: Clark Film Releasing (1978)
PRODUCER/DIRECTOR: Jean Rollin WRITERS: Jean Rollin, Monique Natan MUSIC: Acanthus CAST: Sandra Julien, Jean-Marie Durand, Jacques Robiolles, Michel Delahaye, Marie-Pierre Castel

Son of Dracula
"The first Rock-and-Roll Dracula movie!" England: An Apple Film Production (1974) USA: A Cinemation Industries Release (1974)
PRODUCER: Ringo Starr DIRECTOR: Freddie Francis WRITER: Jay Fairbank MUSIC: Paul Buckmaster CAST: Harry Nilsson, Ringo Starr, Freddie Jones, Suzanna Leigh, Dennis Price

The Strange Love of the Vampires
(*El extrano amor de los vampiros*)

"He's here! Nerve Shattering! Terrifying! Stupefying!" Spain: Richard Films (1975)
USA: NE Distribution (as *Night of the Walking Dead*, 1977)
PRODUCER: Isaac Hernández DIRECTOR: León Klimovsky WRITERS: Juan José Daza, Carlos Pumares MUSIC: Máximum Barratas CAST: Emma Cohen, Carlos Ballesteros, Viky Lussón, Rafael Hernández, Barta Barri

Taste the Blood of Dracula
"They drink his blood and the horror begins!" England: Hammer Films (1970)
USA: Warner Bros. (1970)
PRODUCER: Aida Young DIRECTOR: Peter Sasdy WRITER: John Elder MUSIC: James Bernard CAST: Peter Cushing, Linda Hayden, Anthony Corlan, Geoffrey Keen, Ralph Bates Tender Dracula

Tender Dracula
France: Les Films Christian Fechner (1974) USA: Scotia American (1975)
PRODUCER: Vincent Malle DIRECTOR: Pierre Grunstein WRITER: Justin Lenoir MUSIC: Karl Heinz Schafer CAST: Peter Cushing, Bernard Menez, Alida Valli, Miou Miou, Nathalie Courval

Thirst
"A conspiracy of terror with only one desire" Australia: F.G. Film Productions (1979) USA: New Line Cinema (1979)
PRODUCER: Anthony Ginnane DIRECTOR: Rod Hardy WRITER: John Pinkney MUSIC: Brian May CAST: Chantal Contouri, Max Phipps, Henry Silva, David Hemmings, Shirley Cameron

Twins of Evil
"Which is the Virgin? Which is the Vampire?" England: Hammer Films (1971)
USA: Universal (1972)
PRODUCERS: Harry Fine, Michael Style DIRECTOR: John Hough WRITER: Tudor Gates MUSIC: Harry Robinson CAST: Peter Cushing, Mary and Madeleine Collinson, Damien Thomas, David Warbeck

Vampira
"Count Dracula is having a bloody good time with the year's juiciest playmates!" England: A World Film Services Production (1974)
USA: American International (as *Old Dracula*, 1975)
PRODUCER: Jack Wiener DIRECTOR: Clive Donner WRITER: Jeremy Lloyd MUSIC: David Whitaker CAST: David Niven, Teresa Graves, Nicky Henson, Peter Bayliss, Jennie Linden

Vampire
"No woman can resist him. No man can stand against him. A city trembles when he walks again ... more romantic, more mysterious than ever!"

USA: MTM Enterprises; ABC-TV (1979)
PRODUCER: Gregory Hoblit DIRECTOR: E.W. Swackhamer WRITERS: Steve Bochco, Michael Kozoll MUSIC: Fred Karlin CAST: Richard Lynch, Jason Miller, E.G. Marshall, Jessica Walter, Kathryn Harrold

Vampire Circus
"The Greatest Blood-Show on Earth!" England: Hammer Films (1972)
USA: 20th Century-Fox (1972)
PRODUCER: Wilbur Stark DIRECTOR: Robert Young WRITER: Judson Kinberg MUSIC: David Whitaker CAST: Anthony Corlan, John Moulder-Brown, Laurence Payne, Adrienne Corri, Lynne Frederick

The Vampire Happening
(*Gebissen wird nur nachts; Only Bitten at Night*)
"A satyrical horror comedy of a beautiful woman with bizarre tastes" Germany: Aquila Film Enterprises (1971)
USA: Horizon Films (1974)
PRODUCER: Pier Caminnecci DIRECTOR: Freddie Francis WRITER: August Rieger MUSIC: Jerry van Rooyen CAST: Pia Degermark, Thomas Hunter, Ferdy Mayne, Ingrid van Bergen, Ivor Murillo

Vampire Hookers
"They're a close encounter of a different kind!" Philippines: Cosa Neuva Productions (1978) USA: Caprican Three Inc. (1978)
PRODUCER: Robert Waters DIRECTOR: Cirio H. Santiago WRITER: Howard Cohen MUSIC: Jaime Mendoza-Nava CAST: John Carradine, Bruce Fairbairn, Trey Wilson, Karen Stride, Lenka Novak

The Vampire Lovers
"IF YOU DARE ... taste the deadly passion of the BLOOD-NYMPHS!" England: A Hammer-American International Production (1970)
USA: American International (1970)
PRODUCERS: Harry Fine, Michael Style DIRECTOR: Roy Ward Baker WRITER: Tudor Gates MUSIC: Harry Robinson CAST: Ingrid Pitt, Peter Cushing, Dawn Addams, Madeline Smith, Kate O'Mara

Vampirella (unmade film) England: Hammer Films (1976)
PRODUCER: Michael Carreras DIRECTOR: John Hough WRITER: Christopher Wicking CAST: Barbara Leigh, Peter Cushing

The Vampire's Night Orgy
(*La orgía nocturna de los vampiros*) "When the moon is up the fun begins."
Spain: José Frade Producciones Cinematográficas (1974) USA: International Amusements Corp. (1974)
PRODUCER: José Frade Almohalla DIRECTOR: León Klimovsky WRITERS:

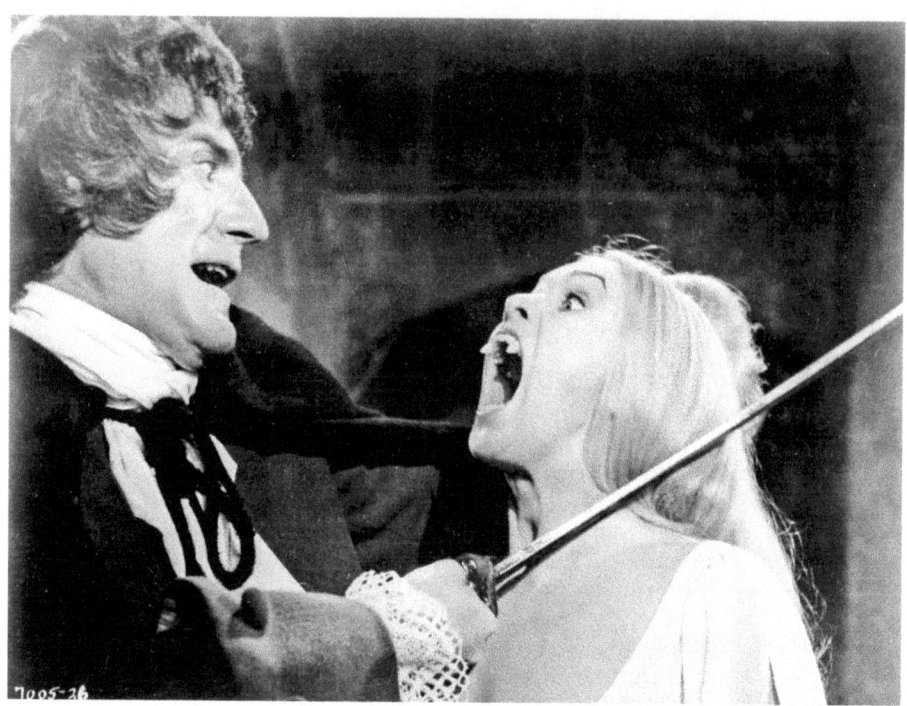

Douglas Wilmer is about to dispatch Kirsten Betts in the exciting prologue to *The Vampire Lovers* (1970).

Gabriel Burgos, Antonio Fos MUSIC: Antonio Ballesteros CAST: Jack Taylor, Dyanik Zurakowska, Helga Liné, José Guardiola, Manuel de Blas

The Vampires of Coyoacán
(*Los vampiros de Coyoacán*)
Mexico: Producciones Filmicas Agrasanchez (1974)
PRODUCER: Rogelio Agrasánchez DIRECTOR: Arturo Martínez WRITERS: Mario Cid, Arturo Martínez MUSIC: Ernesto Cortázar CAST: Mil Máscaras, Superzan, Germán Robles, Sasha Montenegro, Carlos López Moctezuma

Vampyres
"They shared the pleasures of the flesh and the horrors of the grave!"
England: Essay Films Ltd. (1974)
USA: Cambist Films (1975)
PRODUCER: Brian Smedley-Aston DIRECTOR: Joseph Larraz (Jose Ramon Larraz) WRITER: Diana Daubeney MUSIC: James Clarke CAST: Marianne Morris, Anulka, Murray Brown, Brian Deason, Sally Faulkner

Vampyros Lesbos
"A masterpiece of erotic horror"
Spain/West Germany: Fenix Cooperativa Cinematografica/CCC Telecine (1971)
PRODUCER: Artur Brauner DIRECTOR: Franco Manera (Jess Franco) WRITERS: Jaime Chávarri, Franco Manera, Anne Settimó MUSIC: Manfred Hübler, Siegfried Schwab CAST: Dennis Price, Soledad Miranda, Paul Muller, Ewa Strömberg, José Martínez Blanco

The Vault of Horror
"Everything that makes life worth Leaving!" England: Amicus Films (1973)
USA: Cinerama Releasing (1973)
PRODUCERS: Max J. Rosenberg, Milton Subotsky DIRECTOR: Roy Ward Baker WRITER: Milton Subotsky MUSIC: Douglas Gamley CAST: Daniel Massey, Anna Massey, Terry-Thomas, Glynis Johns, Dawn Addams

The Velvet Vampire
"She's waiting to love you ... to death!" USA: New World Pictures (1971)
PRODUCER: Charles Swartz DIRECTOR: Stephanie Rothman WRITERS: Maurice Jules, Charles Swartz, Stephanie Rothman MUSIC: Roger

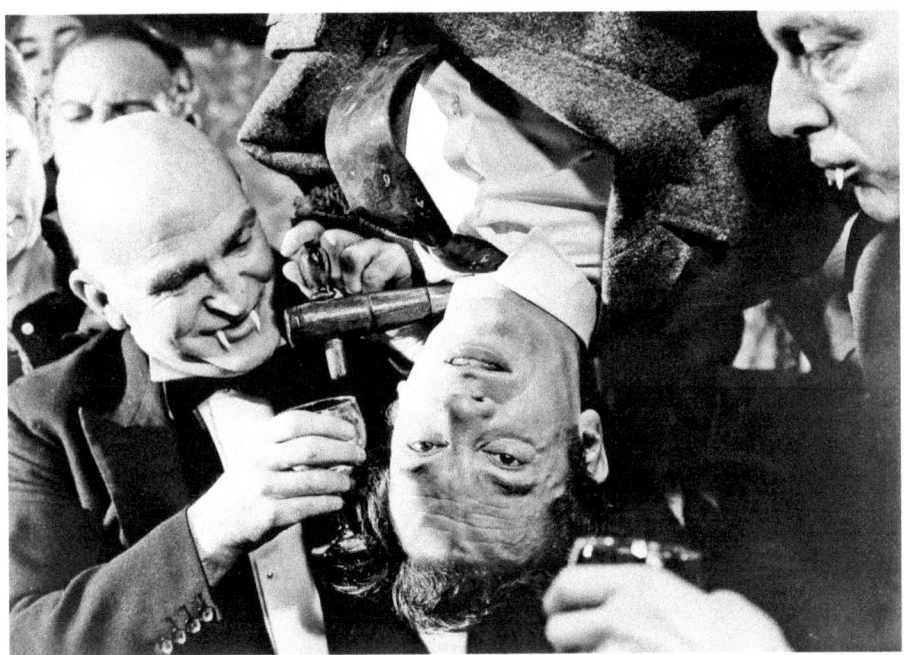

Vampires make a meal of Daniel Massey in *The Vault of Horror* (1973).

Dollarhide, Clancy Grass CAST: Michael Blodgett, Celeste Yarnall, Sherry Miles, Gene Shane, Jerry Daniels

The Werewolf vs. the Vampire Woman
(*La noche de Walpurgis: The Night of Walpurgis*)
"Things happen that have never been seen by human beings. The blood flows like vintage wine." Spain/West Germany: Plata Films (1971) USA: Universal Entertainment Corp. (1972)
PRODUCER: Salvadore Romero DIRECTOR: León Klimovsky WRITERS: Jacinto Molina Álvarez, Hans Munkel MUSIC: Antón García Abril CAST: Paul Naschy, Gaby Fuchs, Patty Shepard, Bárbara Capell, Barta Barri

Zoltan, the Hound of Dracula
"The Blood Lusting Killer!"
USA: Vic Productions; Crown International (as ***Dracula's Dog***, 1978)
PRODUCERS: Albert Band, Frank Ray Perilli DIRECTOR: Albert Band WRITER: Frank Ray Perilli MUSIC: Andrew Belling CAST: Michael Pataki, Jan Shutan, Jose Ferrer, Reggie Nalder, Libby Chase

Bibliography

Arkoff, Sam, with Richard Trubo. *Flying Through Hollywood by the Seat of My Pants*. New York: Carol Publishing Group, 1992.
Benton, Mike. *An Illustrated History of Horror Comics*. Dallas, TX: Taylor Publishing, 1991.
Bruchini, Antonio. *Horror all'italiana*. Florence, Italy: Glittering Images, 1996.
Clarens, Carlos. *Horror Movies: An Illustrated Survey*. London: Secker and Warburg, 1967.
Colacello, Bob. *Holy Terror: Andy Warhol Close Up*. New York: HarperColliins, 1990.
Deane, Hamilton, and John L. Balderson. *Dracula, the Vampire Play*. New York: Nelson Doubleday Inc., 1971.
Edmonson, Roger. *Boy in the Sand: Casey Donovan All-American Sex Star*. Los Angeles and New York: Alyson Books, 1998.
Farson, Daniel. *The Man Who Wrote Dracula: A Biography of Bram Stoker*. London: Michael Joseph Ltd. 1975.
Frank, Alan. *The Horror Film Handbook*. Totowa, NJ: Barnes and Noble Books, 1982.
Hardy, Phil. *The Encyclopedia of Horror Movies*. New York: Harper and Row Publishers, 1986.
Howard, Josiah. *Blaxploitation Cinema*. Surrey, England: Fab Press Ltd., 2008.
Hutchings, Peter. *Hammer and Beyond: The British Horror Film*. Manchester, England: Manchester University Press, 1993.
Hutchinson, Tom, and Roy Pickard. *Horrors: A History of Horror Movies*. London: Hamlyn Publishing Group Ltd., 1983.
Johnson, Tom, and Deborah Del Vecchio. *Hammer Films: An Exhaustive Filmography*. Jefferson, NC: McFarland, 1996.
King, Stephen. *Danse Macabre*. New York: Everest House Publishers, 1981.
Lee, Christopher. *Tall, Dark, and Gruesome: An Autobiography*. London: Granada Publishing, 1978.
McGee, Mark Thomas. *Fast and Furious: The Story of American International Pictures*. Jefferson, NC: McFarland, 1984.
Pattison, Barrie. *The Seal of Dracula*. London: Lorrimer Publishing, 1975. Volta, Ornella. *The Vampire*. London: Tandem Books, 1969.

Index

Abbott and Costello 5
Abbott and Costello Meet Frankenstein 124
Ackerman, Forrest J 26, 133, 199
Adamson, Al 111, 130–136, 154
Adventures of Barrie McKenzie 149
Aguirre, Javier 116
Aller, David 121, 122
Amplas, John 171
Andy Warhol's Dracula 163–165, 203
Andy Warhol's Frankenstein 164
Anulka 77, 78
Aranda, Vincente 60, 61
Aratow, Paul 135
Argento, Dario 102
Arkoff, Samuel Z. 26, 27, 38
Arrow 1
Assignment Terror 113–114, 203
Atlas Comics 201–202
Atwater, Barry 180
The Avengers 22, 30

Badham, John 190, 192
Baker, Roy Ward
Balderston, John L. 5, 153, 190
Band, Albert 172
Bandi, Walter 102
Barry McKenzie Holds His Own 69, 149–150, 203
The Bat People 47–48, 76, 172, 203
Bates, Ralph 12, 13, 56, 57
Bava, Mario 35, 102, 103, 104
Baxt, George 20
Bayless, Peter 146
Beacham, Stephanie 15, 16, 17
Benjamin, Richard 48, 49
Beresford, Bruce 149
Bernard, James 170
Betts, Kirsten 222
Black Sabbath 35, 103, 104
Black Sunday 6, 9, 35, 37, 53, 102

Blacula 7, 36, 43–45, 204
Blaine, Jerry 36
Bloch, Robert 32
Blood 136–138, 204
Blood and Roses 53, 66, 70
Blood Bath 71
Blood Beast Terror 29
The Blood Drinkers 82–83, 204
Blood for Dracula see *Andy Warhol's Dracula*
Blood of Dracula 5, 35, 36
Blood of Dracula's Castle 130, 154
Blood of the Vampire 29
The Blood Spattered Bride 60–61, 204
Bloodsuckers 29–31, 204
The Bloodthirsty Doll see *Legacy of Dracula*
The Bloodthirsty Eyes see *Lake of Dracula*
The Bloodthirsty Roses see *Evil of Dracula*
Blue Demon 92, 93
Blythe, Domini 21
The Body Beneath 136–138, 205
Bonet, Nai 174, 175
Borowczyk, Walerian 68
Boyd, Stephen 144
Brazzi, Rossano 146, 147
Briant, Shane 23
Brides of Dracula 9, 11, 139
The Brides Wore Blood 161, 205
Buffy the Vampire Slayer 154

The Caesars 12
Caged Virgins see *Requiem for a Vampire*
Captain Kronos Vampire Hunter 9, 22–23, 205
Carlson, Veronica 145, 146
Carmilla (novel) 3, 5, 53, 54, 60, 62, 71, 74

Index

Carmilla (play) 55
Carradine, John 79, 80, 130, 131, 133, 135, 136, 174, 175
Carreras, James 13, 20, 25, 54, 55, 57, 63
Carreras, Michael 20, 22, 23, 24, 25, 26, 27, 28
Carson, John 23
Cash, Rosalind 51
Castel, Marie-Pierre 96, 97, 98, 100
Cater, John 23
Chaney, Lon, Jr. 116, 133, 134
Chase, David 160
Chiang, David 24, 26
Chosen Survivors 167–168, 205–206
Clark, Marlene 163
Clemens, Brian 22, 23
Coles, Michael 15, 17, 18
Collinson Twins 57, 58
La Comtesse noire 128
Contouri, Chantel 69
Corlan, Anthony 13, 20, 21
Corman, Roger 28
Corri, Adrienne 21
Count Dracula (1972) 184–185, 190, 206
Count Dracula (1978) 124–128, 206
Count Dracula and His Vampire Bride see *The Satanic Rites of Dracula*
Count Dracula's Great Love 116–118, 206
Count Erotica—Vampire 151–152, 206
Count Yorga, Vampire 15, 36, 38–39, 41, 43, 70, 75, 206
Countess Dracula 21, 63–67, 206
Crain, William 43, 45
Crescendo 15
Croker, Barry 149
Cruise, Tom 2
Crypt of the Living Dead see *Hannah, Queen of the Vampires*
Curse of Dracula 185–186, 207
Curse of Frankenstein 5
Curse of the Vampire 118–119, 207
Curse of the Vampires 10, 83–84, 207
Curtis, Dan 177, 178, 180, 181, 183, 184
Cushing, Peter 11, 15, 16, 17, 18, 24, 25, 27, 30, 31, 32, 55, 56, 57, 139, 143

Daine, Lois 23
Dallesandro, Joe 164, 165, 166
Damiano, Gerard 152, 153
Damon, Mark 76, 104, 105
Dance of the Vampires see *The Fearless Vampire Killers*
Danton, Ray 39, 76
Dark Shadows 7, 66, 177, 181, 200
Daughters of Darkness 66–67, 71, 77, 207
David, Thayer 179
Davion, Alexander, 29, 30, 31
Davis, Robert Hartford 29, 30
Davis, Roger 179

DC Comics 202
Dead of Night 31
Deafula 156, 207
Deane, Hamilton 4, 5, 153, 190
The Deathmaster 39–41, 43, 76, 207
DeCarlo, Yvonne 174, 175
Degermark, Pia 139, 140, 141
de Leon, Gerado 82, 83
Del Toro, Guillermo 3
Demicheli, Tulio 113
de Ossorio, Amando 197, 109, 110, 119
Devils of Darkness 29
The Devil's Wedding Night 104–106, 208
Dickinson, Desmond 30
Doctor Dracula 135–136.208
Dr. Jekyll and Sister Hyde 22
Doctor Terror's House of Horrors 31, 32
Donner, Clive 144
Donovan, Casey (aka Cal Culver) 137
Dor, Karen 114
Dracula (novel) 3, 91, 187
Dracula (1931) 4, 152, 153
Dracula (1973) 181–183, 208
Dracula (1979) 190–195, 197, 208
Dracula (1992) 125
Dracula (2013) 1
Dracula A.D. 1972 15–18, 24, 142, 208
Dracula and Son 141–143, 208
Dracula Blows His Cool 103, 148–149, 209
Dracula Has Risen from the Grave 6, 9, 11, 13, 140
Dracula in the Provinces 147–148, 209
Dracula Prince of Darkness 10, 11
Dracula Prisoner of Evil 128–129, 209
The Dracula Saga 120–121, 209
Dracula Sucks 153–155, 209
Dracula—the Dirty Old Man 151
Dracula vs. Frankenstein 111, 112, 132–135, 209
Dracula Untold 3, 181
Dracula's Daughter 70
Dracula's Dog see *Zoltan the Hound of Dracula*
Dragula 137
Dreyer, Carl 5
Duffell, Peter 32

Ebert, Roger 15, 41, 45, 51, 66, 145, 192, 197
Ege, Julie 26
Ekberg, Anita 109, 110
Elorrieta, Jose Maria 118
Enter the Dragon 24
Evans, Luke 3
Evil of Dracula 87–88, 210

Famous Monsters of Filmland Magazine 26
Fangs of the Living Dead see *Malenka*

Farmer, Suzan 10
Fascination 101, 210
Favorite, Robert 161
The Fearless Vampire Killers 29, 106, 109, 123, 139, 140
The Female Butcher see *The Legend of Blood Castle*
Fennell, Albert 22
Ferrer, Jose 174
Ferroni, Giorgio 103
La Fille de Dracula 128
Fine, Harry 54
Fisher, Terence 53, 56
Forbes-Robertson, John 24, 25
Francis, Freddie 32, 139, 140, 141, 166
Franco, Jess 107, 124, 125
Frankenstein and the Monster from Hell 23
Frankenstein's Bloody Terror 108, 111–113, 210
Frid, Jonathan 177, 178, 179
Fulci, Lucio 147

Gaines, William 33
Ganja and Hess 162–163, 210
Garko, Gianni 103, 148
Gaste, Phillipe 97, 99
Gates, Tudor 54, 55, 57, 59, 60
Gaynor, Gloria 174
Gibson, Alan 15, 17
Gillis, Jamie 153, 154
Goliath and the Vampires 35
Gorey, Edward 190, 191
Grau, Jorge 67
Grave of the Vampire 159–160, 210
Graves, Teresa 145, 146, 147
Greenspun, Roger 15, 32, 38, 44, 45, 56, 73, 159
Grier, Pam 45, 46
Guess What Happened to Count Dracula 157–159, 210
Gunn, Bill 162

Hamilton, Anthony 175
Hamilton, George 48, 49, 153, 214
Hancock, John 7
The Hand of Night 29
Hanley, Jenny 14
Hannah, Queen of the Vampires 47, 76–77, 210–211
Hardy, Robert 69
Harris, Brad 143, 144
Harrison, Sandra 35, 36
Hartley, Mariette 42, 43
Hassell, Imogen 30, 31
Haven, Annette 153, 154
Hayden, Linda 13, 145
Hayes, John 160
Hayles, Brian 28

Hayward, Louis "Deke" 124
Hemple, Anoushka 14, 219
Herzog, Werner 195, 196, 197
Hessler, Gordon 27
Heston, Charlton 51
Hiddleston, Tom 2
Hind, Penelope 31
Holmes, John C. 151, 153, 154
The Horny Vampire 151
The Horrible Sexy Vampire 107–109, 118, 211
Horror of Dracula 5, 6, 9, 11, 183
Horror of Frankenstein 14
Horror of the Blood Monsters 130–132, 211
Hough, John 27
Houghton, Don 15, 17, 24
House of Dark Shadows 178–179, 211
The House That Dripped Blood 31–33, 211–212
Humphries, Barry 149
Hunt, Marsha 15

I Am Legend 50–52
Immoral Tales 68, 211
In Search of Dracula 168–170, 211–212
Incense for the Damned see *Bloodsuckers*
Interview with a Vampire 1, 2, 199
Isbert, Tony 120
It Lives By Night see *The Bat People*

Janson, Horst 23, 205
Jarmusch, Jim 3
Johnson, Artie 48, 49, 214
Jonathan 159, 212
Jones, Duane 162
Jones, Freddie 18, 166, 167
Jordan, Marsha 38, 39
Jourdan, Louis 184
Journey to the Unknown 15

Kali: Devil Bride of Dracula 25
Karloff, Boris 35, 103, 109
Keir, Udo 164, 165
Ken Russell's Dracula 171
Killjan, Bob 38, 41, 45
Kinberg, Judson 20
King, Mabel 162
King, Stephen 187, 188, 199
Kinnear, Roy 13
Kinski, Klaus 125, 196, 197
Kishida, Shin 87
Kiss of the Vampire 9, 11
Klimovsky, Leon 107, 115, 120, 212, 122
Kumel, Harry 66

Lady Dracula 143–144, 212
Lady Vampire 85
Lake of Dracula 86–87, 213
Lampert, Zora 74

Land, Geoffrey 135, 136
Langella, Frank 190, 191, 192, 193, 194
Larraz, Jose Ramon 77
The Last Man on Earth 50
Laughton, Charles 1
Lawson, Richard 45, 46
Lee, Christopher 1, 3, 5, 6, 10–19, 24, 32, 102, 124, 125, 126, 139, 141, 142, 143, 169, 170, 197
Le Fanu, J. Sheridan 3, 5, 53, 71, 74
The Legend of Blood Castle 67–68, 213
Legacy of Dracula 85–86, 213
The Legend of the 7 Golden Vampires 7, 23, 24–26, 82, 213
Leigh, Barbara 27
Leigh, Suzanna 166, 167
Lemora 74–76, 213
Let's Scare Jessica to Death 7, 73–74, 213–214
Lewis, Louise 35
Line, Helga 120, 121, 122
Lips of Blood 99–100, 214
Lom, Herbert 125, 126
Love at First Bite 48–49, 148, 153, 190, 194, 197, 214–215
Lucifer's Women 135, 136
Lugosi, Bela 4, 5, 17, 152, 170
Lumley, Joanna 17, 18
Lust for a Vampire 9, 15, 55–57, 59, 148, 215
Lynch, Richard 186, 187

Macready, Michael 38, 39, 41
The Mad Love of a Hot Vampire 151, 215
Madhouse 38
Madrid, Jose Luis 107
Malenka 109, 110, 215
Margheriti, Antonio 164
Mark of the Vampire 119
Marshall, Phillip 152, 153
Marshall, William 43, 44, 45, 46, 204
Martin 156, 171–172, 215
Marvel Comics 200, 202
Mary, Mary, Bloody Mary 79–80, 215
Máscaras, Mil 93, 94
Maslin, Janet 48
Massey, Anna 33
Massey, Daniel 33
Matheson, Richard 50, 51, 180, 183
Matthews, Christopher 12, 219
Mayne, Ferdy 123, 140
McAndrew, Marianne 47, 48
McGavin, Darren 180, 181
McGee, Vonetta 44
McNee, Patrick 30, 31
Menez, Bernard 142, 143
The Merry Vampires of Vogel 118, 144, 215–216
Meyer, Stephanie 2

Meyers, Jonathan Rhys 1
Milstein, Frederic 21
Miranda, Soledad 126, 128
Moctezuma, Juan Lopez 79
The Monster Club 34
Monti, Aldo 90, 91, 93
Morris, Marianne 78, 79
Morrissey, Paul 163, 164, 165
Moss, Stewart 47, 48
Mower, Patrick 30, 31
Mulligan, Andy 136, 137, 138
Munro, Caroline 15, 27
Murnau, F.W. 3
Murphy, Michael 38, 39
Musgrave, Peter 20
The Mystery of Cynthia Baird 119, 216

Nadler, Reggie 153, 154, 173, 188
Naish, J. Carrol 133, 134
Naschy, Paul 107, 108, 111, 112, 113, 114, 115, 116, 117, 119, 120
Neame, Christopher 15, 16
Nelligan, Kate 192, 193, 194
Neri, Rosalba 104, 105
Night of Dark Shadows 180
Night of the Devils 103–104, 216
Night of the Sorcerers 110, 111, 216
Night of the Walking Dead see *The Strange Love of the Vampires*
The Night Stalker 180–181, 216
Nilsson, Harry 166, 167
Niven, David 145, 146
Nocturna 174–176, 216
Nosferatu: A Symphony of Horror 39, 170, 195
Nosferatu, the Vampyre 195, 216
Nouri, Michael 185
The Nude Vampire 95–96, 100, 217

Ogawa, Ei 85, 87
Old Dracula see *Vampira*
Olivier, Laurence 192, 193, 195
The Omega Man 51–52, 217
One Million Years B.C. 6, 24
Only Lovers Left Alive 3
The Originals 1

Palance, Jack 181, 182
Pataki, Michael 48, 159, 160, 172, 173
Payne, Laurence 21
Peel, David 11
Penny Dreadful 3
Perry, Roger 39, 41, 43, 45
Pertwee, John 33
Philips, Nick 170
Picasso, Paloma 68
Pitt, Brad 2
Pitt, Ingrid 32, 33, 54, 55, 59, 63, 64, 65, 212

Planet of the Vampires 35
Planet of Vampires (comic book) 201
Ponti, Carlo 164
Price, Dennis 58, 129, 166
Price, Vincent 34, 38, 50

Quarry, Robert 38, 39, 40, 41, 42, 45, 160
Queen of Blood 36, 71
Queen of the Damned 69

Rape of the Vampire 95
Rennie, Michael 113, 114
Requiem for a Vampire 97–99, 217
Return of Count Yorga 41–45, 172, 217
Return of Dracula 6
The Return of the Vampire 5
Rice, Anne 1, 199
The Rites of Frankenstein 129
Roberts, Des 157
Robles, German 89, 94
Rollin, Jean 95–101
Romero, George 156, 171
Rosenberg, Max J. 18, 24, 31, 32
Rothman, Stephanie 71

The Sadist with Red Teeth 156–157, 217
Saint James, Susan 48, 49
'*Salem's Lot* 153, 187–189, 199, 218
Salvador, Julio 76
Sangster, Jimmy 56
Santiago, Cirio H. 80
Santo 89, 90, 91, 92, 93
Santo and Blue Demon vs. Dracula and the Wolf Man 91–92, 218
Santo and the Treasure of Dracula 91, 92
Santo and the Vengeance of the Vampire Women 89–91, 218
Santo vs. the Vampire Woman 89, 90
Sasdy, Peter 13, 63
The Satanic Rites of Dracula 17–19, 24, 142, 218
Satan's Black Wedding 170–171, 218
Scars of Dracula 14–15, 125, 170, 218–219
Scream Blacula Scream 45–46, 218–219
Sekka, Johnny 30, 31
The Seven Brothers Meet Dracula see *Legend of the 7 Golden Vampires*
Sex and the Single Vampire 151, 219
Sexula 152, 219
Seyrig, Delphine 66, 67
She 6, 24
She Was a Hippy Vampire 156
Shen, Chen 25
Shepard, Patty 76, 114, 115
Sherman, Sam 111, 112, 132, 133
The Shiver of the Vampire 96–98, 219
Skin, Dez 27
Smith, Cheryl Rainbeaux 75

Smith, Will 52
Smith, William 160
Son of Dracula (1943) 10, 116
Son of Dracula (1974) 166–167, 219
Soto, Talisa 28
Stark, Wilber 20
Starr, Ringo 142, 166, 167
Steckler, Ray Dennis 151
Stensgaard, Yutte 56, 57, 59
Stewart, Robin 25
Stoebar, Orville 7
Stoker, Bram 3, 5, 9, 11, 63, 91, 125, 169, 184, 195
Stoker, Florence 4
The Strain 3
The Strange Love of the Vampires 122–123, 219–220
Style, Michael 54, 56, 57
Subotsky, Milton 31, 32, 34
Superzan 94
Sutherland, Donald 32
Szu, Shih 26

Tagani 130, 131
Tales from the Crypt 32, 33
Taste the Blood of Dracula 11–14, 220
Tate, Sharon 140
Taylor, Robert 113
Tayman, Robert 21
Tender Dracula 143, 220
Terror in the Crypt 53, 102
Thirkell, Arthur 18
Thirst 68–69, 220
Thomas, Damien 57, 58
Thomas, Kevin 23, 57, 197
Thomas, Paul 153, 154
Thompson, Howard 14, 21, 65, 66
Towers, Harry Alan 124
True Blood 1, 3
The Tudors 1
Twilight 1, 2
Twins of Evil 10, 57–59, 104, 220

Uncle Was a Vampire 141, 142

Vampira 144–148, 220
Vampire 185–186, 220–221
The Vampire 5
The Vampire and the Ballerina 6
Vampire Circus 20–21, 65, 221
The Vampire Diaries 1
The Vampire, Happening 139–141, 143, 221
Vampire Hookers 80–81, 221
The Vampire Lovers 24, 32, 36, 53–55, 59, 63, 70, 77, 128.221–222
Vampire Virgins 59–60
Vampirella 26–28, 199, 221
Vampire's Kiss 156

The Vampire's Night Orgy 121–122, 221–222
The Vampires of Coyoacan 93–94, 222
Vampyr 5, 53
Vampyres 77–79, 222
Vampyros Lesbos 128, 223
Varkov, Zandor 133, 134, 136
The Vault of Horror 33–34, 123, 223
The Velvet Vampire 71–73, 223–224
Ventham, Wanda 23
Vernon, Howard 128, 129
Vlad the Impaler 28

Walsh, Edward 42
Warhol, Andy 163, 164
Waterman, Dennis 14
The Werewolf vs. the Vampire Woman 114–115, 224
Wicking, Christopher 26

Williams, Fred 125, 127
Willman, Noel 11
Wilmer, Douglas 222
Winner, Vic 116, 117
Winston, Stan 47, 172
Wohlfahrt, Waldemar 107, 108
Woodward, Edward 31
Wynorski, Jim 28

Yamamoto, Michio 85, 87
Yarnell, Celeste 71, 72
Young, Robert 20, 21

Zabalza, Jose Maria 119
Zelenovic, Srdjan 164
Zerbe, Anthony 51
Zoltan, the Hound of Dracula 7, 153, 172–174, 224

www.ingramcontent.com/pod-product-compliance
Ingram Content Group UK Ltd.
Pitfield, Milton Keynes, MK11 3LW, UK
UKHW021845140426
5217IPUK00022B/1591